ESP and Psychokinesis

A Philosophical Examination

ESP and Psychokinesis

A Philosophical Examination

Stephen E. Braude

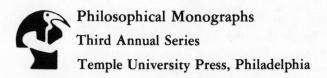

Philosophical Monographs
Third Annual Series
Temple University Press, Philadelphia

Library of Congress Cataloging in Publication Data

Braude, Stephen E.   1945-
    ESP and psychokinesis.

    (Philosophical monographs)
    Bibliography: p.
    Includes indexes.
    1. Extrasensory perception. 2. Psychokinesis.
I. Title. II. Series: Philosophical monographs
(Philadelphia, 1978-   ).
BF1321.B72   133.8   79-27161
ISBN 0-87722-163-4

In memory of my grandfathers,
Morris Braude and Benjamin S. Katz.

Contents

Preface

In the past 100 years the scientific community has lavished an increasing amount of attention on ostensibly paranormal phenomena, and in recent years the scientific examination of such phenomena has gained considerable momentum. Although I do not wish to indulge in lengthy speculations about why this should be so, I cannot help but remark that in a way, the rise in scientific interest in the paranormal is not in the least surprising. As science has continued to widen its scope by developing workable theories covering a broad range of familiar phenomena, the sorts of scientific territories remaining to be charted have become more and more removed from the phenomena familiar to us in everyday life. The great theoretical advances in science, for the most part, no longer have to do (at least directly) with the sorts of mundane macroscopic interactions that occupied so much of Newton's time. Scientific theorizing is now largely devoted to the study of the very small (as in atomic physics and microbiology) or the very large and distant (as in astrophysics).

But in the realm of things inspectable without the aid of microscopes, telescopes, cloud chambers, and so on, there is another range of phenomena to be studied, one whose mysteries cannot so easily be dismissed these days in favor of initially less troubling enigmas attending such humdrum matters as billiard ball collisions. In this realm we find much of the data of parapsychology. And I suggest that at least part of the reason for recent scientific interest in the paranormal has to do with the feeling of many scientists that we have not yet exhausted the important puzzles before our very eyes.

Of course this is only part of the story. As Arthur Koestler is fond of observing (see, e.g., [80]), many scientists have been as much humbled as encouraged by recent scientific advances, particularly those in physics. For example, for all its beauty and utility, quantum physics (and especially the received Copenhagen interpretation) has substantially added to our stock of major perplexities concerning the operations of nature. The so-called 'measurement problem' has provided the physicist and philosopher of science with as deep a set of puzzles (represented, e.g., by Schrodinger's cat paradox, or the EPR paradox) as we have had at any time in the history of science. I also think there is some justification for Koestler's contention that the behavior and properties of the subatomic domain are initially as counter-intuitive as anything proposed by parapsychologists, and that to this extent the physicist who objects to parapsychology on the grounds of its *prima facie* peculiarity seems constrained to heed Benjamin Franklin's injunction, 'Clean your finger before you point at my spots'.

Another, and perhaps more important, reason for the increasing attention paid by the scientific community to ostensibly paranormal phenomena is that in this century parapsychology has begun to establish itself as an empirical science. Although obviously still in its infancy, parapsychology has progressed steadily from the early days of statistical research by gradually refining experimental designs, charting specific research goals, developing the technology to pursue well-defined lines of research, gathering data, and developing more sophisticated (though not always more adequate) conceptual tools. The fruits of these various lines of development have often been extremely interesting, and certainly interesting enough to warrant further investigation. In Part I of this volume I survey some of the best current research. Although I have, unfortunately, had to omit much that is worthwhile, I have tried to indicate the ingenuity and sophistication with which scientists have been probing the domain of the paranormal.

In any event, whatever exactly the reasons for recent scientific interest in the paranormal, as far as my own intellectual orientation with respect to parapsychology is concerned, it should be clear by now that I am sympathetic to the field. I think parapsychology's area of research is perfectly legitimate. Numerous interesting phenomena have occurred in and out of the lab which seem to me clearly to warrant open-minded investigation, empirical and conceptual. Moreover, I am prepared to believe, and in fact do believe, that there are natural forces or processes which science may not at all understand, and which provide at least some of the material for investigation by parapsychologists.

I should add that this is not, as some may think, an especially bold position. I am simply saying that science still has much to learn about nature generally and human beings in particular, and that some of this may pertain to the data of parapsychology. Actually, as Part II of this book (especially II.A.2.) will make clear, I am prepared to go further and maintain that an enormous part of received scientific theory, in particular that area purporting to explain human behavior and cognitive abilities, is disguised nonsense. But of course my more general claim about science does not rest on this criticism. Science may still have plenty to discover about physical and human nature even if the theories I attack in Part II of this book are all on the right track.

As I conceive it, this volume serves two main functions. First I intend it to be a source book for philosophers on the experimental evidence of parapsychology; in fact, in some ways I regard it as a sequel to C. D. Broad's monumental *Lectures on Psychical Research* [24]. Lest that seem intolerably arrogant, I hasten to add that my book is a considerably more modest enterprise than Broad's. But since philosophical theorizing about the subject of parapsychology would be intellectually irresponsible if conducted in ignorance of the data, Broad's book definitely needs to be updated. When Broad wrote his lectures, around 1960, the quantity, quality, and variety of experimental evidence in parapsychology was, despite some undeniably important work, considerably poorer than it is today. Moreover, Broad's discussion of the experimental data concentrated mostly on card-guessing experiments (some of which are now discredited, or at least held to be suspect—e.g., the Soal-Shackleton experiments) and on work conducted in England, giving little attention to the work of J. B. Rhine and his associates and successors. Furthermore, due to recent innovations in automated scoring and generating targets, today's experimental evidence is, for the most part, methodologically cleaner than that surveyed by Broad.

The relative paucity of good experimental evidence also forced Broad to concentrate heavily on anecdotal material. I don't think this material should be discounted; on the contrary, I encourage the reader to study it carefully. And in fact, for reasons outlined in my discussion of experimental replicability (I.A.7.), I suspect that anecdotal material may ultimately be of greater value than experimental data. In any case, the experimental evidence is still important; in fact, by now there is so much evidence of this kind for the various forms of ESP and PK that I shall restrict my attention to this sort of material. One need no longer rely on evidence gathered under non-controlled conditions, subject to the usual charges of faulty memory, mass hallucination, misdescription, and out-right mendacity. The current proliferation of controlled data also provides one reason why I shall have nothing to say about topics concerning life after death (for instance, the intelligibility of the notion of discarnate survival) or such topics as possession, xenoglossy, and ghosts, the evidence for which is still largely anecdotal. I certainly think these topics are interesting and important. But there is now so much to be grasped about ESP and PK alone that, in my opinion, the subject of survival should be treated separately.

The second principal function of this book is to explore the conceptual foundations and some philosophical implications of parapsychological research. As far as the philosophical implications of the data are concerned, I have not been able to bring myself to hazard any big, deep, and sweeping metaphysical claims about the meaning of it all. Personally, I find the data extremely difficult to manage conceptually. I am principally concerned here with presenting the evidence as clearly as possible, hoping to stimulate in philosophically-minded readers fruitful metaphysical speculations. I have, it is true, considered how some of the parapsychological evidence throws certain problems into sharp relief (for instance, problems regarding materialistic/reductionistic theories of the mental); I also present an array of arguments against psychophysical identity theories and mechanistic accounts of the mental. But I do not feel that the evidence of parapsychology is required in order to expose the weaknesses of such positions (though it may help); and the reader looking for large alternative theories (as distinguished, say, from the sketchy remarks made at the end of II.A.2.)—especially theories that can also make clear sense of the data of parapsychology—will be disappointed.

I have tried to write for a fairly wide audience (even though this book is addressed primarily to philosophers). In so doing, I have run certain risks. I would like this book to be useful to students (undergraduate and graduate) as well as to professional academicians (philosophers and non-philosophers). But in order to make it accessible to an audience varying greatly in philosophical sophistication, I have had to face a problem familiar to all teachers. I fear I have written a book too advanced for some readers, yet too elementary for others. For example, many of the exercises in philosophical clarification in I.A. will no doubt strike some professional philosophers as needlessly detailed, while my arguments against mechanism in I.B.4.d. and II.A. may be too advanced and abstract for those unaccustomed to philosophical polemic. Moreover, I am aware that my audience varies not simply in philosophical sophistication, but also in familiarity with the parapsychological literature itself. Many parapsyogists are bound to find parts of this book (especially my survey of the evidence and of certain methodological issues) painfully elementary or cursory. I know of no happy solution to this problem, and trust only that readers will be tolerant of passages aimed at readers at some other level of philosophical or parapsychological proficiency.

My decision to think seriously about the data of parapsychology is relatively recent, and was made in the summer of 1975. I decided then to become part of the community of parapsychologists, in order to learn as much as possible about the latest experimental and conceptual developments in the field. I must thank the many scientists working in parapsychology who have aided me in my attempt to master the data and who have graciously and enthusiastically welcomed me into their fold. I have the utmost respect for the intellectual honesty and flexibility they have shown in encouraging me to express my philosophical perplexities and misgivings about their own theoretical work. Despite my continued efforts to comply with these invitations, I fear I have rendered them less of a service than they have rendered me. Among the many parapsychologists to whom I am indebted, I wish especially to thank the team at SRI (Harold Puthoff, Russell Targ, Edwin May), Charles Honorton, John Palmer, and Charles Tart; also, John Beloff and my colleague Bruce Goldberg, whose suggestions and criticisms have been invaluable in writing the theoretical portions of this book; also Jan Ludwig, for his comments and criticisms of an early draft of the manuscript. For their helpful criticisms and suggestions, and for their willingness to discuss issues with me, I wish also to thank Gerald Barnes, Jule Eisenbud, Michael Hooker, and my UMBC colleagues Thomas Benson, Audrey McKinney, and Alan Tormey. I wish also to acknowledge several very distinguished philosophers, who unlike many other of my colleagues (I'm sorry to say) have displayed the intellectual courage and open-mindedness to support my interest in investigating the subject of parapsychology. In particular I wish to thank Bruce Aune, Roderick Chisolm, Wilfrid Sellars, Hector-Neri Castañeda (who invited me to submit my paper 'Telepathy' to *Noûs* [v.12 (1978): 267-301], which I have revised and woven into the text), and Joseph Margolis, who invited me to prepare this book for

Philosophical Monographs, and whose labors as editor I greatly appreciate. Thanks are due also to Paul Kurtz and Prometheus Press for allowing me to reprint, with revisions, my paper 'On the Meaning of "Paranormal"', which appeared in Ludwig [89]. Finally, I should like to express my gratitude to Wallace and Virginia Reid, owners of the Green Heron Inn in Kennebunkport, Maine, for providing, summer after summer, an atmosphere in which I could collect my thoughts.

My progress in researching and writing this book was aided considerably by several fellowships. These were a Faculty Research Grant for Spring 1977 and Summer Fellowship for 1978, both from the University of Maryland Baltimore County, and a fellowship from the National Endowment for the Humanities for 1979-80.

Fall, 1979

Part I

A. Conceptual Foundations

1. Preliminary Terminological Remarks

The phenomena investigated in experimental parapsychology fall into the now familiar categories of ESP (which includes telepathy, clairvoyance, and precognition) and psychokinesis (PK). As we shall see shortly, these categories may be profoundly misleading, and insistence on a sharp division between them may seriously hinder research. In fact, appreciation of this point alone represents a conceptual milestone in parapsychology, and we would do well to consider the reasons for questioning these familiar categories. Let us begin, then, with a quick survey of the traditional classification of phenomena in parapsychology, and then consider why both theory and practice render it suspect.

But before we embark on this project, a few terminological points merit attention. Most parapsychologists now concede that the term 'extrasensory perception' is an unfortunate expression, since it suggests that the phenomena being picked out are of a perceptual, or quasi-perceptual, nature. Now unless our views of ordinary perception are seriously mistaken (a possibility which ought to be left open), the various forms of ESP apparently involve processes quite different from those of the familiar sense modalities. I am not suggesting that we abandon the term 'ESP'; by now it is too well-entrenched to be usefully excised. But we should be on guard against being seduced into thinking that ESP must be anything like ordinary perception.

Even the term 'parapsychology' is somewhat unfortunate, because it suggests that the proper domain of the parapsychologist is a certain range of *psychological* phenomena, rather than physical or physiological phenomena. In fact, Rhine [118] originally intended to use the term this way. The term 'psychical research', used more widely in Great Britain than in the United States, similarly links this domain with psychology. However, since the phenomena investigated in parapsychology often concern occurrences at the physical and physiological level (for instance, random number generator outputs and moving objects, or blood flow and brain waves), and since the task of interpreting such phenomena may bear directly on the deepest issues in metaphysics, we must be careful from the start about how to characterize them. For at least this reason, C. J. Ducasse coined the somewhat more neutral adjective 'paranormal' to replace 'psychical' and 'parapsychological'. Of course 'paranormal' is not entirely unproblematic; but its difficulties are of a different sort, and will be examined later in II.C.

One final caveat. The forms of ESP and PK are often called *psi abilities*. The use of 'psi' is supposed to designate more neutrally what the more psychologically tinged term 'psychic' signifies. Although this replacement seems unobjectionable (if not especially effective), a certain danger still lurks in the use of the term 'ability'. It is one thing to speak of psi *functioning* and another, of psi *abilities*. If a person accurately described remote locations with great reliability, or moved objects without touching them and without magic, then such performances would properly be described as instances of psi functioning, and the processes involved would properly be labelled 'psi *processes*'. But to speak of psi *abilities*, in connection with ESP and PK, is to risk obscuring an important issue. Although an instance of ESP or PK would presumably be an instance of psi functioning, psi functioning need not involve abilities at all. For example, we do not regard metabolic or gastro-intestinal functioning as kinds of abilities. But for all we know at this stage, psi functioning may be as fundamental a biological activity as these. If so, we would presumably not regard psi functioning as an ability either.

That possibility suggests why talk of psi abilities may be misleading. Many people assume (and even explicitly claim) that psychic superstars are, say, rather like musical virtuosi. We tend to think that musical abilities are not uniformly distributed among the members of the human race, that those who have musical abilities have them in varying degrees of competence, that such abilities are of different sorts (e.g., those of the instrumentalist, the composer, the conductor), and that a person may have one such ability without having another. And many take a similar view of ESP and PK. They would say that not everyone is psychic, that some are more psychic than others, and that not all psychics are psychic in the same way.

But, as I just observed, for all we know psi functioning may be as automatic, as involuntary, and as uniformly distributed among humans as metabolic functioning. It may be something all of us do all the time, simply as part of our repertoire of organic activities, and the processes involved may be as remote from everyday conscious awareness as those involved in metabolic functioning. But if this is so, then we may ask what distinguishes psychic virtuosi from the rest of us? We could plausibly say that psychic superstars are analogous to advanced practitioners of yoga, who can consciously experience, or at least control, biological functions ordinarily imperceptible and beyond human control. If we took this line, then in effect psi functioning would be regarded as no more a skill or talent than spleen functioning. What is marvelous and skillful in a yogi's control of his blood flow, or heart rate, or body temperature is his command of these apparently autonomic processes. The skill involved here is, so to speak, a *meta*-skill. Similarly, psychic superstars would be special, not merely because they function psychically (from this perspective we *all* do), but because of their ability to harness or alter such common functions.

Clearly, the two perspectives sketched above would orient parapsychological research in different ways. For instance, if psi functioning is not universal but is instead confined to a fairly small segment of the human population, there would be little point in trying to garner statistical evidence for psi phenomena by means of randomly selected test subjects. Success with properly selected subjects would not, of course, entail that psi abilities were like musical abilities. The evidence (as I see it) does in fact show that, on the whole, tests involving subjects selected by screening procedures yield better results than tests with randomly selected subjects. But this fact is compatible both with the picture of psi as a gift or talent (like an artistic gift) and with the view of psi as a form of universal human functioning. Psi functioning might well be universal even if few people could control it in ways suitable for laboratory research.

Moreover, if we supposed that all humans function psychically but not necessarily in ways demonstrable in the lab, we might quite naturally ask whether psi processes served some fundamental (possibly continual) subtle organic function. We might even wonder whether we were asking the wrong question in asking: What conditions must obtain for psi to occur? For, if psi were a fundamental and universal organic function, we might ask instead: Why are manifestations of psi so infrequent? Does anything *inhibit* psi? (Do we for instance suppress a continual bombardment of psi information for the sake of our own sanity?) or, Why are we not confronted with more numerous apparent instances of psi functioning? And such questions lead to various others, for instance: Has psi functioning played an important role in evolution? Is it perhaps a vestige of an earlier evolutionary stage in which linguistic communication had not yet developed?

As I read the evidence, we have as yet no reason to prefer either of the two viewpoints sketched. Nevertheless, from time to time, I shall myself speak rather loosely and treat psi as an ability. Indeed, there do seem to be similarities between psi functioning and recognized abilities (especially with respect to conditions under which they are encouraged or inhibited). But for the moment, I simply wish to caution the reader against obscuring this potentially important distinction.

Let us now consider the standard classification of phenomena in experimental parapsychology. I shall provide definitions for each of the familiar categories, but I warn the reader that they should be taken as provisional only. They are intended merely to help us orient ourselves conceptually. Ultimately, we shall see why these familiar categories of phenomena are problematical, if not downright unacceptable.

2. Telepathy

The term 'telepathy' was coined by F.W.H. Myers. Literally, it means 'feeling at a distance'. One might think, then, that all we need to do is to make this definition more precise. But as Broad noted (in 'Normal Cognition, Clairvoyance, and Telepathy' in [23]), we must distinguish telepathic *cognition* from telepathic *interaction*. In telepathic cognition, one individual *A* comes to know what another individual *B* is thinking or experiencing. But for telepathic interaction, we need only posit some sort of causal link between the minds of *A* and *B*, whether or not one of them comes to know anything about the other.* So presumably we may have telepathic interaction without telepathic cognition, though the converse is impossible. Perhaps, then, we should define 'telepathic cognition' along the following lines:

(D1) *telepathic cognition* =df the knowledge of another person's thoughts or mental states gained independently of the five senses.

* Some may regard it as contentious that I treat telepathy as a causal process, rather than as 'synchronistic', and that as a result I beg the question against acausal explanations of psi. I shall argue later, however (in II.B.), that an acausal principle of synchronicity cannot account for the data of parapsychology, that it is not clearly acausal, and that it seems in fact to be unintelligible.

A number of points concerning this definition seem worth making. First, (D1) may be too restrictive in limiting telepathic cognition to knowledge of a *person's* mental states. Some would allow for the possibility of telepathic interaction and telepathic cognition involving lower organisms,* and thus would want to substitute 'organism's' for 'person's' in (D1). I have no quarrel with this adjustment; nothing that follows hangs on it.

Another questionable feature of (D1) is that it takes telepathic cognition to operate independently of just the *five* senses. No doubt some readers would not have been tempted in the first place to relativize telepathic cognition to five senses only. But it is instructive to consider why such a move is ill-advised. Actually, several different issues are involved here. Some might feel that telepathy, if it exists, would operate independently of a range of physiological processes wider than that restricted to the five senses. In fact, (D1) could be satisfied by a number of (admittedly bizarre) cases that we would not countenance as instances of telepathy. Suppose, for example, that A and B are unseparated Siamese twins, and suppose that whenever A is feeling anxious a certain characteristic sequence of neural events occurs in $(A \& B)$'s body, producing a characteristic sensation in B. After a while, B might come to recognize this sensation as the one he feels when and only when A is feeling anxious. But since this bit of cognition about A's mental state is mediated by intrasomatic physiological processes not involving any of the five major senses, B's coming to know that A feels anxious satisfies (D1).

So perhaps we should say that telepathic cognition is the knowledge of another individual's mental states gained independently of *any* sensory information. But this suggestion surely goes too far. It would be question-begging to assume from the start that telepathy is *in no way* sensory,

* See, e.g., the case of Rider Haggard and the dog Bob, *Proc. S.P.R.* 33 (1922): 219ff.

just as it would be to assume that telepathy operates like one of our familiar senses. After all, there is nothing intrinsically objectionable in the *idea* that telepathy has some sort of sensory component. Moreover, there is no ready way to specify in advance which particular set of possible sensory responses telepathy would be independent of, once we allow for sense modalities beyond the big five. So perhaps we should say that telepathic cognition operates independently of the *known* senses. But then, our definition would be useful only as long as we failed to discover a telepathic sense or a sensory component to telepathy. However, this would not clearly be a flaw in our definition. Rather, it would seem merely to reflect the state of our ignorance concerning telepathy.

We might also ask: Should telepathy be construed as something lying forever outside the domain of science? For example, if we discovered some currently unknown type of physiological process which explained this phenomenon, should we say that telepathy had been *explained away*, or should we say that we now know what telepathy is? My own inclination would be to take the latter alternative, and say that we now understand a phenomenon that we could previously describe only with respect to our ignorance.

Moreover, what if it turned out that the evidence supporting the existence of telepathy could be accounted for in terms of *already familiar* sensory processes—processes hardly novel, but whose connection with telepathy had gone unnoticed? The important difference between this situation and the one just mentioned is that, in the former but not here, the explanans is some hitherto unrecognized process. There, we could comfortably label the newly discovered processes as telepathic. But here, we are dealing with processes already familiar from putatively non-telepathic contexts. In this case, I think, we might be justified in saying *either* that we now know what this hitherto mysterious phenomenon (telepathy) is, or that there is no telepathy after all, only another instance of an already familiar physiological process. Which alternative we chose would probably express no more than a preference for a certain linguistic convention. We might continue to speak of telepathy but alter its status from the paranormal to the normal or abnormal, or continue to treat telepathy as a phenomenon involving processes unknown to science but then concede that the class of telepathic phenomena was empty.

With all this in mind, I suggest that we redefine 'telepathic cognition' as follows.

(D1′) *telepathic cognition* =df the knowledge of another person's mental states gained independently of the known senses.

But in fact none of these issues surrounding (D1) seems especially important. They arise simply because, in our ignorance, we can do little more than characterize psi phenomena negatively—as phenomena which, despite superficial similarities to familiar sensory and motor phenomena, seem to be quite different. At this point, we can do little more than say, for example, that telepathy involves a certain kind of interaction-I-know-not-what that is nevertheless distinct from certain related but widely recognized processes. In fact psi phenomena are, if genuine, so little understood and apparently so unreliable in the lab that they cannot even be adequately characterized operationally. Among the obstacles the parapsychologist must face in sorting psi phenomena in terms of experimental operations and outcomes, are: (a) that experimental procedures are ambiguous and do not conclusively discriminate between the familiar categories of phenomena (see I.A.6.), (b) that it is difficult to replicate an experiment in parapsychology, or even to determine when an experiment *counts* as a replication (see I.A.7.); and (c) that experimental results are often surprising—too little is known about psi phenomena to yield, in most cases, accurate predictions about experimental outcomes. We simply lack a detailed (much less a mathematically formalized) theoretical framework in accord with which (as often in .the case of physics) the prediction of experimental effects before their observation becomes feasible.*

In any case, since the main purpose of the definitions I propose is to orient us to the subject of parapsychology, let us be content for the moment with relativizing the forms of ESP to the known senses, and thus let us be content, for the moment at least, with (D1') as it stands. For our immediate purposes this will present no difficulties.

Before leaving the topic of telepathic cognition, I should mention that there is little evidence that telepathy is a form of cognition or, as some put it (retaining the traditional scare quotes), a form of anomalous 'knowledge' (see, e.g., Gauld [58]). There is, however, plenty of evidence for mere telepathic interaction. We shall see in due course that the experimental data are not plausibly interpreted as evidence for a form of paranormal cognition. This does not, of course, make the subject of telepathy any the less interesting philosophically. If no case of telepathic interaction is a case of telepathic cognition, this would only mean that telepathy has less relevance to epistemology than many have supposed, although its relevance to the philosophy of mind would still remain considerable. So rather than linger on a definition of a phenomenon whose existence has virtually no experimental support, and with an eye to avoiding unnecessary disputes over what might count as knowledge, paranormal or otherwise, let us consider how best to define 'telepathic interaction'.

In 'Normal Cognition, Clairvoyance, and Telepathy' (p. 48), Broad defines it as follows:

---

*Rudiments of such a framework have recently been suggested. See, e.g., Schmidt [140], [145] and Walker [187], [188]. Formal theories, of course, still run the risk of incoherence once interpreted. See II.A.3. for a criticism of Walker's efforts. For a grossly unintelligible attempt to formalize the notion of a meaningful coincidence, see Gatlin [57]; and see Braude [20] for a criticism of this paper (for Gatlin's reply and my rebuttal, see *JASPR* 73 (1979): No. 3).

    (D2) *telepathic interaction* =df the supernormal causal influence of one embodied mind on another.

But this is not quite satisfactory. Two terms in (D2) seem initially problematical—namely, 'supernormal' and 'mind'. We needn't worry about the second of these, however. Presumably, we may talk about minds without presupposing any philosophical analysis of what minds are. We may also safely ignore Broad's Cartesian reference to *embodied* minds; at this stage, dualistic assumptions are gratuitous. The use of the term 'supernormal', however, is somewhat more suspicious. We should, at least initially, leave open the possibility that the processes of telepathic interaction are in principle neither different from nor simply more extraordinary than those currently recognized by science. If 'supernormal' were intended to rule out that possibility, it would therefore beg an important question. But if it were not, then the meaning of the term would be correspondingly obscure (I explore possible analyses of the presumably synonymous term 'paranormal' in II.C.).

I think we can avoid this problem with Broad's use of 'supernormal'. The possibility of telepathic interaction derives much of its interest from the fact that we normally assume that a person's mental state cannot produce a change in another person's mental state except by means of processes which at some point involve the operation of one or more of the known (actually, in this case, the *five*) senses. We believe, for example, that my present mental state can cause a change in yours only by means of a causal sequence which at some point involves your sensory contact with your environment (cf. Broad, *op. cit.*, p. 46). We believe that my mental state must first issue in some overt behavior or other *publicly observable* state of mine. Then this behavior or state must have some effect on your body, and thereafter produce some change in your mental state. I may, for instance, change your mental state by talking directly to you, or in virtue of your hearing or reading my recorded or written words (or copies of them), or in virtue of your observing my expressions, gestures, etc. (or reproductions of them), or in virtue of your coming into contact with some object or artifact I produced or used (or reproductions of them).* One reason telepathic interaction is interesting, then, is that the telepathic process is supposed to operate independently of the familiar sensory mechanisms involved in these sorts of complex causal chains.

Of course the sensory mechanisms involved here are those of the five extra-somatic senses. But this does not mean we should say that telepathic interaction is the causal influence of one mind on another independently of those five senses. The reason here is somewhat different than that discussed in connection with telepathic cognition, and concerns the possibility of another form of paranormal interaction. In fact, it bears on a problem we will encounter in defining the forms of clairvoyance. Suppose that *A* wills that the acidity in *B*'s stomach increase, and that subsequently (as a result of *A*'s willing), *B* develops an excessively acid stomach and experiences stomach pain. Since the physiological causes of *B*'s feeling a stomach pain are wholly intra-somatic, this would be a case of one mind's causally influencing another independently of the five (extra-somatic) senses. This also counts as the influence of one mind on another by granting the transitivity of causes. But I prefer to postpone the transitivity issue until the next section. So for the moment, we may tentatively define 'telepathic interaction' as

(D3) *telepathic interaction* =df the causal influence of one mind on another independently of the known senses.

Although there is hardly a philosophical tradition with respect to telepathy, philosophers tend to focus entirely on the possibility of one person's coming to *know* telepathically what another's mental state is. The supposition that telepathy fundamentally concerns this (or at least some) sort of

*The reader may notice that this point is similar to one of Broad's *basic limiting principles* in· [24] :3. See II.C. for a discussion of these.

cognitive process may even explain why telepathy has traditionally been considered to be a form of extrasensory *perception*. But as I remarked earlier, this is at least a partially, and perhaps wholly, misleading approach to the topic. There appear to be interesting forms of telepathic interaction which could not properly be described as cases of cognition. For example, there is evidence suggesting that a person's mental state can produce a *similar* mental state in someone else, independently of channels of communication involving the known senses, and without producing an awareness of the similarity. Thus, A's thought of the Queen of Spades might merely produce in B the thought of the Queen of Spades, or the Queen of Hearts, or Queen Elizabeth. And as we shall see, the possibility of this sort of interaction alone raises important philosophical problems, even though we would not describe such cases as cases of one person's telepathically coming to *know* what another's thought or mental state is.

In fact, as we will soon see, most (if not all) of the best evidence supporting the existence of telepathic processes supports telepathic interaction but not telepathic cognition. Nevertheless, there are significantly different *kinds* of experimental evidence for telepathy. Much of the evidence concerns cases of the sort just mentioned—that is, cases in which an agent's mental state appears to produce a similar mental state in someone else. Let us refer to these as cases of *ostensible telepathic content-simulation*. Clearly, once we grant that there might be telepathic processes in which one person's mental state produces a similar mental state in someone else, and once we grant that these need not be described as cases of telepathic knowledge, then even if the relevant mental states were qualitatively *identical* (although we have no evidence for anything like this), we would not be compelled to describe the second person as knowing the mental state of the first. This would simply be a limiting case of telepathic content-simulation. In the language of Information Theory—which is often employed to describe paranormal goings-on—our case would be the analogue of the transmission of a signal in the absence of noise. Other studies suggest that subjects exhibit subtle physiological responses to telepathic stimuli even though they are not consciously aware of any such interaction. These cases likewise suggest the existence of telepathic interaction without cognition, and may be classified as cases of *ostensible pre-conscious telepathic interaction*. Some of the much-debated experiments in card-guessing may provide evidence for this form of telepathy (see I.B.4.a.), since subjects report that guesses are not based on conscious subjective experiences of the identity of the target. Most of the remaining good cases suggesting the existence of telepathy are cases of *ostensible hypnogenic telepathic interaction*. These concern such phenomena as the inducing of hypnotic trances at a distance, apparently by means of telepathic command or suggestion. Here, too, we seem at best to have a form of telepathic interaction, but no telepathic cognition.

3. Clairvoyance

Parapsychologists often contrast the term 'telepathy' with 'clairvoyance'. Whereas telepathy is supposed to involve a causal sequence between two minds, clairvoyance (literally, 'clear seeing') is supposed to involve a causal sequence running from some physical state of affairs to a mind. Usually this is taken to be a distinction between two forms of cognition. Whereas the object of telepathic cognition is supposed to be a person's thoughts or mental states, the object of clairvoyant cognition is supposed to be a physical state of affairs. But clairvoyance needn't be analyzed this way. In principle, we can distinguish various kinds of clairvoyance corresponding to at least some of the aforementioned kinds of telepathic phenomena.

To begin with, we can distinguish clairvoyant cognition from clairvoyant interaction, and we can formulate tentative definitions of these two classes of phenomena modeled after (D1′) and (D3).

(D4) *clairvoyant cognition* =df the knowledge of a physical state of affairs gained independently of the known senses.

(D5) *clairvoyant interaction* =df the causal influence of a physical system on a person's mental states independently of the known senses.

Again, we do not want to relativize clairvoyance to the five extra-somatic senses only; otherwise, for example, experiencing a stomach pain would count as an instance of clairvoyance. Given our present ignorance once again, our best bet seems to be to relativize the definitions to known sensory processes and to be prepared to revise them, once we discover how to explain the phenomena in question.

We may now distinguish some forms of clairvoyant interaction corresponding to some of the forms of telepathic interaction already classified. Suppose, for example, that an event—say, a fire in a house (or a person drowning)—is an immediate causal antecedent of a person's having, at some remote location, a mental image of a house on fire (or of a person drowning). These would seem to be cases of *ostensible clairvoyant content-simulation*. Or, suppose that a person exhibits subtle physiological responses—but not conscious responses—to remote physical events (like a light flashing in another room). These would be examples of *ostensible pre-conscious clairvoyant interaction*, and there is, as we shall see, evidence for this sort of phenomenon (see I.B.3.c.). Without trying to provide a complete list of possible forms of clairvoyant interaction, let us simply observe, therefore, that —as with telepathy—there may be forms of clairvoyant interaction that are not also forms of clairvoyant cognition.

Regrettably, the distinction between telepathy and clairvoyance—useful as it may have been in the early stages of conceptualizing parapsychological phenomena—is far from clear. For example, if we compare (D1') with (D4), and (D3) with (D5), we must concede that telepathy may prove to be a *special case* of clairvoyance—if, that is, as reductionistic materialists insist, mental states are simply kinds of physical states. On the other hand, if the idealists are correct in taking the physical world to be a construct out of inner episodes, then clairvoyance would turn out to be a special case of telepathy. At this stage, however, we needn't take a stand on such global metaphysical issues, and so we may tentatively accept the traditional distinction between telepathy and clairvoyance.

There is, however, a different way of challenging the distinction. It is a familiar fact that we often come to know another person's mental state by observing his bodily states (e.g., his behavior, gestures, expressions, etc.). But if we can *clairvoyantly* come to know these sorts of things about a person, then it seems we can clairvoyantly come to know a person's mental states. Thus, A might know that B is feeling angry by knowing clairvoyantly how B is acting, and while most of us would not regard this as a case of *telepathic* cognition, it does satisfy (D1'). As for non-cognitive interaction, suppose that B imagines himself laughing, and suppose further that this causes B to laugh and that B's laughing causes A, at some remote location, to have an idea of B laughing. Although most of us would not regard this as a case of telepathic interaction, it nevertheless satisfies (D3).

A similar situation plagues our definitions for clairvoyance. Suppose, for example, that A comes to know that B's house is on fire as the result of coming to know telepathically that B knows that his house is on fire. Although this case satisfies (D4), most people would take it to be an example of *telepathic* cognition. Or, suppose that B clairvoyantly comes to know that a certain house is on fire, and that his resulting mental image of a house on fire causes a mental image in A of a house on fire. Although B's mental image is a causal consequence of some clairvoyant interaction, A's mental image results from telepathic interaction with B. Nevertheless, since the house on fire causes A's mental image, then even though there is no clairvoyant interaction between the fire and A, this case satisfies (D5).

Here the transitivity of causes permits certain undesirable non-proximate causal sequences to satisfy our definitions. So what we need is a way of confining attention to appropriate *direct* or *immediate* causal sequences.* I propose, therefore, that we recast our definitions as follows, in order to block (in a way clear enough for our purposes) problems arising from the transitivity of causes, and also to reflect the dependence of paranormal cognition on paranormal interaction.

(D6) (a) *telepathic interaction* =df the direct causal influence of one person's mental states on those of another independently of the known senses.

(b) *telepathic cognition* =df knowledge gained through telepathic interaction concerning the mental state of the agent in the interaction (or knowledge inferred from this).†

(D7) (a) *clairvoyant interaction* =df the direct causal influence of a physical system on a person's mental states independently of the known senses.

(b) *clairvoyant cognition* =df knowledge gained through clairvoyant interaction concerning the cause of the interaction (or knowledge inferred from this).

The point of the parenthetical additions to (D6b) and (D7b) is to allow for the possibility of *inferential* forms of telepathic and clairvoyant cognition. For example, (D6b) would be satisfied by a case in which *A* correctly infers what *B* is thinking or feeling on the basis of some *other* bit of

---

*I want to resist the temptation to refine this point any further. However important, in other contexts, it may be to examine the notion of direct or proximate causation, such an enterprise would be incommensurate with the limited importance of our definitions—which, as we may recall, were merely intended to help delineate our subject for fruitful discussion.

†I follow the custom of calling the person who initiates the telepathic causal chain (the 'sender') the *agent*. The term 'agent', unfortunately, seems to presuppose a *radiative* or *energy-transfer* view of telepathy, in which the agent *sends* some sort of signal to the *percipient* (another unfortunate term, presupposing—oddly enough—a *perceptual* rather than radiative or transmissive model of telepathy).

telepathic cognition about B (e.g., that B is in mental state ϕ, because he is known telepathically to be in state ψ, which (let us say) presupposes state ϕ). Similarly, (D7b) would be satisfied by a case in which A correctly infers the occurrence of some remote state of affairs on the basis of some other bit of clairvoyant cognition (e.g., A might correctly infer that B's house burned to the ground because he acquired clairvoyant knowledge of a subsequent newspaper headline reporting the event). (D7b) is also satisfied by the case mentioned earlier, in which A comes to know what B is *feeling* on the basis of clairvoyant knowledge of B's overt behavior. But that seems unobjectionable; we simply do not want this case to satisfy (D6b).

Another line of attack on the distinction between telepathy and clairvoyance concerns the larger issue of *experimental ambiguity* in parapsychology. Since, however, it is an issue sufficiently important to warrant separate treatment (see I.A.6.), I shall pass over it for now and return to it shortly (by which time, mercifully, we shall no longer be interested in framing definitions). Meanwhile, let us complete this brief survey of the traditional categories of psi phenomena.

4. Precognition

Perhaps the first thing we must note is that the loose and popular ways of talking about precognition are extremely misleading. First of all, many events tentatively classified as precognitive are not *cognitions* at all. This should come as no surprise, having already noted that telepathy and clairvoyance seem to be non-cognitive. It may even be that precognitive events are simply a subset of the set of telepathic and clairvoyant events. We can, therefore, reject at once one customary way of defining 'precognition'—namely, as 'the non-inferential knowledge [or, even less plausibly, as the *perception*] of some future state of affairs'.*

---

*E.g., B. Brier [21] defines it as 'perception of an object or event which in the future' (p.x).

Secondly, people frequently treat precognitive phenomena as *experiences* of some kind. If we confine ourselves to the sorts of incidents described in anecdotal reports of apparent spontaneous precognitive events—unusually vivid dreams, or waking visions or hallucinations—that characterization is somewhat reasonable. But in the laboratory setting the evidence for precognition often has little or nothing to do with notable experiences on the part of the subject. Instead, it may merely consist of time-displaced correlations between a series of guesses and a series of target cards—for instance, the Soal-Shackleton experiments (see I.B.4.a.). Generally speaking, when the experimental evidence for precognitive ESP involves time-displaced hits between call and target sequences, subjects report no unusual experiences at all (the calls are often made in rapid succession), much less experiences which appear to the subject to be forecasts, or to be about the future (*prospective* experiences, to use Broad's terminology, as contrasted with *retrospective* experiences). In fact, even in successful laboratory studies of apparently precognitive dreams, or in ganzfeld-type precognition tests (see I.A.6. for a description of ganzfeld stimulation), the subject's experiences are typically not about the future—that is, nothing in the experiences themselves 'refers', or points to the future, or strikes the experient as having to do with the future. It is true that the content of the experience is often judged to correspond in intriguing ways to some later event, but that is another matter (see I.B.3.d., and e.g., Krippner *et al.* [86], [88], and Ullman *et al.* [182]). It is not very promising, therefore, to define 'precognition' in terms of some sort of precognitive experience or conscious awareness of the future.

Still, even though a precognitive event need not necessarily terminate in an awareness or a precognitive experience, it seems safe to say that it will terminate in a mental state of some kind or perhaps just a bit of behavior (e.g., a 'guess' about the next card to be turned up or the next lamp to light). In other words, it seems safe to say that a precognitive event produces a state of a *person*. This is hardly an earth-shattering revelation, but it suggests that we can give at least a preliminary *causal* characterization of precognition, in terms of precognitive *states*, somewhat as follows:

(D8) State *s* of person *P* is precognitive =df a causal condition of *s* is some state of affairs occurring later than *s*.

One striking feature of (though not necessarily a flaw in) (D8) is that (D8) does not distinguish precognition from retroactive PK or, for that matter, retroactive clairvoyance or telepathy. This may even be viewed as a virtue by those who regard the traditional divisions of psi phenomena as arbitrary or otherwise unsupportable (see the discussion of experimental ambiguity, in I.A.6.), or by the proponents of currently popular *observational theories* (see I.B.2.e.), according to which all psi phenomena reduce to retroactive PK.

The possibility of including precognitive phenomena under one or more of the other categories of psi phenomena is worth pursuing, since there seem to be two distinct traditions in parapsychology regarding the relationship of precognition to other forms of ESP. According to one, precognitive phenomena are distinct from, and independent of, such psi phenomena as telepathy and clairvoyance. For example, Broad takes this approach in 'The Notion of "Precognition"' (in Smythies [152]: 165-196). He writes:

> If the admitted facts of a case of ostensible precognition could be certainly or plausibly explained in any one, or any combination, of the following ways, we should decline or hesitate to call it a case of *genuine* precognition. The alternative explanations . . . may be divided into (a) those involving nothing but *normal* factors; (b) those involving factors which are *abnormal*, but not paranormal; and (c) those involving *paranormal* factors (p. 182).

Broad's examples of paranormal explanations of ostensibly but not genuinely precognitive events include the following. Person *A* might seem to know precognitively what *B* will do; but this might be due to *A*'s telepathic knowledge of *B*'s disposition or intention to perform that action. Or perhaps *A* unwittingly desires *B* to perform that action, and *A*'s unconscious desire acts telepathically (or psychokinetically) on B as a kind of hypnotic suggestion.

Interestingly, it seems not to have occurred to Broad that the various forms of ESP might have precognitive *modes*— which brings us to the tradition opposing the one represented by Broad. That tradition refuses to admit that precognition is a phenomenon distinct in principle from other forms of ESP. Adherents hold, for example, that telepathy and clairvoyance are sometimes precognitive. In fact, they often claim that all forms of psi phenomena (including PK) are temporally independent in some sense or exhibit a relevant kind of time-displacement. As far as I can tell, this is now the dominant position, and represents a shift away from the position adopted by Broad, which used to dominate. The change is probably due to the fact that recent experimental data have eroded the old idea that psi phenomena generally have a preferred temporal direction. For one thing (as we shall see, in I.B.2.), even PK seems in some cases to be retroactive. For another, many find it arbitrary to place temporal restrictions on the other forms of ESP. Recall that we were able to provide preliminary characterizations of telepathy and clairvoyance without assigning a specific temporal direction to telepathic or clairvoyant phenomena. Nothing in our definition of 'telepathic interaction', for example, precludes B's mental state at t causing A's mental state at some $t' < t$.

Some might object to this tolerance of backward causation on *a priori* grounds, arguing that our concept of causality is such that causal connections can run *only* in the familiar forward direction. On this view, the evidence for precognitive telepathy or clairvoyance cannot justifiably be construed as evidence for unusual sorts of causal connections. I suggest, however, that we can justifiably take an event E to be a causal condition of E' if the occurrence of E is a necessary condition of the occurrence of E'. Also I recommend that we be sufficiently open-minded to allow for the possibility that, in some cases, the necessary conditions of an event E, may occur *after* that event. Although I cannot defend this point at length here, I can at least lay my cards on the table and say that, in my view, the notion of a causal condition of an event is simply that of a necessary condition. Events have many such conditions, and which ones we designate as causes will always reflect our interests of the moment. In other words, for any event, there is no one necessary condition (or set of conditions) which, independently of any and all contexts deserves to be considered the event's cause. In any case, it seems to me that the notion of a necessary condition for an event E is not covertly temporal. One familiar way of unpacking the notion is in terms of an undefined—but apparently atemporal—concept of *impossibility* (presumably *empirical*, rather than logical impossibility in this case), as follows:

E is necessary for E' =df. It is impossible both that E does not occur and that E' occurs.

Here, the issue of the temporal ordering of the two events does not arise.*

In any case, despite its somewhat controversial implications regarding the concept of causality, this second and more recent tradition, taking precognition to be a mode of telepathy and clairvoyance rather than a distinct phenomenon, is the one I shall follow in this book. So when we look more closely at the data later, the evidence for precognition will not be treated separately from the evidence for the other forms of ESP. But I do not intend by this to minimize the importance of time-displaced psi effects. Indeed, there is reason to believe that such effects may be more pervasive and more fundamental than anyone (until recently) has anticipated. For example, in some of the 'remote-viewing' experiments conducted at the Stanford Research Institute (see

*I realize that this position is contentious. But I cannot explore in detail here the entire issue of the intelligibility of the notion of backward causation. There already exists a substantial body of literature on this topic, and for those who wish to explore this issue and its relation to parapsychology, I suggest, as an introduction, Beloff [12], Brier [21], [22], Broad [*op. cit.*], Ducasse [43], [44], Dummett [45], and Mundle [101].

I.B.3.d.), subjects have been asked to describe a randomly selected remote target *currently* being visited by a team of outbound experimenters, while in others subjects are asked to describe a target which the outbound team *will* visit *after* subjects' descriptions are recorded. Results of both sorts of experimental arrangements show that subjects tend to perform better in the precognitive version of the experiment. Assuming these studies provide evidence for ESP, this may indicate that it is easier to use precognitive ESP than real-time ESP.* Furthermore, the scientists at SRI have found that subjects do best in remote-viewing experiments when they are given feedback after the test by being taken to the remote target. One interpretation of this seriously entertained at SRI is that subjects do best in describing remote targets when they can rely on precognition of their subsequent visit to the target location.

In any case, having decided to treat precognitive events as a subset of telepathic or clairvoyant events, (D8) now turns out to be unnecessary. Similarly, we needn't frame a definition for precognition's mirror phenomenon, *retrocognition*, since retrocognitive phenomena would just be another subset of the set of telepathic and clairvoyant phenomena. In retrocognition, the temporal direction of the causal link is the familiar one; retrocognitive states would be produced by some previous event without the mediation of familiar sensory processes. Moreover, like precognitive states, retrocognitive states need not be cognitions.

But I do not want to discard (D8) before conceding openly its most controversial feature—namely, its reliance on the notion of backward causation. For many readers, this feature of (D8)—and presumably of any definition of 'precognition'—is reason enough to consign precognition to the conceptual

---

*For whatever the testimony of famous psychics is worth, Ingo Swann, one of the most thoroughly tested of contemporary psychic superstars, told me in conversation that he finds precognitive ESP easier than real-time ESP. For a sample of the work done with Swann, see Targ & Puthoff [164] and Schmeidler [132]. See also Swann's own book [163].

dust-heap. For the moment, however, let me suggest that that reaction may be premature. Later, we shall review what seems to be remarkable evidence for a kind of retrocausation. This evidence strongly suggests that the acceptability of the idea of retrocausation may not be purely a philosophical issue, and it reminds us that here, as elsewhere, we may need to adjust our thinking to what we discover about the world.

Incidentally, in the paper mentioned earlier, Broad objects not only to a retrocausal account of precognition. It seems he objects to *any* sort of causal account of precognition. For Broad, if event X is a precognition of a later event Y, then (a) it cannot be a chance occurrence that Y follows X, and (b) 'there can be no influence, direct or indirect, either of X on the occurrence of Y or Y on the occurrence of X, and ... X and Y cannot both be causal descendants in different lines of causal ancestry, of a common cause-factor W (p. 194). The point of condition (b) is to rule out *any* causal link (normal, abnormal, or paranormal) between X and Y. Although Broad is not entirely explicit, his intuition seems to be that a precognized event cannot be a causal consequence of its precognition, either directly (in which case Broad might call it PK) or through some common causal ancestor. Broad never defends this intuition; nevertheless, we can sympathize with the idea that precognition would not involve temporally orthodox causal connections. On the other hand, Broad also feels that Y cannot be a causal condition of X, since, at the time of X, Y is just an unrealized possibility, and as such it has no causal consequences at all.

Whether or not we share Broad's intuitions, we can see why he regarded the notion of precognition as internally problematical. Conditions (a) and (b), above, cannot jointly be satisfied. If (b) is satisfied—that is, if there is no causal connection between the precognitive event X and the event Y of which X is a precognition, then Y's following X can *only* be fortuitous; hence, condition (a) cannot then be satisfied.

Broad's view clearly hinges on the rejection of backward causation. But, as I have suggested, our position ought to be responsive to the striking *prima facie* evidence, recently collected, for the existence of retrocausal connections. Moreover, many feel that Broad's view that future events are unrealized possibilities is incompatible with modern physics, which treats time as an inseparable component of a four-dimensional spacetime continuum. They would claim that physics compels us to regard world history as existing in its totality in some timeless sense, and that the unrealized quality of future events is a function of the epistemic limitations of human consciousness and not a mind-independent feature of nature. This is an issue I prefer merely to mention at this point—and then set aside. The interpretation of modern physics and the reality of temporal becoming are matters that warrant a detailed treatment beyond the scope of this book.* For the moment, then, let us waive the issue of the intelligibility of precognition and retrocausation, and continue our survey of the traditional arsenal of parapsychological concepts.

5. Psychokinesis (PK)

Sometimes called 'telekinesis', this is popularly known as the phenomenon of *mind over matter*. Literally, 'psychokinesis' means 'motion produced by the mind'. The reader probably knows the sorts of things that would count as instances of apparent PK, if only from watching recent movies which portray people carrying out paranormal vendettas by willing objects to move in fatal trajectories or willing people to explode. Experimental PK, alas, is somewhat tamer. If one tried to define 'PK' clearly, it would be tempting to say it was the non-motor causal influence of a person (or organism) on a physical system. But this would not do, because it would allow the following inadmissible case.

*But see Werth [192] for a discussion of precognition and the block-universe, as well as other approaches to the explanation of precognition.

Suppose that a person A causes a remote building to explode by means of a sensitive triggering device attached to his body, activated as soon as A's body temperature (or, say, the electromagnetic energy measured on his scalp) exceeds a certain threshold. A's causing the building to blow up would be a form of non-motor and non-muscular influence on the building; but it would surely not be a case of PK.

We might, therefore, try defining 'PK' as 'the causal influence of a person (organism) on a physical system s without any physical interaction between the person's (organism's) body and s'. The trouble with this, however, is that it makes the PK process non-physical *by definition*. Since it seems possible that we might discover physical processes which account for the data of PK, it would be premature to legislate against a physicalist construal of PK. The reader will recognize that this issue is similar to that mentioned in connection with defining the forms of ESP as non-sensory. So perhaps we should follow a strategy similar to that endorsed in the case of our earlier definitions.

(D9) *PK* =df the causal influence of a person (organism) on a physical system s without any known sort of (or scientifically recognized) physical interaction between the person's (organism's) body and s.

It is an obvious pitfall of (D9) that, if PK turns out to be a physical process, and if we later discover what the process is, then either we shall have to alter our definition of 'PK' or else admit that there no longer is any such phenomenon as PK. This parallels the difficulty faced earlier in relativizing telepathy and clairvoyance to sensory processes *known* to science (see the discussion of (D1) in I.A.2.). But since (as before) we can define the major categories of psi phenomena only in terms of our ignorance of the processes involved, the fact that (D9) might become obsolete is, after all, not a defect of that definition.

On the assumption, then, that (D9) will do for our present purposes, some comments are in order. As with the earlier definitions of 'telepathy' and 'clairvoyance' (which threatened to collapse into one another depending on whether our deeper metaphysical commitments were materialistic or idealistic), the relation of PK to the other categories of psi phenomena depends on certain large metaphysical issues. For example, if the physicalists are correct in maintaining that mental events are nothing but physical events, then all cases of telepathy and some cases of clairvoyance turn out to be cases of PK. Thus, an apparent telepathic interaction in which A's mental state causes a change in B's mental state proves to be a case of A's producing a change in a remote physical system. For that matter, it is also a case of a physical system's producing a change in someone's mental state, and so counts as a case of clairvoyance as well.

From the dualist's perspective, moreover, ordinary mind →body interaction may count as a form of PK. In fact, many parapsychologists are dualists, and take mind →brain interaction to be a (or *the*) fundamental form of PK (see Eccles [47] and Popper and Eccles [112], and Beloff's review of the latter [13]). Although it does not make PK less mysterious than does the view that PK effects are always external to the PKer (after all, we must still bridge the gap between the mental and the physical), the dualist's thesis does raise some distinctive questions. If, for example, PK were a pervasive factor in the exercise of human volition (as it would be if mind →brain interaction were a form of PK and also an essential component in the exercise of volition), then we might well ask why PK effects are *localized* almost exclusively in the brain. Why, in other words, should it be easier to exert PK influences on our brains or bodily parts than on the compass needle before us on the table? What typically constrains the range of PK effects?

Actually, we do not know that such effects *are* localized in this way, assuming PK effects do exist. For all we know, every time we exercise a volition, we may be causing PK effects on subatomic systems outside our bodies (perhaps only in our immediate vicinity). Since the best recent evidence for PK has to do with changes produced on the subatomic level, this possibility cannot be ruled out. Still, there are similar puzzles to be considered. For instance, if, in mind →body PK, mental events directly and constantly cause macroscopic physical changes like arm or leg movements, then why should *external* macroscopic PK effects be so infrequent? But even here we must be careful. We do *not* really know that external macroscopic PK effects (assuming they exist) *are* infrequent. Such effects may be occurring all the time, but in ways that fail to attract attention (as they do, for example, in poltergeist phenomena, where for instance, objects suddenly fall off shelves or fly across the room). Still, another question remains: Why should external macroscopic PK effects be more difficult to produce *intentionally* than, say, the raising of one's arm? We *do* know that star PK subjects have much more difficulty producing modest external effects (like moving small objects) than producing bodily movements.

But we are getting ahead of ourselves. These questions may be pursued more profitably after reviewing the evidence for PK, and after taking a more critical look at the continuing debate among materialists, idealists, dualists, and the rest. After all, we have not yet considered whether it is really plausible—or even intelligible—to treat mind→brain interaction as a form of PK.

Rhine, by the way, has suggested that ESP and PK are twin phenomena—that is, two aspects of one general psi process or phenomenon, analogous to the sensory and motor aspects of the central nervous system. But, intriguing as it is, this idea may not be entirely supported by the evidence, which to some extent suggests that ESP is not akin to a sensory phenomenon, or PK, to a motor phenomenon. However, it is *not* outrageous to think that ESP and PK may simply be different manifestations of some general psi phenomenon, and we should keep this possibility in mind. In fact, Rhine coined the expression 'GESP' (*general* ESP) in the belief that finer-grained divisions of ESP-type phenomena may not be experimentally or theoretically justified. And many parapsychologists follow the lead of Thouless and Wiesner

[178] in distinguishing only two classes of phenomena, ψ_γ (psi-gamma) and ψ_κ (psi-kappa). These expressions are coextensive with 'ESP' and 'PK', respectively, but many feel that the Greek terms are the more theory-neutral.

This fuzziness around the borders of the traditional categories of psi-phenomena brings us to the general topic of the experimental justification for these divisions. As we will see, experimental procedures do not render these borders any clearer.

6. Experimental Ambiguity and Purity

A *pure* experiment in parapsychology is an experiment that tests for one and only one psi phenomenon. Experimental purity, however, comes in varying degrees, and the completely pure experiment may be a theoretical impossibilty. Important ambiguities plague not only the concepts, but also the experimental procedures of parapsychology. Several related issues arise here. But the best way to begin may be to consider some paradigmatic difficulties confronting researchers at the end of the nineteenth century and the beginning of the twentieth. In some ESP tests performed during that period, one person (the *agent*) would concentrate on a drawing or a card, and another (the *percipient*),* separated by some means from the agent, would at a specified time try to reproduce the drawing, or identify the card. Some of these tests yielded seemingly impressive results—which were taken as an indication of the existence of mental suggestion (telepathy), until it was discovered that equally impressive results could be obtained in the absence of the agent. Researchers consequently realized that the earlier experiments in thought-transference had been ambiguous. If they indicated the exist-

*As I have already noted, these are unfortunate terms, suggesting that telepathy is either radiative or perceptual. But they are by now fairly well-entrenched members of the philosophical/parapsychological lexicon, and having acknowledged their theoretical dangers, we may now (hopefully) use them with the correct caveats in mind.

ence of some hitherto unexplained phenomenon, it might have been clairvoyance rather than telepathy. In fact, even the later experiments—those appearing to test only for clairvoyance—were plagued by a related ambiguity. The impressive results of those tests appeared to be explainable in principle as due to *precognitive* knowledge of the *subsequent* recording of the order of the cards in the unexamined deck, or of the subsequent examination of the sealed envelope containing the target drawing. In general, one could not be sure whether, in a successful test of clairvoyance (or telepathy), psi was operating in a real-time or in a precognitive mode.

These considerations highlight the principal difficulty in designing pure experiments for telepathy. In order to insure that the extraordinary external influences affecting the percipient's mental state originate in the mind of the agent, it is crucial to avoid recording the target objects or the score of hits and misses. So long as there exists an independent record of what the target objects are, or which guesses were successful, impressive test results can easily be attributed to a phenomenon other than telepathy—for instance, precognitive clairvoyance of the test results. An attempt at a pure telepathy experiment, in which no recorded account of targets and guesses was permitted, has actually been made (see McMahan [94]), but it failed to yield very impressive results. In fact, an impressive test of this sort would still fail to satisfy those determined to test for psi phenomena under strict controls. Presumably, such controls must be public in a way that is ruled out from the start by such tests.

A further ambiguity in telepathy experiments bears on determining who the agent is. To put it somewhat roughly, it is not clear whether telepathic interaction should be construed as a process in which the percipient *invades* the privacy of the agent's world of experience (much as one might invade the privacy of a secret room), or as a process in which the agent *injects* thoughts into, or somehow alters, the flow of the percipient's mental life. The percipient seems to play a more active role in telepathic interaction in the former case; in the latter, the agent seems to be doing the work.

Moreover, as I suggested earlier, precognitive ESP seems *prima facie* to be experimentally indistinguishable from some form of PK, since (i) ostensible precognition may sometimes be analyzed as retroactive PK, and (ii) since there seems to be no way in general of ruling out the possibility that the ostensibly precognitive state of the percipient directly or indirectly caused the ostensibly precognized, later event to occur. Actually, (ii) may not be very troublesome applied to the anecdotal literature. If S dreams at t of some monumental disaster occurring at some $t'>t$, and if we have grounds for believing that S's dream instantiates some psi phenomenon, it may be more reasonable to suppose that S precognized the disaster than that he caused it by dreaming. Is it, for example, plausible to suppose that PK operates on such a scale that a maritime disaster, an earthquake, or World War II could have been caused psychokinetically by anyone's precognitive dreams or visions? Furthermore, Meehl [95] has recently proposed a way of distinguishing precognitive telepathy from agent-PK in at least some types of ESP experiments. This particular ambiguity, then, may not be as serious as some think.

To sum up: Tests designed to elicit evidence for telepathy also provide, in principle, evidence for clairvoyance. Moreover, it is difficult to distinguish experimentally between real-time and precognitive modes of psi. And the results of at least some tests for ESP may also be accounted for in terms of PK (including retroactive PK) affecting experimental equipment, or the brain, of someone connected with the experiment.

Perhaps an even more annoying type of experimental ambiguity concerns the so-called *experimenter effect* in parapsychology. Suppose we are testing a subject for ESP or PK, and suppose that our test results are positive and significant. How can we tell whether the subject exhibited some psi ability, or whether the experimenter did? In other words, how do we rule out the possibility of experimenter PK—for example, on the brain of the subject in an ESP test, or on the PK targets in a PK test? After all, both experimenter and subject are likely to be motivated to see the test succeed, and if the subject can enlist the services of some psi ability (consciously or unconsciously) to produce certain desired results, so presumably can the experimenter.

Some might argue that the use of double-blind experimental designs would resolve this particular ambiguity, since, presumably, the experimenter would be ignorant of the desired outcome. But since tests for psi phenomena presuppose the possibility that such phenomena occur, we must also allow for the possibility that precautions taken in double-blind experiments can be circumvented by the use of experimenter-psi. In general, double-blind procedures rule out only normal means of information-acquisition.

But a case in which the experimenter rather than the (official) subject produces extrachance scores is only one possible sort of experimenter effect. In fact, in some ways it is the least insidious, because significant extrachance scores buttress the experimental evidence for psi even if we are not sure *who* is responsible for the good scores. It is, however, also possible that the experimenter (say, through an unconscious wish to fail or to discredit a colleague's work, or perhaps because of certain personality traits) may somehow influence scores negatively, by 'cancelling out' a subject's psi effort so that scores hover around chance levels. Such an effect (whether normal or paranormal) would clearly complicate the process of interpreting experimental evidence for ESP and PK, since it would interfere with the demonstration of psi within an experiment as well as within a *series* of experiments designed to replicate an earlier successful experiment (see the discussion of replicability in the next section).

Of course, experimenter effects need not be paranormal. But·since we are entertaining here the possibility of psi phenomena, we should be prepared to admit that some experimenter effects in orthodox psychology (see, below, the discussion of the *Rosenthal effect*) might even be due to the operation of some psi ability. And even if we rule out experimenter psi as a way of influencing test results in parapsychology, we should not ignore or underestimate the role of less exotic experimenter effects. Influence may still be exerted through the experimenter's attitude toward the experiment (whether he is a believer or a skeptic) or toward the subjects (whether or not he likes them), or simply through his general personality (whether, e.g., he is enthusiastic, pleasant, compassionate, supportive, or, conversely, negative, cold, stiff, and unrelating) or through the way his personality 'fits' with that of his subjects (e.g., whether they are comfortable with him). On the reasonable assumption that psi abilities, like other human abilities, may be stimulated or inhibited in different psychological environments, we would expect that some researchers might be unable to create an environment conducive to demonstrations of psi. It would not be surprising, for example, if an experimenter's deep (and possibly unconscious) hostility toward parapsychology (or perhaps toward a scientist whose work he is trying to replicate) affects his behavior in ways that make the experimental environment less congenial to the subject. Also, the quality of experimenter/subject interaction might affect the subject's general state of mind so as actually to inhibit psi functioning. As Arthur Koestler has observed [80], it would not be at all surprising if psi functioning were as sensitive to context as, say, penile erection in the human male.

It may even be such experimenter influences that explain why John Beloff and his associates at the University of Edinburgh have so consistently failed to obtain positive results in parapsychology experiments. (I invite the reader to corroborate this by reviewing the Edinburgh team's research reports, in *Research in Parapsychology*.) Although some successful experiments by British parapsychologists (like Carl Sargent) have begun to erode the view that, *in general*, the British cannot get positive results, and although there seems to be no official or systematic data on the different success rates of American and British parapsychologists, the apparent disparity between research in Britain and the United States has been notorious enough to prompt Beloff to comment.

> . . . when it comes to the phenomena, the Atlantic does seem to represent some kind of a *divide*. There have been occasions this year when, getting together with my friends at the Society for Psychical Research in London, we have asked one another, in mournful tones, whether perhaps ESP is not just something that happens in America! ([8] : 197).

Interestingly, although parapsychologists recognize the importance, for psi functioning, of the experimental environment, there is as yet no general agreement as to what sort of environment elicits the best performance, or (to put the point in the jargon of Information Theory) best reduces 'noise' in the channel. For example, two rather different approaches are exhibited by the research teams at the Stanford Research Institute and Maimonides Hospital, in Brooklyn. In their *remote viewing* experiments at SRI (see I.B.3.d.), scientists feel that a soothing, relaxed, and *familiar* environment best reduces psychic noise; subjects are accordingly provided a comfortable and softly-lit room. The room contains comfortable chairs and a large comfortable sofa, and the subject may sit wherever he or she wishes, or even recline on the sofa (or, I suppose, on the floor, although to my knowledge no one has elected to do so). The director of parapsychological research at Maimonides Hospital, Charles Honorton, takes a quite different approach. He also believes that the general experimental environment should be congenial and supportive; but he favors the use of more exotic means of placing the subject in a psi-conducive state. For example, he uses biofeedback techniques in conjunction with a form of sensory alteration called *ganzfeld* stimulation (see also I.B.3.d.), which a subject undergoes while sealed alone in an electrically-shielded, sound-proof and shock-proof chamber. Although the subject gets to remove his shoes and recline in a reclining chair, he also has ping-pong ball halves taped over his eyes and listens to white noise played over headphones.

Between the diffused light resulting from the ping-pong balls and the hissing of the white noise, the subject is presented with a relatively homogeneous visual and auditory field. The purpose of this is to quiet major sources of sensory stimulation and (through the resulting reduction in potentially distracting patterning) to allow other mental processes to emerge more clearly. Unlike the SRI experiments, in which subject and experimenter continue to interact face to face even while responses are being given, at Maimonides, relaxed interaction with the experimenter is usually suspended during ganzfeld stimulation, or is at least conducted via intercom as the subject listens to the experimenter's voice through headphones. But the researchers at SRI, while they do not deny that ganzfeld stimulation can enhance psi functioning (in fact, the evidence supports the utility of this method; see Honorton's reviews of ganzfeld research [69] and [70], and Palmer's review in Krippner [85]: 114ff.) nevertheless feel that ganzfeld stimulation is too unusual and introduces its own kind of noise.*

I will not attempt to resolve this disagreement. Both SRI and Maimonides Hospital boast successful experiments, and so it does not seem that either procedure uniquely leads to success or failure. Furthermore, the experiments at neither of the two locations were identical in all features save the environment in which subjects gave their responses. I would suggest, then, that we need more data before pronouncing either method better than the other.

Another reason for exploring the possible influence of the experimenter's attitude on test results concerns the so-called

---

*My own experience, in being tested at Maimonides Hospital, was that ganzfeld stimulation was extremely distracting. But I was tested only once in this way; and I would not be at all surprised if, after one or two more such experiences (which, by the way, I found to be great fun), the peculiar features of this artificial condition would no longer seem distracting. In fact, according to Honorton and the Maimonides subjects I have interviewed, this is what veterans of the ganzfeld experience report.

sheep-goat effect. This effect was first tested for in the early 1940s by Gertrude Schmeidler (see Schmeidler & McConnell [133]). Schmeidler divided her subjects into two classes, those who accepted the possibility of ESP under the test conditions and those who did not. Members of these classes she labelled, respectively, 'sheep' and 'goats'. Schmeidler found that sheep score more positively than goats on card-guessing tests. Although many of the numerous replication attempts have failed to confirm Schmeidler's results, about one-third of them have succeeded (according to Palmer's survey; see [102], [103], and his essay in Krippner [85]); moreover, all significant sheep-goat differences have been in the predicted direction (that is, there have been no statistically significant results in which goats scored higher than sheep).

Now, if the subject's attitude may influence the result of a psi experiment, then since we cannot in principle rule out experimenter influence, we must admit the possibility that the attitude of the experimenter may significantly affect the experimental outcome as well. And since we apparently cannot rule out the possibility of experimenter psi, in principle at least the experimenter must be counted as much a subject of the experiment as the (official) subject, and his attitudes and predispositions as well as the subject's must, in principle, be taken into account.*

Another reason for conceding the possibility of experimenter effects in parapsychology is the reasonably well-documented existence of such effects in orthodox psychological research. Not only is there evidence that the sex, behavior, and personality of the experimenter can affect an experimental outcome with a subject, but there is also evidence that the experimenter's *expectations* concerning research results also affect the experimental outcome. This effect of experimenter expectancy is called the *Rosenthal* effect, named after the psychologist Robert Rosenthal (see [127], [128]; and

---

*See the next section for futher remarks about sheep/goat results and the concept of negative psi.

Martin [92] for a philosophical discussion of this effect), who first attempted to demonstrate such effects experimentally.* In one well-known experiment conducted by Rosenthal and his associates, subjects were asked to rate photographs of human faces according to a numerical scale supposed to gauge the degree to which the subject felt the person in the photograph was experiencing success or failure. The scale ranged from −10 (extreme failure) to +10 (extreme success). Half the experimenters were led to believe that the 'correct' results would hover around +5, while the other half were led to believe that the 'correct' result would be approximately −5. Each experimenter was given exactly the same instructions to read to subjects, and was not permitted to deviate from the script. In this experiment, and even more dramatically in replication attempts, subjects scored in the direction expected by their experimenters. In all cases, the differences between the scores of the two experimental groups were statistically significant. In the original experiment and its two replications, the probabilities associated with the differences between the two scores were .007, .0003, and .005, respectively (see Rosenthal [127]:143ff).

In another famous series of experiments, experimenters were provided with groups of rats which they were told had been bred to be maze (or Skinnerbox)-bright or maze (or Skinnerbox)-dull; and the experimenters believed that their tests were designed to confirm the success of this selective breeding. But in fact, the rats had not been selectively bred for their dullness or brightness. Groups of rats assigned to the different experimenters were selected so as to mini-

---

*Rosenthal's results have been challenged on methodological grounds by other psychologists (see, e.g., Barber [3], and Jensen [73]). But even Rosenthal's critics tend to admit that some tests for experimenter expectancy effects are sound and that such effects do exist. For simplicity, then, I will sidestep the methodological issues surrounding Rosenthal's work, especially since the alleged flaws in his work are not ineliminable problems in his basic experimental designs, but are sometimes merely due to the improper application of experimental procedures. Procedural lapses aside, then, Rosenthal's experimental designs and results are still useful for illustrating the points I wish to make.

mize differences between them (each group had two males and three females, and the mean age was 12-13 weeks). Which groups were to be labeled dull or bright was decided randomly. Nevertheless, the rats believed by their experimenters to be bright outperformed those believed to be dull (Rosenthal [127]:158ff).

Results similar to these were obtained in a test (known now as the *Pygmalion* experiment) involving elementary school children. Rosenthal describes the experiment as follows.

> All the children in an elementary school were administered a non-verbal test of intelligence, which was disguised as a test that would predict intellectual "blooming." There were eighteen classrooms in the school, three at each of the six grade levels. Within each grade level, the three classrooms were composed of children with above average ability, average ability, and below average ability, respectively. Within each of the eighteen classrooms, approximately 20% of the children were chosen at random to form the experimental group. Each teacher was given the names of the children from her class who were in the experimental condition. The teacher was told that these children had scored on the "test for intellectual blooming" such that they would show remarkable gains in intellectual competence during the next eight months of school. The only difference between the experimental group and the control group children, then, was in the mind of the teacher.
>
> At the end of the school year, eight months later, all the children were retested with the same IQ test. Considering the school as a whole, those children from whom the teachers had been led to expect greater intellectual gain showed a significantly greater gain in IQ than did the children of the control group. ([128] : 260; see also [127] : 410ff).

Without trying to decide how, exactly, experimenter expectancy leads to desired test results, I should mention a possibly important feature of the experiments in photograph rating. The first replication attempt differed from the original in an important respect. In the original experiment the stimulus photographs were held, one by one, before the subject so that they could be rated. And of course the experimenter holding the photos had already been led to expect the ratings to be of one sort rather than another. But in the first replication the photos were mounted on cardboard and labelled, so that the subject could evaluate the photographs without looking at the experimenter and then just call out the rating. The reason for doing this was to reduce the likelihood that the subject was receiving subtle sensory cues from the experimenter—for example, from his hand as he held the photos, or from his face, which in the first experiment would have been in the subject's field of vision during the rating process. It was by means of such extremely subtle sensory cues that the horse Clever Hans had been able to perform his apparently astounding feats of intelligence (see Pfungst [106]). In spite of these additional precautions, however, this particular experiment showed the largest rating biases of the three. Although this result does not lead directly to cosmic conclusions about the nature of the experimenter influence in such experiments (much less their paranormal nature), it nevertheless strongly suggests that such influence is quite unlike that which Pfungst discerned in the case of Clever Hans. From the first replication, it appears that experimenter expectancy led to biases in the ratings, even though experimenters did not handle the stimulus material and they were not always in the subject's field of vision. Clever Hans, on the other hand, lost his 'abilities' when his interrogator, or the experimenter, was located outside the horse's field of vision. I am not suggesting that the next natural conclusion is that experimenter psi (e.g., PK) accounts for the biases in the ratings. Still, this remains a live option, depending on the strength of the evidence for various sorts of PK, or perhaps telepathy (as in the Soviet studies in telepathic suggestibility, described in I.B.4.c.).

One final complication: if the so-called *observational theories* of psi (see I.B.2.e.) are correct in maintaining that all psi influence reduces to a form of *retroactive* PK, then we should expect to be able to find evidence of *retroactive* experimenter effects. Recent studies by Broughton [25] and

Sargent [131] have tested for this, Sargent's results (in a test for retroactive experimenter *expectancy* effects) are especially suggestive.

In any case, having now considered various respects in which the results of psi experiments are ambiguous, it should come as no surprise that these ambiguities complicate the process of evaluating attempts to *replicate* such experiments. But this evaluation process is both enormously complicated and important, and deserves a section to itself.

7. Experimental Replicability.

Critics of parapsychology—and, in fact, sometimes even its defenders—often claim that the major obstacle to this field's acceptance by the scientific community at large is its failure to produce a repeatable experiment. I want now to examine this claim. I shall argue, first, that it rests on a naive conception of what experimental repeatability is, in both parapsychology and science generally; second, that it fails to take seriously the nature of parapsychology and the reasons why it should, *in principle*, be difficult to repeat experiments in this field; and third, that once we see how loose a notion experimental repeatability is, the claim that there have been no repeatable experiments in parapsychology is at best highly questionable.

It is clear enough why so much emphasis is placed on the replication of experiments, both in parapsychology and in orthodox science. Replication is considered the principal means of legitimizing experimental results. The underlying idea is that if an experiment E gives a certain result, while replication attempts do not reproduce that result, we have good reason to regard E's result as scientifically unacceptable or inconclusive. If continued attempts to replicate E fail to duplicate E's result, we have, it would seem, *prima facie* evidence for taking that result to be due to a flaw in E's experimental design, or to experimenter negligence or incompetence, or perhaps even to chicanery. As a rule, then, only experiments whose results can be repeated are considered genuine and reliable; in this way experimental repeatability serves as a kind of demarcation criterion between science and non-science. Thus, according to the common wisdom, if a field like parapsychology claims to be scientific, but cannot design repeatable—and hence reliable—experiments, we simply must refuse to accord it the status of a science.

It seems to me, however, that experimental repeatability is at best only a very crude demarcation criterion. First of all, criteria of, and reliance on, repeatability vary from one science to another. These differences are especially pronounced when we compare behavioral with non-behavioral sciences. But even in non-behavioral sciences, the relative importance of, or reliance on, experimental repeatability varies—for example, as between geology and physics. And in parapsychology, criteria of repeatability may be so difficult to apply—or even formulate—that the results of replication attempts may not be a reliable guide to its status as a science. Moreover, if psi phenomena really have some of the features they appear or are alleged to have, then the notion of a successful replication in parapsychology turns out to be far from clear, and repeating an experiment in parapsychology may not be nearly as straightforward a matter as some have suggested.* My remarks here are inspired and guided by some first-rate and philosophically sophisticated papers by a British sociologist of science, H. M. Collins [30], [31] (see also, Ransom [116] for a discussion of repeatability and a survey of other criticisms leveled against parapsychology).

In order to see just how crude the notion of experimental repeatability is, let us begin by asking: In what respects can replication attempts differ from the original experiment? It is clear, first of all, that no replication attempt can ever be *exactly* the same as the original, if only because of changes in the time and place of the experiment. But of course such

---

*See, e.g., Flew's extremely superficial treatment of the issue of repeatability in [52].

differences tend to be accompanied by differences in the general conditions of the experiment, or the experimental environment. These may include differences in the actual participants. But even if the participants remain the same, we can expect changes in their attitude or mood, or even in the condition of the experimental apparatus required (especially sophisticated, sensitive, or delicate equipment), all of which may vary subtly or dramatically from one test to another.

To some extent, similar differences between experiments and their replication attempts may be found even in the hard sciences. In physics, an experiment conducted at laboratory L with a certain kind of particle accelerator may be replicated at laboratory L' with a different design of accelerator. In microbiology, experiments conducted with microorganism M in solution S may be replicated by studying M in a different solution S' (which may have been more convenient to use, but whose differences are treated as not making a difference); in fact, even a different microorganism M' may have been substituted, and its differences discounted. And of course despite the expectations of the replicating scientist, it is always possible that such differences between experiments can lead to differences in experimental outcome. In physics, for example, some of the inevitable differences between experiments and their attempted replications may account for the mixed results of efforts to carry out the crucial experiment suggested by Einstein, Podolsky and Rosen, which addresses the issue of whether the world can be said to be in a fixed state independently of any observer (see [48]). In fact, various attempts to test this famous thought experiment have not even studied the same particles. One uses proton pairs, and the others, photons.* Yet they are all considered versions of the same experiment. If one of these experiments supports the predictions of quantum mechanics—against Einstein *et al.*, then the other experiments will, if they also support those predictions, be considered repli-

Scientific American 239 (July 1978): 72f.

cations of the first. The differences between these may be ignored, then, if their results agree, but those same differences may be deemed both relevant and important if these different experiments produce relevantly different sorts of results.

Although replication attempts in parapsychology may differ from one another in respects similar to those in the hard sciences, the problems of repeatability in parapsychology are for the most part more akin to those in the behavioral sciences, and have to do with the ways in which (possibly inevitable) differences concerning the *participants* are relevant to the outcomes of an experiment and its replication attempts. Let E_1 be our original experiment, and let E_2 be a replication attempt. Among the inevitable differences between E_1 and E_2, accompanying those of time and place, will be differences in the state of mind of the participants. Now assuming psi exists, it is reasonable to suppose that the manifestation of psi, like ordinary behavioral phenomena, is critically dependent on the state of mind of the subject and of those around him. Presumably, then, just as they may alter the outcome of experiments in psychology, variations in the psychological environment or atmosphere may affect the results of experiments in parapsychology. From the very start, then, parapsychologists face the problem that the ability to manifest psi phenomena may be as context-dependent and as fragile as such ordinary abilities as the ability to be witty, or sensual, or of being able to shoot free-throws. In effect, then, the experimental outcome of E_2 may differ from that of E_1 simply in virtue of ordinary psychological changes in the subject or experimenter, perhaps due even to such mundane things as changes in the weather, or something one of the participants read that morning in a newspaper.

What is extremely important about all this—for the hard as well as the behavioral sciences—is that (as I mentioned above) when, despite the inevitable and potentially relevant differences between E_1 and E_2, scientists agree that E_2 successfully replicates E_1, such (actual) differences will be *discounted*. So the notion of replication is rather loosely used in science. Moreover, since such differences cannot be avoided and may well lead to a difference in outcome for two experiments, we must concede as well that the *failure* of E_2 to achieve the same results as E_1 does not automatically discredit or even cast serious doubt on E_1. The situation changes somewhat when a *series* of replication attempts fails to produce the results of the original experiment. But as I shall show in more detail below, even this would not automatically discredit the original experiment.

Those who insist on the importance of experimental repeatability might protest that these concessions simply amount to a refusal to be scientific—or else constitute a tacit admission that parapsychology (perhaps like much, if not all, of psychology proper) is not a genuine science. They might argue that, even admitting inevitable differences between E_1 and E_2 and the fact that, in practice (even in the hard sciences), many such differences may be ignored, one could still specify, in principle, the respects in which E_1 and E_2 must be similar if E_2 is to count as a replication of E_1. Thus Spencer Brown remarks,

> We want results which are not only consistent in one experiment, but which can be observed to recur in further experiments. This does not necessarily mean that they must be repeatable at will. A total eclipse of the sun is not repeatable at will; nevertheless it is demonstrably repeatable—we can give a recipe for its repetition. And this is the minimum we look for in science. We must be able to give a recipe (from 'Discussion' in Wolstenholme & Millar [199] : 44).

But this hope that such general criteria (or recipes) of repeatability are specifiable, I will now argue, is nothing more than wishful thinking. Not only does it ignore certain interesting facts about the ways scientists actually operate, as well as most of what is interesting about experimentation in parapsychology, but it also ignores some extremely important philosophical truths.

Perhaps the best way to approach this topic is to consider various sorts of reasonable possible differences between an experiment and its replication attempts, and then see whether we can sensibly specify ground rules which lay down which such differences are admissable.

Differences in the Domain of Phenomena. Suppose that psi experiment E_1 is conducted at time t, and that we search through all the activities occurring after t to see whether any count as replications of E_1. As Collins observes, one might think that we should reasonably reject, first, all those activities that do not concern the phenomena of parapsychology at all. But how do we do this, if (as some maintain) psi phenomena manifest themselves in the most rudimentary sorts of physical phenomena? Some contend that such things as cell differentiation and embryonic development are actually functions of paranormal occurrences at the cellular level (see Randall [115]). Moreover, there is now a large body of evidence suggesting that humans and other animals can affect subatomic processes (see I.B.2.). If these suggestions are true, or even just reasonable, then we cannot be sure when psi phenomena are occurring and when they are not.

But let us not get bogged down so soon. Let us suppose that we have some idea which activities occurring after t are experiments (and not merely preliminary observations) and, of these, which concern the domain of phenomena investigated in E_1. And now let us consider various additional possible differences between these experiments and E_1.

Differences in Design. In what ways may the experimental design of E_2 differ from that of E_1? This question concerns much more than mere differences in experimental apparatus, or in time, place, and mood. Apart from such differences, we may still wonder whether, for instance, experimental protocols must be the same if E_2 is to replicate E_1. Sometimes, of course, differences in apparatus may require differences in experimental design, but even if we ignore this class of differences, exact duplication of experimental protocols is not a requirement either in the behavioral sciences or, to some extent, in the hard sciences. Parapsychology follows their lead in this regard. In both parapsychology and psychology, E_2 may differ from E_1 with respect to such things as the method of stimulating, or eliciting a response from, a subject, providing a subject with feedback, evaluating responses from a subject, or in the type of interaction permitted between experimenter and subject, or even in the type of response required of the subject. In the actual life of the experimenting scientist such differences between experimental designs may be regarded as unimportant. It seems, then, that there may be a range of allowable variations in design between an experiment and its replications. Certainly there are no clear criteria for specifying the limits of this range, much less for specifying them in advance.

With respect to the importance actually given these kinds of differences in psi experiments, Collins observes an interesting conflict within parapsychology itself. Some parapsychologists aver it to be *desirable* that replication attempts employ different designs from those used in E_1. They argue that the evidence for psi phenomena is as good as it is, precisely because the phenomena have been demonstrated under more than one sort of experimental situation. From this point of view, confirmatory experiments in parapsychology perhaps should not—or at least need not—be replications of experimental designs. On the other hand, many (and perhaps even some of the same) parapsychologists would not hesitiate to dismiss negative results of experiments which employed designs different from their own.

Of course these two positions are not incompatible. Although it is possible (and even desirable) for psi phenomena to be demonstrated by different means, departures from a successful experimental design may nevertheless omit something essential to the demonstration or manifestation of the phenomena. After all, so little is known about psi phenomena (assuming they exist) that we cannot say in advance which deviation in design will affect the experimental outcome, or whether the outcome will be affected positively or negatively.

But now, let us suppose that we are clear about how the designs of E_1 and E_2 may differ permissably, and let us consider what other sorts of differences may be tolerated.

Differences in Participants. So far we have considered cases where the participants in experiments E_1 and E_2 are the same. But we may wonder, for example, whether the results of E_2 would carry more weight as a replication if the *subjects* of E_1 and E_2 had been different. On the assumption that most people are incapable of manifesting psi abilities either dramatically or reliably enough for laboratory studies, it is clear that not just any random person can serve as a good subject. Although obtaining similar results with different subjects may strengthen our confidence in E_1's results, we must leave open the possibility that the subject of E_1 is unique, or that the subject/experimenter combination of E_1 works uniquely well. So it looks as if E_2 can successfully replicate E_1 whether the subjects are the same or different. At least, there seems to be no general requirement that we must observe here.

But what about the experimenter? Must the experimenter in E_2 be the same as the experimenter in E_1? Ordinarily in science, a replication attempt is considered successful and convincing when it is conducted by someone *other* than the original scientist. Popper, for example, writes, 'any empirical scientific statement can be presented (by describing experimental arrangements etc.) in such a way that *anyone who has learned the relevant techniques* can test it' ([111]: 99, emphasis added). Beloff concurs.

> One rule that science insists upon is that no new discovery be admitted to the general body of scientific knowledge until it has been checked and corroborated by some independent investigator. Only thus can we insure against the fallibility of the individual worker. In parapsychology, however, although we pay lip service to the principle of repeatability, we indulge in every manner of special pleading in order to cover up our failure to honour it . . . if we want to be treated on a par with the other sciences, then we cannot flout the very criteria that are used to distinguish the genuine from the pseudo-science ([7]: 131-132).

In parapsychology, however, it may be unreasonable to insist that replications be successfully conducted by someone other than the original experimenter. Although successes by different experimenters would be desirable in most cases, we should perhaps weaken the *demand* for such replication, in light of the possibility of an experimenter effect in parapsychology (including the possibility of experimenter PK), and of the widely acknowledged existence of experimenter effects in orthodox psychological experiments. Presumably, it is possible that only a few experimenters are capable of producing an environment conducive to good psi demonstrations, either generally or with specific subjects. But if so, then we should not *insist* that replication attempts always be conducted by a different experimenter from that in the original experiment.

Moreover, taking this possibility seriously is not just a way of letting parapsychology off the hook. In fact, the situation we are envisioning, in which only a few experimenters may be able to create psi-conducive environments, has important analogues in familiar life situations. Most people are aware that they can reveal certain sides of themselves to, or that they feel free or able to do certain things with, certain other people only. For example, some people sing, tell jokes, or act sexy only with those in whose company they are extremely comfortable. But even if we ignore the more intimate or more vulnerable sides of ourselves (one may not, after all, feel it to be scary or revealing to demonstrate psi abilities), there may still be certain sides of ourselves which only a few people are able to encourage or stimulate. For example, perhaps only a few people will excite in us a certain kind or style of humor. Perhaps in the company of most people I feel like joking in the manner of certain night-club comedians, while with a small circle of friends I tend to manifest a more Oscar-Wildeish sense of humor. Or perhaps with some people my humor tends to be gentle and compassionate, while with others it tends to be hard, cutting and sarcastic.

I see no reason to deny that a similar situation might obtain in parapsychology—that certain experimenters might be able to make subjects feel all right about demonstrating psi abilities, or that they might be uncommonly or uniquely able to inspire their subjects. The evidence is certainly compatible with the idea that psi manifestation is a fragile ability, and that relatively few experimenters can create psi-conducive environments, and that certain subjects can work with certain experimenters only. But in that case we must concede that merely mastering the relevant techniques may *not* qualify a scientist to replicate a parapsychology experiment; and we may not, in advance of actual efforts, be able to determine who can repeat a certain experimental result. The experimenter, we may recall, is (in principle) as much a subject in psi experiments as the official subject; and, if psi abilities are not uniformly distributed among humans, then changing experimenters, like changing official subjects, may be fatal to replication attempts. This is, actually, how many would explain the fact that Helmut Schmidt is more successful than anyone else in replicating the experiments of Helmut Schmidt (see I.B.2.).

Furthermore, if experimenter psi or a less exotic experimenter effect may obtain, due say (as in psychology), to the expectations, attitude, or character of the experimenter, then we might even *expect* different results from replication attempts by different experimenters. In fact, as I mentioned earlier, the rather notorious failure of many British parapsychologists to get positive results may even support the existence of such an experimenter effect. Thus, if the British really do tend to exert a negative experimenter effect, it would be counter-productive to seek British replications. And of course an analogous problem may obtain on a smaller scale—for example, perhaps all those at a certain laboratory exert such an effect (the results from Edinburgh seem to demonstrate something like this).

For these reasons, it is tempting to suppose—at least with experimenters whose biases are well-known—that we could predict the appearance of such effects and, using our successful predictions, thereby evaluate the results of replication attempts. But the situation may be more complicated than this. If an experimenter may (perhaps by PK) influence the outcome of an experiment through unconscious or subconscious biases or desires, we may never reliably control the experimenter effect in parapsychology. If not, then even incorrect but inductively well-supported predictions of an experimenter effect would not necessarily discredit a particular experimental design or result.

Suppose, for example, that successful experiment E_1 is conducted by a parapsychologist who regularly obtains positive results in his experiments. If replication attempt E_2 is conducted by a similarly successful parapsychologist—to make things simple, assume the test subjects to be the same—it might be reasonable to expect E_2 to yield positive results as well. But suppose that the results of E_2 do *not* duplicate the positive results of E_1. This hardly warrants the conclusion that the results of E_1 are spurious. After all, the replicating scientist might have had a bad day. He may have been feeling negative or irascible; perhaps he did not 'hit it off' with the subject; or perhaps he was harboring an unconscious desire to discredit a colleague's work. In fact for these reasons, even *repeated* failures by the replicating scientist need not conclusively discredit E_1.

Thus, when we consider the possibility that the state of mind of the experimenter may be causally—and in particular, psychokinetically—related to the experimental outcome, and when we realize that the experimenter's influence or psi functioning may be long-term or short-term, and may be unknown to the experimenter and to all others, we cannot help but appreciate the difficulty in determining, in particular cases, whether the experimenter's attitude or interests render him unable to serve as a replicating scientist. For example, there is no way to be sure whether his presence would tend to suppress or cancel out the subject's psi activity. Such considerations frustrate all our attempts to specify general criteria of experimenter appropriateness in replication attempts. In fact, as we have seen, we are not even entitled merely to insist that the experimenter in E_1 be different from the one in E_2. E_2 can count as a replication of E_1 whether or not the experimenter is the same in both cases.

Interestingly, Collins tries to state one sort of general requirement concerning experimenter appropriateness. He argues that 'the greater the social and cognitive separation of [the original experimenter] and a repeating scientist, the greater the value of a positive replication' ([30] : 7). In other words it is presumably preferable for replicating scientists to have a kind of social or theoretical distance from the original scientist. Ideally, perhaps, the replicating scientist should not be a student of, or a strong sympathizer with, the original scientist. A skeptic's replication of E_1, for example, may be judged more convincing than replication by one of the original scientist's students who, as it happens, is also a firm believer in the paranormal. (To concede this, of course, is not to demand that replications be conducted only or principally by skeptics.)

On the other hand, if the cognitive and social distance between the two scientists is too great—for example, if the replicating scientist is an adversary of the original scientist and hopes for negative results in order to discredit him—then such results may reflect the replicating scientist's state of mind more than flaws in the original experiment. So perhaps all we can say, seeking a rough measure of experimenter appropriateness, is that the replicating scientist should be as emotionally detached from the experiment as possible, and that he should have no particular investment in getting a certain kind of result. Of course, this is hardly very helpful, since it is ridiculous to expect total detachment from any scientist who has any interest in his work. And in whatever respects a scientist wavers from this virtually unattainable total neutrality, he runs the risk of inadvertently influencing the experimental outcome.

Differences in Kind of Result. An especially vexing problem in the attempt to distinguish successful from unsuccessful replication attempts concerns the topic of positive and negative experimental results. On the surface, one would think that once we have decided that the design of E_2 copies that of E_1 (even though there may be no general criteria for determining this), all we need to do is to see whether E_2, like E_1, yields positive results. But in parapsychology, the very notion of *positive experimental results* is extremely unclear.

From one point of view, the result of an attempt to replicate E_1 is negative when it fails to produce significant deviations from mean chance expectation over a series of trials. From another point of view, however, E_2's failure to produce significant scores needn't undermine the legitimacy of E_1, since the absence of such deviations in E_2 may be a manifestation of either experimenter incompetence or a persistent experimenter effect. In this last case, moreover, the failure to get significant results might actually be regarded as a kind of positive result itself—evidence for the occurrence of a psi phenomenon in which the experimenter inhibits or cancels out the results of the subject's psi functioning. In this way we could interpret the failure of the Edinburgh parapsychologists to get significant results as positive (albeit not very conclusive) evidence for the existence of psi phenomena.

A related, but more important, phenomenon with respect to which the distinction between positive and negative results has been blurred is that of *negative psi*, or *psi-missing*. For many years, extending through Rhine's early work at Duke University, only one kind of quantitative measure of psi abilities was recognized. In order to demonstrate psi, subjects in quantitative experiments had to score significantly and consistently *above* chance levels. Some experimenters, however, noticed that certain subjects scored significantly and consistently *below* chance levels, and it appeared to many that such deviation from chance scoring might furnish a new sort of evidence for psi phenomena, a kind of *psi-missing* rather than psi-*hitting*. This conjecture was also supported by evidence for the *sheep/goat* effect (see I.A.6.).

The notion of psi-missing is rather curious, and merits a short digression. Some have maintained that we can best interpret these consistent below-chance scores as resulting from the subject's using some psi ability (presumably subconsciously) in the service of producing poor scores, perhaps to discredit parapsychology, or for some other reason.* In such cases the subject might use ESP to identify the correct target in order to be sure to 'guess' the wrong one. Otherwise, it seems, there would be no way of ensuring the continued below-chance scoring, and scores would hover around chance levels.

Rhine, however (in [121]), has argued that psi-missing may not be a function simply of the subject's *motivation* to produce low scores. He observes that psi-missing often occurs under conditions of *stress*. For example, in studies conducted in India (Rao, Kanthamani and Sailaja [117]), subjects tested before an important interview showed significant psi-missing, although positive scores were obtained in post-interview sessions. Rhine suggests that, while under stress subjects may inadvertently alter whatever subconscious 'strategy' or procedure they employ when using ESP (e.g., instead of responding to the first idea that comes to mind, they may wait for the most vivid one, or they may modify guesses in order to avoid the appearance of *patterns* in their calls). Thus, a 'change of method' (as he calls it) may account for negative deviations. But whether these 'methods' do or do not involve the use of any psi ability requires further probing.

First of all, the idea that psi subjects employ subconscious —and often maladaptive—calling strategies has been explored in another context by Tart (see I.B.3.e.). This idea strikes me as at least reasonable, and perhaps even plausible. Certainly, there is nothing objectionable in supposing that a person's behavior can be guided by goals and strategies of which he is not consciously aware. Consider, for example, people who tend to behave in a manipulative or controlling way, or who tend to draw attention to themselves. Such people are

---

*In a series of experiments conducted by Dukhan and Rao [46], some meditation students showed significant psi-missing when tested prior to meditation and significant psi-hitting after meditation. Some have suggested that the psi-missing was due to a subconscious desire to demonstrate the value of meditation. Rhine's suggestion (see text, below) seems more plausible to me, however.

often genuinely unaware consciously that their behavior shows such regularities, and particular instances of such behavior are usually unconsciously improvised in immediate response to the behavior of others. In general, *how* the attention-getter (say) draws attention to himself is not something planned in advance. He may not even be consciously aware of the need for attention, and what he will feel is required in a particular case in order to draw attention to himself is not (barring precognition) something he knows in advance. Yet his spontaneous behavior may be so successfully designed to command our attention that we could reconstruct his behavior plausibly as the result of a process of calculation. And of course sometimes a person's behavioral strategies may not be well-adapted to his situation. For example, behavior designed to get attention or produce friendly responses in others may produce avoidance behavior (as psychologists often like to call it) instead. Since these sorts of unconscious or subconscious behavioral strategies are familiar components of behavior, it is plausible to suppose that, in making calls on ESP tests, one may likewise be guided by unconscious strategies which (like behavioral strategies generally) may vary from one situation to another and be either successful or unsuccessful.

In the case of psi-missing in *PK* tests, of course, appeals to *calling* strategies are out of the question. We may, however, be able to appeal to something more like a *strategy of attack* or a *game plan*. Just as in tennis, say, a player might vary the way he approaches or spins the ball, or just as he might vary broader matters of strategy like playing aggressively rather than letting the opponent make the mistakes, and just as differences in these different sorts of strategy can lead to different sorts of results, a PK subject may similarly have different ways of engaging in a PK task which likewise lead to differences in experimental outcome. A tennis player's serves may tend to be long because the player hits the ball early in his swing. An adjustment in his swing, however, or in the way he throws the ball, may cause his serves to fall in-bounds with greater regularity. I am not, of course, suggesting that we take this analogy too literally. For example, PK may not require an *effort* in anything like the sense in which tennis serves require an effort. Yet PK, like a tennis serve, may nevertheless be something a subject *does* or initiates, and that has different forms or modes. So it seems reasonable enough to suppose that PK efforts, like tennis serves, are not all of a kind, and that differences in effort can lead to differences in result. Just as a tennis player may tend to hit long serves, a PK subject may exercise PK in a way that tends to produce −1s rather than +1s on a random number generator (in a test situation where +1s count as hits).

Notice, though, that subconscious strategies can only be part of the story in explaining persistent non-chance scores. Even if it is plausible to attribute subconscious strategies or changes in strategy to subjects in psi experiments, appeals to such strategies do not seem to explain why subjects' scores should be statistically significant, especially over a long series of trials. If a subject uses no psi ability during a test, one would think that test scores would be at chance levels or would tend to reduce to chance levels as the number of trials increased, *no matter* what strategy the subject was using. Concentrating just on *calling* strategies for ESP tests, a certain strategy (say, basing calls on one's most *vivid* idea) may, for a time, produce non-chance results. But unless the strategy is somehow linked to an appropriate psi ability— for example, if one's most vivid ideas tended to be produced by ESP of the target, or, on the contrary, if one's *first* idea tended to be of the target while the most vivid tended to be distinct from it—then we could not very well expect *consistent* non-chance scores, positive *or* negative. Appeals to calling strategies alone, then, seem unlikely to explain more than short-term deviations from chance. The statistical properties of a subject's strategy-based calls may be such that statistical artifacts result from matching those calls against a random target sequence. But presumably such artifacts would not persist for long. (Of course, how to decide when a series of trials is sufficiently long is a thorny issue, and I have no suggestions for clearing it up.) Thus, consistent non-chance scores over a long series of trials is not plausibly explained solely by appeal to fortuitous correlations between a subject's calling strategies and the target sequence. Changes in calling strategies may explain why—say, before and after an important interview—subjects change the direction of their scoring. But again, by itself, this does not strengthen the case for psi abilities; such strategy changes could explain short-term changes in the subject's scores *independently* of any psi ability. When, however, non-chance scores continue to persist over a series of trials, it becomes more plausible to suppose there is some link—perhaps only a contingent link— between the subject's calling strategies and a psi ability.

Moreover, it is important to remember that the links between a subject's calling strategy and his psi functioning may be no more than contingent. Once we admit this possibility we can move away from the suggestion that the subject is subconsciously *using* his psi abilities to attain a certain desired result. For example, he may subconsciously base his calls on his first idea, and, unbeknownst to him, it may just happen that the first idea is the one which *in this particular subject* (but possibly not in others) is produced by ESP. In another subject, it may be that his second idea, or his most vivid idea, is usually produced by ESP. And such regularities in psi functioning may or may not correspond to regularities in strategy-based calls in a way that produces non-chance correlations. So the similarity between the calling strategies of two subjects need not correlate with the similarity of their test results, even if both subjects rely on the operation of psi for their non-chance scores.

I think, then, that we may agree with Rhine that psi-missing need not be explained by reference to the subject's motive to score poorly and his use of some psi ability to achieve the desired result. If the degree and persistence of the negative deviations suggest that psi is operating, we might appeal instead to the subject's subconscious calling strategies (and the corresponding strategies for PK) and possibly accidental connections between those strategies and the subject's psi functioning. And since a person's strategies need not rest on a motive to obtain a negative result (or to obtain any

kind of result), and since the connection between the strategies and psi functioning that accounts for the non-chance
scores may be no more than accidental, Rhine's suggestion
has the virtue of being able to explain psi-missing without
positing either suspiciously artificial motives for achieving
negative results, or a kind of subconscious psychic cunning
in using psi to achieve the results.

Unfortunately, however, since the strategies involved may
be highly variable and impossible to identify with any accuracy, even for a single subject, it is not clear just how much
the appeal to such strategies really explains. Tart, who has
searched his data for fine-grained evidence of calling strategies, has suggested, for example, that a subject may unwittingly avoid making the same call twice in a row, guided by
the common but mistaken belief that the probability of
independently generated random targets depends on the
identity of the target generated previously. But since in a
sequence of randomly generated numbers (say), the same
number may occur in pairs, triplets, or even larger sets, the
use of such a strategy would of course tend to prevent psi-
hitting, even if it did not lead to detectable or significant
psi-missing. By analyzing the subject's call sequences, a
strategy like this would be relatively easy to detect. But a
subject may be employing other strategies as well (for example, waiting for the most vivid idea); and the preference given
to one strategy over another may vary continually, thereby
complicating (probably hopelessly) the process of determining the nature of the subject's contribution to the experimental outcome and the extent to which psi is operating, if it
is operating at all. About the most we can do, perhaps, is
retreat to the familiar position that deviations from chance
(positive or negative) should simply be as great as possible.
The greater the deviation, the more likely that complexes of
calling strategies do not account entirely for the results.

Moreover, some might be suspicious about the suggestion
that psi functioning may produce both positive and negative
deviations from chance. They might see it as an attempt to
eschew rigorous criteria of replicability in favor of loose

criteria which render psi experiments virtually unfalsifiable. In order to offset this suspicion, we should observe that an analogue to psi-missing occurs in ordinary life situations. Consider the case of Jones, whose unusual sensitivity and perceptivity account for his success in dealing with people. Many people enjoy Jones' company because he is extremely responsive to their changing moods; he always knows how to act in a way that makes his companions feel comfortable in whatever psychological state they find themselves. Occasionally, however, Jones takes a strong dislike to someone, and while he is not malicious, the sensitivity he uses so supportively and compassionately in other circumstances, he uses with people of this sort very differently. With people he dislikes, Jones might overtly convey his disapproval, but even more subtly, he might behave so as to make them feel uneasy without actually displaying his disapproval. For example, in talking with Smith, whom he dislikes, Jones might use his ability in order to detect when Smith is feeling insecure or uncomfortable, and then act in ways designed to exacerbate this condition. Smith might, for instance, betray in very subtle ways that he is uneasy about a certain topic, and Jones may continue to discuss this topic in ways that he knows Smith will not perceive as designed to make him feel uncomfortable. The reason I suggest there is an analogue here with psi-missing is that Jones' sensitivity can be used to produce two quite different sorts of effects—to make people feel either comfortable or uncomfortable. And since people are notoriously prone to self-deception and may not be especially introspective, we needn't suppose that Jones is consciously aware of how he communicates his antipathy to those he dislikes. So if there is an objection to the notion of psi-missing, it cannot be because there is something wrong in principle with the notion of a certain ability or sensitivity being used (wittingly or unwittingly) to achieve different results under different conditions.

What I think begins to emerge from all this is that it is as reasonable to regard psi-missing as a genuine psi effect as it is psi-hitting. Another possible source of support for this comes from the well-known *placebo effect* in medicine, where changes in a patient's *expectations* concerning the effectiveness of treatment seem to be causally related to profound changes in his physiological and psychological functioning. There is by now a considerable body of evidence confirming that placebo effects are sometimes dramatically more powerful than those of the drugs that might ordinarily have been used (see Frank [56] and Shapiro [150], [151]). But if a patient's physical well-being can improve or deteriorate in accord with his expectations, other causal links between his expectations and his organic functioning may obtain as well—some pertaining to ESP and PK scores. If a patient's expectations can issue in profound physiological changes, it seems reasonable enough that they can initiate organic changes that influence psi functioning and affect the outcome of psi experiments. Just as a patient who expects his condition to deteriorate may get what he expects, so, too, a subject who expects to score poorly on an ESP test may score poorly, and in both cases, the negative results may be mediated by physiological or psychological changes produced by the subject's negative expectations.

In any case, returning to the issue of successful replications, we have observed that at least some kinds of negative results may count as *positive* evidence for the existence of psi phenomena. So since negative scoring or psi-missing may be a function of some psi ability plus appropriate psychological dispositions (which may not be experimentally discernible), it is no longer clear whether negative results in attempting to replicate experiment E_1 tend to disconfirm E_1's positive results. A great deal depends, for example, on whether our original experiment aims (or *should* aim for) positive deviations or merely for extra-chance scores (positive *or* negative). And to make matters worse, if we allow for the occurrence of both psi-hitting and psi-missing either in a single experiment or in a series of related experiments, the *combined* result of the scoring may iron out these different sorts of deviations. The total score may, then, actually hover around chance levels, thus further obscuring the possible presence of psi phenomena. Some statistical tests might reveal which chance scores resulted from the interaction of psi-hitting and psi-missing, but some results might not be susceptible to such analysis.

Connected with all this is the statistical issue of what counts as an appropriate level of significance for deviations from mean chance expectation. According to the *Journal of Parapsychology*, the results of a psi experiment are usually considered significant when the probability of the result is .02 (odds against chance, 50 to 1) or less, and a probability of .05 (odds 20 to 1) is still regarded as suggestive. In fact, often a *good* parapsychological experiment is significant only at the .01 or .001 level (odds against chance, 100 to 1 or 1,000 to 1, respectively). I am not competent to assess this convention. But it is worth noting that these criteria are at least as stringent as those demanded in the other social sciences, including psychology. Furthermore, many psi experiments, as we will see, achieve levels of significance much greater than these.

Still, many experiments do not, and the skeptic or the parapsychological fence-sitter may well wonder whether scores significant, say, at the .01 level might not be the result of statistical artifacts of some kind. An intuitively satisfying tenet of probability theory is that not even small deviations from chance will persist over extended trials, if the deviations are merely chance effects. Very roughly, the idea is that if small deviations in trial runs are genuinely chance results, they will tend to disappear as the number of tries increases. Similarly, in tossing an unbiased penny, we should expect the ratio of heads to tails to converge toward 1 the more times we toss the coin. But when the statistical significance of scores hovers around the .01 level, we can always wonder whether the series of trials was long enough to iron out normal statistical artifacts.

Some recent studies in the matching of more than 70,000 digits from random number tables lend support to this concern (Hardy *et al.* [63]). For example, the combined result of two experiments which together contained 49,600 pairings (trials)—a number greater than the number of trials found in many 'successful' psi experiments—showed a *negative* deviation of 211. The odds against this occurring are 1,250 to 1; and had this been the data for an ESP test, the result might well have been regarded as good evidence of psi-missing. Furthermore, these studies showed that successful pairings of digits tended to occur in patterns similar to so-called *position* effects, in which a subject tends to score better in specific segments of the trial run—say, in the first and last parts of the run.

Somewhat opposed to these findings is an experiment, conducted in the 1930s, in which shuffled decks of ESP cards were matched against each other to simulate ESP tests. One deck would represent the targets and the other would represent the calls. In more than 100,000 pairings, the number of 'hits' proved to be *not* statistically significant (see Warner [190]). Shortly thereafter, an even more extensive experiment was carried out (see Greenwood [61]). This test involved half a million trials of matching calls from highly successful card-guessing experiments against shuffled ESP decks. Again the results were at chance levels. It remains unclear, then, how much weight we should assign to less-than-amazing deviations from chance in ESP and PK tests, and thus how much weight we should give to apparently successful replication attempts significant at the .01 or .001 level.

Accordingly, some parapsychologists have sought more subtle and more fine-grained statistical measures of the existence of psi phenomena—for instance, *differential* effects arising from variations in the experimental conditions. Thus, if the subject scores above chance under one set of conditions but at or below chance under slightly altered conditions, this fact might be taken to reveal not only the existence of some psi phenomenon, but also something of its character. When we later examine Tart's hypothesis of *trans-temporal inhibition* (I.B.3.e.), we shall see a rather different sort of refined analysis of the data. In any case, these more refined statistical measures by no means avoid all the problems I have been discussing. For example, even in measuring differential effects, we may still wonder whether we have selected an appropriate level of significance for difference measures. The measurement of differential effects does not by itself settle the question of what constitutes positive results in parapsychological experiments.

Before leaving this topic, I should at least mention one very interesting position that has attracted some in their efforts to explain deviations from chance in psi experiments. Believing that statistical methods have been correctly employed, but generally skeptical about the existence of psi abilities, they have proposed that something may be amiss in the foundations of probability theory itself (see Spencer Brown, [155] Hardy *et al.* [63]). This is an intriguing idea; but it cannot be examined here. In fact, considering how valuable probability theory has been in such areas as quantum physics, I shall adopt the position (if only to see where it leads) that, with respect to successful quantitative experiments in parapsychology, we have more grounds for questioning received views about the limits of human abilities than we have for questioning the axioms of probability.

Rate of Success. Even if we could decide what counts as a copy of the design of E_1 and what counts as a positive result, the question remains: In a series $E_2 \ldots E_n$ of attempts to repeat E_1, how many members of that series must yield positive results for E_1 to be considered successfully replicated? Since one isolated apparently successful replication attempt may always be a fluke, and since in practice not all attempts to replicate an experiment succeed, this question is obviously important.

One widely accepted (and perhaps the standard) criterion in the behavioral sciences is that 5 percent of $E_2 \ldots E_n$ can be expected to give significant positive results by chance alone. Now whether this measure of significance is sufficiently stringent is a matter I do not propose to settle here. For one thing, assuming that psi phenomena are genuine, then if they are really as fragile and reticent as (from a sympathetic point of view) they appear to be, it is not clear how many successes we should expect—especially when we consider the possibly crucial role played by the experimenter. In any case, we should keep in mind that some experiments in parapsychology have been replicated (even on a conservative estimate) well beyond the 5 percent level. Honorton, for example collected data on replication attempts for several years, and claimed at one point [71] that the PK experiment first reported by Schmidt in 1970 (Schmidt [136]) had by that time received 54 replication attempts in 7 different laboratories,* 65 percent of which (i.e., 35/54) were significant at the .05 level, 35 percent of which were significant at the more stringent .01 level, and 20 percent of which were still significant at the .001 level. In another paper [70], Honorton reports similar figures for work conducted at Maimonides Hospital (although these figures may need to be revised in light of the recent criticism of Kelly [78]). The remote viewing experiments at SRI are also receiving independent replications (see I.3.d.).†

---

*Many of these other experiments differ in major details from Schmidt's original experiment. Yet Honorton and others consider the experiments to be replication attempts and, in some cases, successful replications. This series of experiments may thus prove to be a valuable source of data for those interested in examining in more detail how the parapsychological community (or the scientific community generally) uses the concept of replication.

†I should add that the reason the replication figures are as impressive as they are is not due to selective reporting of positive results, which is often the case in other areas of science. In fact, Honorton observes that the Parapsychological Association is the only affiliate organization of the American Association for the Advancement of Science to have a *policy* against the selective reporting of positive results. This is why the parapsychological journals and especially the annual proceedings of the P.A. contain numerous reports of apparently unsuccessful experiments (which account for much of the tedium one is likely to experience in surveying the laboratory data). Moreover, although, on the null hypothesis that 5 percent of replication attempts would give significant positive results by chance alone, the odds against obtaining 35/54 significant experiments is 50 billion to 1, even if we assume that for each of the 35 significant replication attempts there are 10 unreported failures (a highly unlikely possibility considering how little parapsychological experimentation is actually being conducted), the 35 successes would still be significant with odds against chance of more than 2,000 to 1.

Curiously, if *every* member of $E_2 \ldots E_n$ were to give positive results, the parapsychological community would view the series with suspicion, no matter how statistically impressive its successes. In part this may be because we expect statistical distributions in the behavioral sciences. But more specifically, many expect some replication attempts to fail when the participants in the replication attempts are different from those in E_1. They would argue that psi abilities, if they exist, are likely to be as variable and as unevenly distributed as other more familiar abilities (like the ability to be seductive, or the ability to be calm in the face of danger, or the ability to hit accurate tennis serves), and that this should be reflected in the variability of scores in psi experiments. From this point of view, a completely successful series of replication attempts may suggest either a major flaw in experimental design or chicanery. If this position is reasonable, then even a statistical measure of replication success requires some amount of qualification. We would have to agree not only on when the rate of success falls within chance levels, but also on that point *past which* further successes become suspicious.

Philosophical Considerations. To lend a somewhat broader perspective to this discussion, we should also observe that some difficulties in determining when an experiment has been repeated are not peculiar to the scientific enterprise or to the process of experimentation. Rather, they are instances of the more general problem of determining when *any* sort of event has been repeated. These problems, in other words, concern the general concept of *recurrence*, and even more fundamentally, the concept of *similarity*. Suppose that A tells a certain joke and that his telling of the joke, J, is very funny. But suppose that B, who is not as gifted a comedian as A, tries to tell A's joke, but that he uses different words than A uses, and that his inflection and timing are such that his joke-attempt J' is not funny. How, then, do we answer the question: Is J' a recurrence of joke-attempt J? The important thing to observe here is that this question has *no* simple or straightforward answer. There are perfectly acceptable reasons for answering it either affirmatively or negatively.

Some might say that although B told the same joke as A, he did not do so with the same (or perhaps any) comedic skill. On the other hand, some might claim that, since A and B uttered different strings of words, and since J' was not funny, A's joke had *not* been repeated by B.

The important point to grasp here is that neither response is intrinsically better than the other. Whether we take B's performance to replicate A's performance depends on what is appropriate for the context in which the question arises. Suppose people are taking turns telling jokes at a party, and that it is expected that each will tell a different joke. If B were to tell his joke we might feel justified in complaining that he did not tell a new joke, and, in fact, that he merely told A's joke rather poorly. On the other hand, suppose the party guests are playing a different game, in which each has to memorize and repeat verbatim what his immediate predecessor says. Suppose, then, that A tells his joke and that B, whom we may suppose is mnemonically handicapped, tries unsuccessfully to repeat A's performance. Even if the *content* of what A and B said was similar—so that B succeeded in producing a *version* of A's joke—B's performance (the string of words produced in the manner produced) would not count in this context as a replication of A's performance. We can imagine even more stringent requirements of replicability. Suppose B is studying the comedic arts, and that his task is to repeat, *not* just the same words as those of his teacher A, but also A's inflection and timing (and note, criteria of sameness for inflection and timing are not hard and fast—we needn't suppose, for example, that A and B have voices of the same quality). In this context, what B does will not be a recurrence or replication of what A does, if B manages to get only the words exactly right.

The moral of all this is that whether or not B's verbal performance constitutes a recurrence of A's joke telling, J is not simply a function of formal features of what A and B do and say. In one context B's sequence of words may count as a recurrence of J, while in another it may not.

The situation is, to some extent, similar in scientific experimentation. Whether E_2 replicates E_1 is not strictly a function of the formal features of the two experiments, and may depend in part on the social and professional contexts in which they are embedded. I have already observed that replication attempts will inevitably differ in some respects from the original experiment, but that in the ordinary course of the established sciences, such differences tend to be discounted when a replication attempt is deemed successful. In parapsychology, however, the very same sorts of differences are regarded as potentially relevant to the experimental outcome, although even in parapsychology such differences may also be discounted when replication attempts are deemed successful. The extremely important point (to which these observations have been leading all along) is simply that whether or not the differences between E_1 and E_2 are to count as relevant is *not* determined independently of the decision as to whether one is or is not a replication of the other. Scientists tend to regard many such differences as important only if the outcomes of the experiments differ. Before knowing the results of E_2, then, it is pretty much an open question whether the differences between E_1 and E_2 matter. Of course, scientists may claim in advance that the differences do not matter, but if the replication attempt fails to give the same results as the original experiment, this judgment may be retracted.

Moreover, as I explain in more detail below, the importance we attach to formal differences between E_1 and E_2 is also a function of certain larger considerations concerning the status of the science itself. In a context where parapsychological experimentation generally is suspect, for instance, and in which positive results of E_1 are automatically open to suspicion, the status of E_2 will be far less clear than in a context in which the existence of psi abilities or the legitimacy of parapsychological research is taken for granted. This is one big reason why the questions we have been considering regarding experiment repeatability arise *in principle* in other more established sciences, but rarely arise in practice.

It would be a waste of time, then, to seek purely formal criteria for experiment repeatability. The formal features of E_1 and E_2 cannot by themselves determine whether the latter replicates the former—just as the merely formal features of the performances of A and B cannot themselves determine whether B has told the same joke as A. And when we add to this the observation that inevitable and perhaps intangible differences between an experiment and attempts to replicate it may lead to differences in experimental outcome (in physics as well as in parapsychology—although especially in sciences dealing with human subjects), and when we consider the difficulties of trying to state general criteria of replicability, it becomes increasingly unreasonable to expect formal criteria of replicability to be of much use. Nevertheless, replication attempts in parapsychology may be evaluated on a case-by-case basis, and some replication attempts may be—and in fact seem to be—sufficiently convincing despite difficulties in specifying general criteria of replicability.

In order to bring this discussion to a close, let us consider briefly to what extent appeals to replication attempts support the claim that some ostensibly new or unexplained phenomenon is a genuine phenomenon. Here again, I am indebted to the penetrating work of Collins.

Suppose that our original scientist (OS) conducts experiment E_1, and that E_1 appears to give evidence for the reality of some hitherto unrecognized phenomenon P. And suppose that our replicating scientist (RS) conducts an experiment E_2 in an attempt to replicate the work of OS. The question I want us now to consider is: When the legitimacy or genuineness of P is in question, of what value is E_2?

Suppose, first, that both E_1 and E_2 yield positive results, which seem *prima facie* inexplicable in terms of ordinary processes, and seem to suggest the existence of some strange new phenomenon P. Now, if there is genuine doubt whether P is even possible (e.g., if we can doubt whether such a phenomenon as telepathy is possible), numerous questions, raised already in connection with E_1, are bound to carry over to E_2. Those who question the reality of P may (already) have wondered about the integrity of OS or his experimental design. If, say, a flaw in the design of E_1 could account for the positive results of E_1, then perhaps a similar flaw may account for the positive results of E_2. So, even if RS gets the same sort of positive result in E_2 as OS got in E_1, this would not settle the issue of whether P was a genuine new phenomenon. It would show only that certain experimental results could be repeated not that a certain *explanation* of them ought to be accepted. On the other hand, suppose that RS gets negative results in E_2. These results will, again, be inconclusive. If we have doubts about the soundness of E_1 and the genuineness of P, then the negative results of E_2 and the discrepancy between the results of E_1 and E_2 will not settle the issue of whether P is genuine. If we are not certain how to assess E_1, our results will leave open the question of whether the results of E_1 are spurious, or whether those of E_2 are.

It seems, then, that when attempting to establish experimentally the existence of some novel phenomenon P, questions concerning such things as competence of the experimenter or integrity of experimental design are inevitably live questions. But since these questions carry over from E_1 to its replication attempts, to rest the defense or rejection of claims for the reality of P on appeals to replication attempts seems question-begging. Perhaps the most we can say is that when the results of replication attempts are *consistently* positive (or negative), we have good *presumptive*—though not conclusive—evidence that the phenomenon tested for is (or is not) genuine.

This situation may not be quite as bleak as it sounds, since similar problems afflict every science that attempts to establish experimentally the existence of some novel phenomenon. In parapsychology, of course, these problems are rather more acute, since unlike such established sciences as physics, the legitimacy of the field itself is continually being challenged, and parapsychology lacks a clear theoretical framework which can be used to generate *in advance* of experimentation, detailed predictions about the nature of novel phenomena. We may expect, then, that as the theoretical foundations of parapsychology become more organized, unified, and sophisticated, certain questions concerning the value of replication attempts will recede into the background.

One last point: Jule Eisenbud [49] has suggested that parapsychology's failure to design experiments that are as reliably repeatable as those in other areas of science may be a function of large-scale or cosmic constraints on psi functioning. Although he regards dramatic laboratory evidence for psi as a kind of chance occurrence, he does not deny the existence of psi functioning. Rather, he argues that psi functioning may be such that it tends to operate in all of us, but unobtrusively, and that occasional dramatic occurrences of psi in the lab are random fluctuations in what, *by its very nature*, is a non-dramatic range of phenomena. For this reason, Eisenbud suggests that we should abandon the quest for greater repeatability in parapsychology, since persisting in it is tantamount to trying to upset the laws of psi functioning, which generally keep the manifestations of psi hidden from public view. Eisenbud thus opposes the view of parapsychological experimentation according to which the experimenter tries to uncover, or tap into, the underlying laws of psi functioning in such a way as to obtain reliably repeatable demonstrations of psi. He maintains instead that the underlying laws are such that demonstrable psi is a kind of deviant event in nature, and that larger natural forces tend to balance out its occasional overt manifestations.

A similar position has been expressed by Crumbaugh [35], who writes,

> the enigmatic and illusive [sic] way in which psi capacities avoid being pinned down causes me to suspect that if they do exist as valid phenomena they also bear characteristics which may make it forever impossible to demonstrate them by the criteria of mechanistic science (White [194] : 433).

I think this general position deserves to be taken seriously, although Eisenbud and Crumbaugh (especially Eisenbud) state this view in a way that makes it seem as if there were some mysterious feature of psi itself which makes psi difficult to pin down. Some might see this as an effort to explain the mystery of psi by reference to an even greater mystery. Still, if psi exists, and if it is really difficult to test for experimentally, it may be difficult for rather ordinary sorts of reasons. A clue to all this may come from a comparison of parapsychology's replication score card with those of other areas of science. I don't have data on this, but my impression is that while parapsychology boasts far fewer replications than the 'hard' sciences, it compares less poorly with (but still worse than) the biological and behavioral sciences—at least in certain areas of experimentation. This suggests that the difficulty of repeating psi experiments may have less to do with those cosmic matters proposed by Eisenbud (according to which replication failure represents a kind of operation of the laws of probability) or with some peculiar feature inherent in psi phenomena as (Crumbaugh suggests), and more to do with the variable nature and behavior of organisms generally, and human beings in particular. There are numerous kinds of behavior, like the ability to control one's feelings, or the ability to be witty, or seductive, or poetic, or the ability to draw inspiring lessons from everyday occurrences, which would presumably be difficult to test for under rigid laboratory conditions, and which are manifested in day-to-day life only under certain kinds of conditions. And it still seems to be a very live hypothesis that psi functioning may be an unusually fragile phenomenon, even for this class.

B. The Data

1. Introduction

I do not pretend that the following survey of the experimental evidence for ESP and PK is comprehensive. For one thing, I shall concentrate on successful experiments rather than apparent failures. Moreover, I have chosen to describe the details of many experiments rather than simply report results, and this has further reduced the amount of work I have been able to summarize. Still, I shall try to convey to the reader enough of the flavor of current research to enable him to appreciate how much psi experimentation has changed since Broad's survey in the early 1960s. For those who want to investigate the data in greater detail (which I encourage), I suggest reading the annual reports of the proceedings of the Parapsychological Association, which appear in a series of books called *Research in Parapsychology* (published annually by Scarecrow Press, Metuchen, N.J.). Many of the papers cited and listed in the bibliography were presented at the most recent annual conventions of the P.A. and will eventually appear in that series. I also urge the reader to scan the major parapsychological journals, especially the *Journal of the American Society for Psychical Research*, the *Journal of Parapsychology*, the (British) *Journal of the Society for Psychical Research*, and the new *European Journal of Parapsychology*. I also recommend some books containing detailed surveys of the data. See, for example, Krippner [84], [85] and Wolman [198].

Traditionally, skeptical objections to parapsychological research have been of two sorts, one of which I believe is worthless, the other—although important—has been rather successfully undermined by recent methodological advances. The worthless criticism focuses on the integrity of experimenters. Since successful laboratory experiments have been conducted and replicated by numerous researchers in different laboratories and even in different parts of the world (admittedly not as often as one would like), those critics who claim that many, or all of the positive results in psi experiments are explained by chicanery have found themselves impugning the characters of an unreasonably large number of respected persons, and have sometimes been driven to advance a ludicrous 'conspiracy' theory. Some cases of experimenter fraud have of course been uncovered, but the parapsychological community seems very sensitive to the issue and also open and responsible in its housecleaning.* A variant of the worthless attack holds that the results of parapsychological experiments must be rejected so long as fraud is *possible*—whether or not positive evidence for it obtains. In fact, Hansel [62] takes this position in his sweeping attack on parapsychology. But it is surely too strong. In a good survey of objections to parapsychological research [116], Ransom offers a suitable response.

The important question is not whether cheating was possible in a certain experiment, but whether or not someone actually cheated. If cheating did not in fact occur, the fact that the experimental design made cheating possible is of no concern. It is only because we may have no way of knowing whether someone actually cheated that we have to adopt the next best standard, that of considering the possibility of cheating. But, though we cannot have proof of whether someone cheated or not, we can have evidence one way or the other. Is there any direct evidence of fraud? Is there any direct evidence of an honestly conducted experiment? In short, if you have

*See Rhine [122], [123]. As the case of the late Cyril Burt reminds us, experimenter fraud is not limited to parapsychology; when it occurs, the experimenter, and *not* his entire discipline, is discredited. See Wade [186].

a situation where fraud or ESP are the only explanations for an experimental result, the result is evidence for (not proof of) ESP to the degree that the evidence for an honestly conducted experiment outweighs the evidence for fraud; and it is evidence for (not proof of) fraud to the degree that the evidence for fraud outweighs the evidence for an honestly conducted experiment (White [194]: 406-7).

The more serious form of criticism concerns the integrity of experimental designs. Some have maintained that test conditions permit sensitive subjects to pick up extremely subtle sensory cues which would account for their outstanding scores. Parapsychologists generally concede that a number of the more successful experiments of this century are vulnerable to this criticism—even if the alternative methods of information-acquisition suggested seem rather far-fetched. But some classic experiments (e.g., the Pearce-Pratt clairvoyance tests; see I.B.3.a.) still seem methodologically 'clean'. Furthermore, some critics have objected to the methods of generating target sequences, and have protested that the ordering of targets is not genuinely random. But a considerable number of recent experiments employ ingenious innovations in electronic target generation and mechanical scoring, which have robbed this line of argument of much (if not most) of its force. We shall examine these new experimental procedures below.

In fact, I intend to begin my survey with an examination of the evidence for PK, because that research introduces at once these important methodological innovations and their effect on the character of much research in parapsychology, including research in ESP.

2. PK

a. History of Research

In order to place recent experimentation against an appropriate background, I shall first briefly summarize the history of laboratory research in PK. In the mid 1930s, J. B. Rhine began conducting quantitative experiments in PK (see Rhine & Rhine [125], and Rhine [119]). The principal method used was to release dice while a subject made a concentrated effort at wishing or willing that a particular side turn face-up. Although the results of these experiments were often impressive and interesting, the tests suffered from various methodological weaknesses. In some, inadequate precautions were taken against target-bias, not only in the dice themselves, but sometimes in the choice of targets. For example, some subjects were allowed to choose their own target (i.e., die face), and they frequently chose the number 6, which in pitted dice is the lightest side and thus the one most likely to turn face up. In others, there were inadequate checks on recording errors, and some experiments permitted inappropriate statistical procedures like optional stopping. Furthermore, even though hand-thrown dice were replaced by the presumably cleaner methods of using cup-thrown and machine-thrown dice, none of these methods could be trusted to produce random falls. Similar problems in ensuring random falls of targets plagued PK experiments in coin-tossing and flipping.

Then in the 1950s, a new method for testing PK was introduced, called the *placement* method. The idea was to have the subject try to influence test objects so that they would move in a certain specified *direction*. For example, in some tests (Cox [33], [34]), dice were made to roll down an incline onto a table, which was divided by a line down the center. The subject's task was to try to influence the dice to move to the right or the left of the line. The experimenters hoped that such a procedure would enable them to detect and measure the magnitude of a PK *force*. In this respect, the tests were not successful (see Forwald [55] and J. Rush's review of Forwald [129]); now, the hypothesis that PK is mediated by a kind of emanative force is considered dead in most quarters, particularly given the startling results of recent research with random number generators.

Perhaps the most serious and nagging problem with die-face or placement tests in general is that dice, coins, and so on are not ideal tools for this kind of quantitative study. The physics and mathematics of rolling dice, for example, are so complicated that we have no idea, really, to what extent such a process is random. The outcome of a die-fall depends not only on such things as the die's initial position and the physical properties of the tumbler, but also on matters that cannot adequately be controlled and compensated for, and which frustrate attempts to predict accurately the statistical properties of a series of such falls. For one thing, we do not really know to what extent the material out of which the dice are made can affect the outcome of a roll of the dice. Moreover, the unpredictability of such an outcome increases the more the dice are shaken and the more they are allowed to tumble. And part of the general unpredictability of dice rolls would seem to be a function of quantum indeterminacy, since certain relevant experimental conditions, like internal oscillations of the die, atomic vibrations on the incline surface, and the motion of air molecules colliding with the die, cannot be measured with sufficient precision to permit an accurate prediction of the die fall. Thus, we may be better off trying to measure a PK effect on a simpler system, one whose statistical properties are more reliable and predictable.

b. PK and RNGs

Accordingly, recent PK research has charted a new direction. One of nature's most elementary random processes is radioactive decay. For example, atomic nuclei in the radioactive element Strontium-90 decay *spontaneously* after an average life of 30 years. It is not that the atoms age, or that anything occurs which causes them to decay. The way most physicists understand the process is that radioactive decay is a genuine random occurrence typical of events at the atomic level. Moreover, this randomness is of an especially deep kind, since on the received (Copenhagen) view, there is literally nothing which is the cause of the decay of an atom of Sr-90. We can, of course, predict with considerable accuracy how many such atoms will decay in a given period of time. But there is no basis in principle for predicting when particular decays will occur. Now, if all this is true, then atomic decay could provide PK researchers with a paradigm natural random process to use in their experiments, one whose statistical properties are well known and not subject to the vagaries and complexities of dice rolls and coin tosses. Moreover, this process is extremely difficult to influence by such ordinary physical conditions as electromagnetic fields and temperature changes, and is thus relatively immune from various forms of human interference, either inadvertent or intentional.

Although he was not the first to test for PK on quantum processes, the parapsychologist who pioneered psi research using radioactive decay is the physicist Helmut Schmidt. Originally, Schmidt used atomic decay to generate targets in a precognition experiment; we shall consider this experiment later (I.B.3.b.). Schmidt's first use of radioactive decay to test for PK proceeded as follows. Schmidt designed a binary random number generator (RNG), an electronic 'coin-flipper', which produced random sequences of heads and tails in the following way. When an atom of Sr-90 decays, it emits an electron which is registered on a Geiger-Müller tube (i.e., Geiger counter). This event then stops a high-speed two-position counter (a million hz square-wave oscillator), which oscillates between the head and tail positions one million times per second. Atomic decays occur about 10 times per second, but the actual times between decays is indeterminate. So there seems to be an equal chance of the counter's stopping in the head or tail position. Control runs of Schmidt's RNGs invariably bear this out.

In Schmidt's PK tests, the subject tries to make the RNG produce an excess of, say, heads. In his first PK experiment [136], Schmidt places the subject in front of a display panel with nine lamps arranged in a circle; the panel is connected to the coin-flipper located in another room. One lamp is lit at a time, and the light jumps in the clockwise or counter-clockwise direction around the circle depending on whether, respectively, the RNG produces a head (+1) or a tail (−1). In a standard test run of 128 numbers (which, at the target generation rate of 1 per second, takes about 2 minutes), the subject, who is instructed to concentrate on the display panel (rather than the RNG), tries to influence the light to move clockwise around the circle. The sequence of numbers produced by the RNG is recorded manually, and also mechanically on paper punch tape, thus reducing the risk of human error or chicanery. Between runs, the machine is left running, in order to insure that it is behaving randomly when the trials are not in progress. Sometimes, the outputs from the RNG to the display panel are reversed, so that an excess of heads cannot be attributed to a bias in the RNG.

For his pilot study with this equipment, Schmidt's subjects were selected on the basis of their availability, rather than for any supposed psi ability. To his surprise, the subjects—although instructed to make the light move clockwise—showed a tendency to score negatively. That is, the light walked counterclockwise around the circle and the RNG favored −1s instead of +1s.

To confirm this unexpected result, Schmidt selected 15 of the most negative scorers and, as before, instructed them to concentrate on scoring positively. But after 32,768 trials, the negative scoring persisted, with odds against chance of 1,000 to 1. In his second confirmatory study, Schmidt used two subjects, K.G. and R.R., who were believed to have psychic abilities. In preliminary tests with these subjects, K.G. scored unusually high, while R.R. scored unusually low. Schmidt attempted to confirm this finding by having each subject complete 50 runs of 128 trials each. The difference in their scoring persisted. Both subjects were instructed to concentrate on making the light move in the clockwise direction, but while 52.5% of K.G.'s 6,400 trials were +1s, only 47.75% of R.R.'s jumps went clockwise. Since the odds against this, or a larger, difference between the two scores is greater than 10 million to 1, it seems that this result cannot be attributed to chance.*

---

*Schmidt recognized that in principle the success of these experiments could be attributed to *precognition* on the part of the experimenter or subject. Schmidt writes, 'Since the sequence of generated numbers depended critically on the time when the test run began, and since the experimenter, in consensus with the subject, decided when to flip the start switch; precognition might have prompted experimenter and subject to start the run at a time which favored scoring in a certain direction' ([136]: 181).

From the point of view of efficiency, Schmidt's PK tests left something to be desired. Sessions were held only when subjects felt ready, and since the degree of concentration required for the trial runs apparently exhausted subjects rather quickly, the actual collection of data was very slow. In order to improve efficiency, Schmidt designed a high-speed RNG so that more trials could be conducted before the subject experienced fatigue (see [138]).

This new RNG was, like its predecessor, a binary RNG (i.e., a coin-flipper). But instead of using radioactive decay as a source of randomness, Schmidt used an electronic noise generator, which selects a target whenever the generated noise exceeds a certain threshold amplitude, and which can produce faster sequences of random numbers than Sr-90.* Furthermore, Schmidt thought he might now be able to test for *bursts* of PK activity, even if they lasted for a fraction of a second, since so many random events would be generated in a very short interval.

The new RNG could produce up to 1,000 random events per second, although Schmidt used the machine at only two generation speeds, a low speed of 30 events per second and a high speed of 300 events per second. The number of trials per test run was (at the low speed) 100 and (at the high speed) 1,000. So the test runs were about 3 seconds long. Scores, as usual, were recorded both manually and mechanically (see [138]:108 for a description of the two methods of automatic recording), and the RNG was tested successfully for randomness by being allowed to run unattended for long periods of time (usually overnight) for 20 nights.

---

*In correspondence, Schmidt explained the operation of this RNG rather concisely, as follows: 'A diode conducts current in one direction and blocks it in the other direction but when the voltage gets too high, a current flows even in the blocking direction because of some breakdown effects. This breakdown effect shows strong chance fluctuations, observable as voltage fluctuations between the two sides of the diode. Whenever the voltage passes a certain limit, a threshold detector is activated and this *event* (with the proper setting of the threshold) occurs randomly in time, much like the events registered in a Geiger counter'.

In these tests, the experimenter decided whether the subject should aim mentally at producing +1s or −1s. What registered on the feedback display as a hit thus depended on this prior decision by the experimenter. The two numbers were used as goals equally often. To insure psychologically favorable test conditions, Schmidt provided his subjects with immediate feedback of their results, and the feedback varied between two types, auditory and visual. In the auditory mode, hits and misses were represented as clicks in stereo headphones, hits in the right ear, and misses in the left; and subjects were instructed to concentrate on making clicks appear in the right ear. At the low speed, subjects were able to discern the individual clicks. But at the high speed, this was not possible; increased hits and misses appeared rather as volume increases in noise in, respectively, the right and left ears. Subjects would thus concentrate on increasing the volume of the noise in the right ear. In the visual feedback mode, subjects were instructed to make a needle on a pen chart recorder fluctuate to the right. The magnitude of the fluctuation from the center was proportional to the difference between generated hits and misses. The visual differences between the two speeds was much less than the corresponding auditory differences, especially after Schmidt reduced pen sensitivity for the fast speed. This allowed for the comparison of PK performance at different generation speeds under visually near-identical conditions.

After encouraging preliminary tests, Schmidt conducted a confirmatory experiment with ten subjects who completed 400 trial runs (of 100 trials each) at each speed, for a total of 40,000 trials at the low speed and 400,000 trials at the high speed. Differences between results of the two types of feedback were insignificant. The overall results are shown in Table 1.

From a practical point of view, the experiment was quite successful, since PK effects were apparently demonstrated over a large series of trials within a 'pure test time' of only 20 minutes (400 test runs × 3 seconds). Schmidt suggests that the difference in the hit rate at the two generation

Table 1. PK results at target generation speeds of 30 and 300 events per second.

Trial speed	No. of trials	Hit rate	Odds against chance
30/sec	40,000	51.6%	7×10^9 to 1
300/sec	400,000	50.37%	4×10^5 to 1

speeds is plausible, on the assumption that, at the lower speed of 30 events per second, the subject is able to concentrate better on individual random events. The lower hit rate at the higher speed suggests that efficiency in PK testing cannot continually be increased by speeding up the rate of generating targets.

Schmidt's suggestion about the subject's concentration, though hardly outlandish, must be treated with caution. Some evidence gathered in PK and ESP experiments suggests that concentration by the subject may not be as important as one might think; or, at least, that the concentration required need not be directed at a presumed psi-task. We shall consider the evidence shortly.

c. Retroactive PK.

By now, the reader should have some sense of the sophistication of Schmidt's PK experiments. We may turn, therefore, to some of his most peculiar results, particularly his astonishing *prima facie* evidence for retroactive PK. Let us begin by briefly considering an experiment designed by Schmidt which suggests that PK success is independent of the complexity of the PK task (see [139]). In this experiment, subjects were tested on RNGs having different degrees of internal complexity. The *simple* RNG was one of Schmidt's coin-flippers. The *complex* RNG was also a binary RNG, but it selected a $+1$ or a -1 by first generating 100 binary random events (at the rate of 30/sec) and then taking the 'majority vote'. In the case of a tie, no decision was made and the test went on to the next trial. The generator displayed only the majority decision, and the information about the details of the 100 individual trials was lost.

Subject and experimenter were located in one room; the two RNGs, in a non-adjacent room, and each trial began by having the subject press a switch which triggered both generators. During the experiment, trials were randomly alternated between the two RNGs, and neither experimenter nor subject knew which RNG was active for a given trial. Moreover, to insure that subjects could not sensorially distinguish which RNG was active through differences in feedback, a 3-second delay was added to the simple generator, so that both RNGs would take about 3 seconds to produce a binary decision. Subjects were seated in a chair facing two differently colored lamps, corresponding to the two binary choices. Outputs to the lamps were periodically reversed as a further safeguard against generator bias. The subject was instructed to visualize the color of the target lamp, and then to try to make that lamp light up.

What is especially interesting about this experiment is that statistically significant scores were obtained with each generator *when it was the target*. The highest scores were obtained with the simple generator, but the difference between the two scores was not statistically significant. The data shows that the simple RNG, which was left running even when it was not active in the experiment, operated at chance levels when its outputs were not targets. This suggests that the subjects (or perhaps the experimenter) had some non-conscious way of determining which RNG was active so that they could selectively influence it.

The fact that statistically significant scores were obtained with two internally different systems under psychologically identical conditions suggested to Schmidt what he has called the *equivalence hypothesis*. Roughly, this hypothesis states that, under the same psychological or sensory conditions, PK can affect *any* two RNGs to the same degree. Schmidt puts this more elaborately as follows.

Consider two binary random generators whose decisions are based on indeterminate quantum processes. Let each generator be mounted inside a 'black box' with one trigger input and two output lines carrying the binary decisions. Assume that the two systems behave alike so that they are, for the physicist, undistinguishable from the outside. Then the equivalence hypothesis states that the two systems are also undistinguishable by PK experiments, i.e., that they are affected by PK efforts in the same manner ([144]: 538).

As Schmidt recognized, one of the far-reaching implications of the equivalence hypothesis is that two output-indistinguishable systems will be equally susceptible to PK influence, *no matter when the processes affected by PK occur.* Schmidt puts the point this way, with respect to an imaginary experiment.

Compare the following two black box random generators. The first black box contains our electronic coinflipper, which is activated once per second by a timer, so that two output jacks receive binary random signals at this rate. The other black box contains an identical coinflipper activated at the same rate. The generated signals, however, are not sent directly to the output jacks but rather stored on an endless magnetic tape from which they are, 24 hours later, played back to the output jacks. Then each of the signals which emerge from this generator at the rate of one per second, was internally generated 24 hours earlier.

These two black box generators are, from the outside, undistinguishable, and if we take the equivalence hypothesis seriously, then they should work equally well in any PK experiment. Note, however, that if the subject succeeds in a test session with the second system, if the subject obtains significantly more heads than tails, this requires that the internal electronic coinflipper developed a bias for heads 24 hours before the subject made his PK effort ([144]: 538).

This apparently outrageous consequence of the equivalence hypothesis is what Schmidt's experiments in retroactive PK seem to confirm (see[142]).

These tests are important and merit detailed treatment. After some suggestive preliminary studies using pre-recorded targets, Schmidt conducted a series of three experiments, the first two of which were very successful and the third of which gave non-significant results. I shall describe only the first two. The third experiment is very interesting, but different in so many ways from the first two that its failure to yield significant results does not detract from the earlier successes. It warrants further study, however, since it may reveal crucial experimental variables relevant to PK success.

The first experiment with pre-recorded targets. This experiment had two parts, a conventional part using momentarily-generated targets, and a part using pre-recorded targets.

In the conventional portion of the experiment, Schmidt used an electronic RNG so designed that the probability of obtaining a hit was 1/64 and the probability of obtaining a miss was 63/64. Each run of the RNG lasted until a hit was obtained, and since the probability of a hit is 1/64, the average run length (i.e., the number of trials needed to obtain a hit) was 64. At the trial generation rate of 10 per second, the average run time would thus be 6.4 seconds, assuming the RNG was behaving randomly (which it was, giving an average run length of 64.48 over 4,000 runs). When a hit was obtained, the RNG stopped and the hit was displayed as a weak click in a pair of headphones. Counter readings indicating the length of each run were recorded manually as well as mechanically on paper punch tape.

What Schmidt wanted to do in this part of the test was to increase the hit probability, and thus reduce the average run length. The subjects were not told of this goal, however. They were instructed to listen carefully for the weak clicks so that they would not miss any of them, and they were encouraged in this task by being asked to imagine the clicks as being associated with some real-life situation, like listening to faint bird sounds in the forest. Schmidt hypothesized that the subjects' active concentration on, and expectation of, the next click (or hit) would activate a PK mechanism so that the next click occurred earlier than would be expected on the hypothesis of chance.

For the pilot study, 20 subjects contributed 20 runs each. The average run length for the 400 hits was 54.23 rather than the chance level of 64.0. Thus, at the trial generation rate of 10 per second, the average waiting time per click was 5.42 seconds rather than 6.4 seconds. This result is significant at the .001 level. 30 subjects participated in the confirmatory study, again contributing 20 runs each. For the resulting 600 hits the average run length was 55.34, also significant at the .001 level.

Although Schmidt hypothesized that the subjects' concentration on the next hit would subconsciously activate a PK mechanism, he realized that such a mechanism might also be activated by the subjects' eagerness to please the experimenter, or that positive results might be attributed to experimenter PK. In any case, given the RNG's performance in control runs, the abnormally low run length of the test sessions appears to be a PK effect.

The revolutionary part of Schmidt's experiment was identical to the conventional part, with the important difference that the random sequences of hits and misses which appeared in the tests were not generated during those tests, but were generated and recorded on tape earlier, in the absence of both experimenter and subject. Nobody examined these sequences until they were played back during the test sessions.

The sequence of events for this part of the experiment ran as follows. First, the RNG was automatically activated, and hits and misses were, respectively, recorded as signals on a stereo cassette tape in the right and left channels. After each run (i.e., after a hit was obtained), the generator stopped for ten seconds while the number of trials (i.e., the length of the run) was recorded on paper punch tape. Thus two independent records were made of the generator output, one on magnetic tape and another on paper punch tape.

Two 60-run sequences were generated in this way, the first labelled A and the second, B. Ten such pairs of sequences were recorded, and for each test session, only one member of each pair was used, the other serving as a control sequence. The decision as to which member of each pair was to be the test sequence was made after the target generation but before inspection of the content of the tape. Test and control runs were thus generated under identical conditions, and before a decision had been made as to which runs would be which.

The results of this portion of the experiment match those of the conventional portion. 30 subjects again participated; and for the total of 600 runs, the average run length was 56.37, again significant at the .001 level. The control runs, however, evaluated after the test sessions, showed no significant deviation from chance, the average run length being 63.08.

The results of the two experimental arrangements thus produced very similar ostensible PK effects. Apparently, the production of such effects did not depend on whether targets were generated during or before the test. Since the only apparently relevant difference in the conventional and unconventional portions of the experiment was that, in the latter, targets were generated before the test, and since the conventional portion suggested that PK activity occurs *during* the test, it seems that, in tests with pre-recorded targets, the activity of the subject during the test (or, perhaps, the activity of the experimenter) is a causal condition of the earlier nonrandom behavior of the RNG. The only relevant difference between test and control tapes was that the former were played back to a subject making a kind of PK effort.

Those sympathetic to the existence of psi phenomena, but wary of backward causation, may wish to propose another explanation. The least outrageous possibility is that the experimenter (or perhaps the subject) unconsciously used precognition *before* target generation to determine (a) when exactly, the 60-run sequences would be generated, and (b) which of these sequences would be chosen as test sequences, and then (c), again unconsciously, the experimenter (or subject) used PK during target generation to produce nonrandom behavior in the RNG just for the test sequences. A variant of this account would (a) have the experimenter (or subject) use real-time clairvoyance to know when the 60-run sequences were being generated, while (b) using precognition to know which sequences would be test sequences; and then (c) use PK to influence the generator at the appropriate time.

We may well question, however, whether these alternative (*super-psi*) explanations are any easier to swallow than the retrocausal interpretation of Schmidt's results. In some ways, actually, they seem harder to accept, since they require *three* different psi performances rather than one. Moreover, each of these accounts relies on the operation of precognition. In fact, the first requires two precognitive achievements in addition to a PK achievement. But if we question the retrocausal account in virtue of its reliance on retrocausation, the accounts relying on precognition would, presumably, be doubtful for the same reason. Moreover, the precognition required would be of an extremely refined sort, more impressive than any psi ability demonstrated (as far as I know) in other contexts by experimenter or subjects—in fact, more detailed and accurate than any for which we have experimental support. But if Schmidt's experiments demonstrate retroactive PK, the PK required would be no more startling (in terms of effectiveness of refinement) than that demonstrated in the conventional part of the test. The only difference between the two seems to lie in the temporal direction of the PK effort. Hence, the most promising alternative paranormal explanations of Schmidt's results seem less promising in some respects than the retrocausal explanation.*

I should mention that, from a certain perspective, a super-psi hypothesis does not seem all that far-fetched (although, to those who judge the above super-psi hypotheses to be extravagant, such a perspective will no doubt also seem extravagant). Suppose we take the view that a person's mind can

---

*An interesting philosophical defense of retrocausation, too complicated to be examined here, has been offered by Brier [21], [22], and takes its inspiration from Dummett [45]. Its central thesis is that there is a difference between *affecting* the past and *changing* the past. Only the latter, Brier claims, seems to be impossible.

and does affect his external environment with the same degree of refinement and persistence used to affect the body, as in cases of biofeedback, hypnotic suggestion (for example the raising of welts on the skin), the placebo effect, and other continual psychosomatic processes. Perhaps we always take an active role in literally shaping or causing the events around us, though not by the familiar forms of agency; and perhaps this explains why some people are lucky or unlucky, or why some people experience more coincidences than others. Perhaps, just as we may be continually controlling our body's health through subtle mental influence, and just as this might explain why some people are perpetually healthy or sick, we might also be continually exerting an effect on our physical environment as a whole. If so, psi functioning would seem to be more refined and sophisticated than any of our crude laboratory tests reveal; perhaps we underestimate its power because we seek out only its least interesting manifestations. (In fact, in II.B., I suggest that one viable approach to a causal theory of meaningful coincidences may be that coincidences are the genuine external physical effects of unconscious mental processes.)

It is important to remember, moreover, that even if Schmidt's experiments provide evidence for retroactive PK or some other kind of super-psi, it may be *experimenter* PK or psi rather than subject PK or psi. Reinforcing this point somewhat, two parapsychologists at the University of Edinburgh (see Millar and Broughton [98]) attempted in two experiments to replicate Schmidt's second experiment in retroactive PK (to be described below), but got nonsignificant results. This is interesting since it is well-known, first, that Edinburgh parapsychologists do not usually obtain significant results in psi experiments, and second, that Schmidt does. In fact, Schmidt may be a very strong psi source. In an experiment he conducted using cockroaches (see [137]), Schmidt hypothesized that the insects would use PK to influence the output of an RNG in order to receive *fewer* than chance levels of electric shocks. But in fact, the cockroaches received more shocks than were predicted on the hypothesis of chance. Schmidt, as it happens, dislikes cockroaches. So, as a number of parapsychologists have observed,* unless we are to suppose that the cockroaches enjoyed the shocks and used PK to increase their frequency of occurrence, the experiment suggests PK activity on Schmidt's part—presumably, expressing his aversion to his subjects.†

The second experiment with pre-recorded targets. This experiment may be viewed as a variant of the one described above, using RNGs operating at low and high speeds. You will recall that scores in that test seemed to be dependent on the generation rate of targets, with lower scores occurring at the high generation speed of 300 events per second. The conditions for both auditory and visual feedback, however, were not the same for the two speeds, although the visual feedback conditions were virtually the same. But according to the equivalence hypothesis, and also according to a theoretical model of psi developed by Schmidt (see [140], [141], [145]), the experimental outcome ought not to depend on the method of target preparation, so long as the conditions for feedback do not vary as well. In part, the second experiment was designed to test this conjecture.

The important features of the experiment are as follows.

(i) The test runs were arranged so that momentarily generated targets were alternated with pre-recorded targets.

---

*See, e.g., R. L. Morris, 'Parapsychology, Biology, and ANPSI', in Wolman [198], and J. R. Rush, 'Problems and Methods in Psychokinesis', in Krippner [84].

†At the time of writing, further reports of attempts to replicate Schmidt's work are trickling in. J. W. Davis and M. D. Morrison [37] failed to get positive results, and later failed again (see Morrison and Davis [100]). Schmidt, however, has had continued success with pre-recorded targets. In a test conducted with J. Terry (Terry and Schmidt [173]), he obtained weak positive results. But in some ingenious experiments in which the subjects tested themselves at home (Schmidt [143]), he obtained rather strong results. He continues to obtain positive results, which he has reported at the P.A. Convention (Schmidt [146]).

Schmidt felt that this procedure would enable him to make a more direct comparison between conventional and retroactive PK than was possible in the previous test—for which the two sorts of PK were tested on different occasions.

(ii) The pre-recorded targets were generated and recorded at what, in the earlier test, had appeared to be somewhat too fast a speed—namely, the high speed of 300 events per second. The twist in this case was to be that, when the targets were played back during the test runs, they were played at the speed of 10 per second. Schmidt hoped this arrangement would test the hypothesis that the experimental outcome was not a function of the conditions at the time the targets were generated, but instead a function of the conditions during the presentation to the subjects of target-feedback.

(iii) In the first experiment in retroactive PK, the scores obtained with and without time displacement were approximately the same. However, Schmidt's theoretical model suggested that, under conditions of time displacement, subjects' scores could be improved through *repeated* playback of the pre-recorded targets—at least so long as the subject was unaware that the same targets were being replayed. If the subject were aware of this procedure, he might feel that a genuine PK effort would be futile when the targets were repeated. To test this, Schmidt presented each pre-recorded target *four* times to the subject. The repeated targets were embedded between momentarily generated targets and repeated at different sections of a test run—in order to reduce as much as possible the likelihood of subjects' detecting that targets were being repeated.

Subjects were given visual and auditory feedback simultaneously. They were instructed to move a fluctuating needle to the left as far and as long as possible, which yields a display corresponding to an excess of generated tails (−1s) over heads (+1s). Coupled with the visual display was a variable frequency sound generator. Deflections of the needle to the left or right corresponded, respectively, to a decrease or increase in the frequency of the sound. The subjects were asked to try to lower the frequency, mentally.

The actual structure of a test run was as follows. Before a run was actually begun, and while the experimenter was talking to the subject, a sequence of 128 binary random numbers was generated at the rate of 300/sec. and stored in a computer memory. In addition, the sequence of heads and tails was also recorded on paper punch tape, for the purpose of a permanent record. Experimenter and subject did not at this stage know what the 128 numbers were; the subject did not even know (at least by normal means) that a target sequence had been recorded. Subjects thought all their targets were momentarily generated. After the 128 numbers had been generated and recorded, a sequence of 256 events was presented to the subject at the rate of 10 per second. The even-numbered events in this sequence were generated on the spot; however, the odd-numbered events came from the computer memory of the pre-recorded sequence. Subjects thus received a mixture of momentarily generated and pre-recorded targets. The experimenter received no feedback of targets during the test.

After the run of 256 events, there was a 15 second intermission to enable the subject to look at his score on the display counter, and also to print the score on paper punch tape. Then, another sequence of 256 events was presented to the subject, using the same 128 pre-recorded targets for the odd-numbered events in the sequence. This procedure was then repeated two more times, so that by the end of the test each subject had been presented with 512 momentarily generated targets and 128 pre-recorded targets presented four different times.

At the end of each group of four runs, the memory of the 128 targets was automatically read and the numbers of heads and tails printed (once again) on paper punch tape. There were thus two different records on paper punch tape of the pre-recorded sequences of targets, which allowed Schmidt to verify that the memory content had not been changed during the test (so far as we know, nobody has yet been able to use PK to change an already punched tape). For purposes of control, the randomness of the RNG was rechecked (it had been tested successfully for randomness in the earlier test using two speeds). Also, as a standard precaution against generator bias, generator outputs were alternated after each session.

Some of the main results of this experiment are given in Table 2. The scoring rate of 50.815% with the momentarily generated targets is only marginally significant (at the .05 level), although this rate is not to any statistically significant degree lower than the rate of 51.6% obtained at the slow speed of 30 events per second in the earlier two-speed test, conducted under psychologically similar feedback conditions.

Far and away the most interesting result was the much higher scoring rate of almost 53% on the repeated pre-recorded targets. Moreover, comparing the scores, for each of the 20 subjects, with momentarily generated and pre-record-ed targets, we see that the difference between those scores is significant at the .025 level. The second experiment, then, seems *prima facie* to confirm the existence of PK on pre-recorded targets. It also supports the hypothesis that there would be an *addition effect*—i.e., that repeated feedback of the pre-recorded material can increase the scoring rate. This is especially interesting when viewed against the earlier test in which targets were generated *and played back* at the rate of 300 per second, and for which the scoring rate was 50.37%. Since, in this test, all targets were displayed at the rate of 10 per second, this fact lends support in turn to the idea that the experimental outcome depends more on conditions during the test than on conditions during target generation.

Until more experiments of this sort are conducted, one must, to say the least, be circumspect in interpreting these results. On the face of it, the different playback speeds and the repeated playback of targets seem to be causally relevant to the different scores. But if so, then the only way to ac-comodate this fact would seem to be to admit backward causation; for we must explain how the slower playback speed, or repeated playback, aids in producing the *earlier* nonrandom output of the RNG. We can resist admitting backward causation, of course, by arguing that the correla-

Table 2. Main results of the second experiment with pre-recorded targets.

	Momentarily generated targets	Pre-recorded targets
Number of trials	20,480	5,120
Deviation from chance	+167	+151
Scoring rate	50.815%	52.95%
Odds against chance	20 to 1	2,000 to 1

tion between test scores and different playback speeds (for example) are not what they appear to be. But then, we must still explain why those correlations obtain; we seem only to have traded one mystery for another.

If, however, we take the bold step of allowing backward causation (if only to see where it leads us), then at least we can make some reasonable conjectures about the role of slow or repeated playback. As far as the apparent causal efficacy of slow playback is concerned, the most reasonable conjecture (given the current state of ignorance) is perhaps that, at the slower display speed, subjects are able to concentrate better (consciously or subconsciously) on individual events. Perhaps even at the display rate of 10 per second, subjects miss some of the individual events, so that they attend to certain of them for the first time only during repeated playback. This is at least compatible with Schmidt's hypothesis that success depends more on conditions during the test than on conditions during target generation. In any case, further experiments in which pre-recorded targets are played back and repeated *at even slower speeds* might shed additional light on this matter. With respect to the apparent causal efficacy of repeated playback, it is tempting to say (as I have just suggested) that the repetitions simply allow the subjects to attend to relevant information missed (for one reason or another) on previous playbacks of targets. Although these conjectures hardly clear up the major mystery of apparent backward PK, at least they introduce no further major mysteries. These are, in fact, just the sorts of things we would say if we were concerned rather with causal connections running in the familiar temporal direction. So if these speculations are hard to swallow, it is primarily because we have difficulty accepting the idea of retrocausation.

Let us now pass from reviewing the details of Schmidt's work to a brief review of some other PK research. Findings resulting from some recent work connect in rather interesting ways with Schmidt's own results, and are often surprising in themselves.

d. Further PK Research

Many studies in PK, as well as in ESP, suggest that subjects are more likely to obtain above-chance results when they do *not* actively try to affect the experimental outcome. That is, a state of *passive attention* or expectation often seems more conducive to successful scores than a state in which the subject makes a conscious effort to succeed. For this reason, subjects in psi experiments are often asked merely to *wish* for good results at the beginning of an experiment rather than attempt consciously to *make* something happen.

This apparent finding is consistent with what we know about the operation of biofeedback and the efficacy of placebos. Biofeedback research has established that ordinary persons can learn to control, voluntarily, numerous physiological processes customarily regarded as involuntary—for example, skin temperature, brain wave frequency, and even the activity of a single cell (see Basmajian [4], [5], and Green and Green [60]: 31-32), simply by observing feedback displays which monitor these processes. Research has shown that these self-regulatory activities are most effective when the subject simply desires the intended result and allows it to occur, rather than striving or exerting a conscious effort. Two leading biofeedback researchers, Elmer and Alyce Green of the Menninger Foundation, call this *passive volition*. The mechanisms of successful self-regulation through biofeedback are not at all well-understood. But enough is known about the surface aspects of its operation to make comparison with ESP and PK performance illuminating and to lend some credibility to the idea that passive volition is conducive to psi functioning.

The efficacy of placebos also appears to provide evidence of the power of passive volition. Placebos are pharmacologically inert; yet patients who believe that the substances have curative properties frequently experience remission of symptoms at least as good as that provided by orthodox treatment. Recently, there have been reports of the discovery of pain-inhibiting substances (endorphins) produced in patients who, after taking a placebo, experience remission of pain. But contrary to naively optimistic reports in the media, this discovery clears up none of the large mysteries surrounding the placebo effect. For one thing, it leaves unanswered the major question: In what way is the placebo causally connected to the brain's secretion of an endorphin? Furthermore, the placebo effect has been demonstrated with respect to symptoms other than pain. For example, Jerome Frank, of the Johns Hopkins University (see Frank [56]), has reported on the placebo treatment of warts—painting warts with a brightly colored dye and telling patients that the warts will disappear as the dye wears off. He observes that this treatment is as effective as any other, including surgical excision. The relevant fact is that patients do not consciously attempt to will the wart away. Rather, they expect it to disappear, and then it does.

Though certainly interesting in itself, the apparent efficacy of passive volition or expectation in psi experiments connects in a provocative way with a growing body of evidence that PK success is not dependent on subjects' knowing (at least by normal means) what system or kind of system they are supposed to influence. We have already observed one example of this phenomenon in Schmidt's experiments with RNGs having different degrees of internal complexity. The simple system, we may recall, was one of Schmidt's conventional binary RNGs, whereas the complex system chose heads or tails by taking the majority vote of 100 rapidly generated binary events. Subjects did not know which of the two RNGs was active for a given trial. Nevertheless, their concentration on a certain target color for the feedback display correlated with non-chance behavior of the very RNG that was active.

A further experiment conducted by Schmidt, this time with Lee Pantas (Schmidt and Pantas [147]), provides additional evidence that successful PK subjects need not know what system they are supposed to influence, and that success in a PK test does not even depend on the subjects' knowing they are being tested for PK. Tests were performed on a machine which could be switched between two different types of internal circuitry by the flip of a switch. The subject never knew (at least by normal means) which version of the machine was operating; psychologically, both seemed the same to the subject. This arrangement allowed for the comparison of results with physically different machines under psychologically equivalent conditions.

The machine in question was a smallish box with four horizontally displayed colored lamps, and a button below each lamp. The machine operated in an ostensibly precognitive and an ostensibly PK mode. I say 'ostensibly' because neither arrangement was free of the sorts of ambiguities discussed earlier, in I.A.6. The precognitive circuitry could be used to test for PK, and the PK circuitry for precognition. Nevertheless, the circuits were quite different. To clarify the import of the experiment, I shall therefore describe the circuitry first.

The precognitive circuitry was similar in operation to Schmidt's standard binary RNG using Sr-90 as a source of randomness. The subject was instructed to press the button of the lamp he thought would light next. When the button was pressed, the next electron from the decay of the Sr-90 to register on the Geiger counter would stop a modulo-4 (i.e., 4-position) counter driven by a high speed oscillator. Depending on which of the four positions the counter stopped in, the corresponding lamp would light. Although this design seems to test for precognition, it is clear that nothing in the arrangement prevents the subject from using PK to stop the counter in the position corresponding to the button pushed.

The second circuit arrangement seems, on the face of it, to call for a kind of PK by the subject, although a certain form of precognition is not ruled out in principle. The difference between the two arrangements was that, in the second, a logic circuit was introduced into the machine. It operated as follows. If the modulo-4 counter stopped at a 1, 2, 3, or 4, the lamp which lit was respectively, 1, 2, 3, or 0 steps to the right of the button pushed (think of this as a form of circular counting, so that one step from 4 is 1). Thus, if the subject pressed button 2, and the counter stopped at 1, lamp number 3 would light, and the subject would score a miss. Obviously, the only way to score a hit with this arrangement was to have the counter stop at 4, since only then would the lamp lit not advance from the number of the button pressed. It seems, then, that in order to score a hit, the subject must use PK to make the counter stop at 4. Actually, the same result could be obtained if the subject had a precognitive (not necessarily conscious) waiting strategy, so that through precognition he would know when the counter would stop at 4, and wait until the appropriate time to press a button. (This strategy strikes *me*, at least, as less plausible than conventional PK, since it seems to require extremely high-precision clairvoyance and button pushing.)

In any case, despite the switching from one sort of circuitry to another, the external behavior of the machine remained the same; subjects could not tell the difference between the precognitive and PK versions of the test. The principal experimenter (Schmidt) knew in every case which of the two circuits was in use (thus raising the spectre of experimenter PK), although neither co-experimenter nor subjects knew that the experiment involved two different types of tests. Results in both the precognitive and PK modes were statistically significant—at the .01 and .0005 level, respectively, and the difference between the two scores is not itself statistically significant. What is most important is that the instructions given subjects were the same in both cases, and in no case did subjects think they were participating in a PK experiment. This experiment provides, then, some evidence—by no means conclusive—that not only is PK success independent of subjects knowing the technicalities or identity of the system they must control, but also that PK success is independent of subjects knowing they are in a PK test.

We may recall that, in Schmidt's first experiment with retroactive PK (in both the conventional and unconventional portions of the experiment), subjects were not informed they were participating in a PK test. They were merely instructed to listen for the next click in their headphones; Schmidt hypothesized that their expectancy would trigger some subconscious PK mechanism.

Another example along these lines comes from an interesting experiment conducted by R.G. Stanford *et al.,* in which subjects apparently biased the output of an RNG when, unknown to them, their fate depended on what the output was. First, subjects were assigned a boring task to do. Unknown to them, an RNG was generating away in another room. The experiment was arranged so that if, during a prescribed period (while he was engaged in his boring task), the RNG produced a certain above-chance outcome, the subject could leave his boring task and enjoy a pleasant one. Subjects were also later given a conventional PK test.

Interpreting the results of this experiment is complicated somewhat by the fact that the two data collectors in the experiment obtained quite different sorts of results. One of them got nonsignificant scores under both conditions (unintentional and intentional PK), and the other got above-chance scores under both conditions. This suggests that the difference in the two sets of scores is at least partly the result of an experimenter effect. Still, 8 out of 40 subjects escaped their unpleasant task. This number, although marginally significant, is more impressive if we suppose that the first data collector was able to inhibit the performances of his subjects. However, it is not clear whether we are entitled to this conjecture.

Stanford has conducted a number of other experiments designed to demonstrate unconscious psi functioning (not necessarily PK), in order to deal with contingencies not known to subjects by ordinary means. While often ingenious, these experiments were complicated and have failed to produce results as impressive as Schmidt's. It is hard to know at this stage whether Stanford's marginally significant results should be attributed (a) to his theoretical model (which may be so profoundly incorrect as to promote experimental designs doomed to fail), (b) to complications or flaws in the experimental designs themselves (whether or not the theoretical justification for them is acceptable), or (c) to a negative experimenter effect on the part of Stanford or his associates. Still, his experiments repay careful attention (see also, e.g., Stanford *et al.* [159], and Stanford and Stio [160]), and I encourage the reader to consult them.

e. Theoretical Issues.

Summing things up thus far, there is a growing (if not always coercive) body of evidence that success in PK experiments does not depend, or depends very little, on subjects' knowing (at least by normal means) such apparently relevant facts as the nature, mechanics, or existence of the PK target system, or even whether they are being tested for PK. There is evidence, also, as I observed above, that subjects tend to perform best when they do not actively try to affect the experimental outcome. And when we add these to the results of Schmidt's experiments, we begin to get a rather surprising picture of PK. In fact, to some, it begins to look as though success in PK tasks might be accomplished without any form of computation or information-processing by subjects. In other words, the evidence may point away from what Stanford calls the *cybernetic* model of PK.

Lately, the idea that PK violates a cybernetic model has received considerable attention in parapsychology. There are two main reasons for this. The first concerns the recent emergence and development of various speculations lumped together under the heading of *observational theories*. These offer an analysis of psi functioning quite unlike that suggested by conventional models—an analysis that seems consistent, in fact, with a good deal of otherwise puzzling evidence. The second concerns the influence of a certain line of thinking championed most conspicuously by Stanford [156],

[157]. Stanford has been arguing for the *prima facie* incompatibility of the evidence for PK not only with a cybernetic model of PK, but also with a more general 'psychobiological' model of psi, which treats ESP as a form of sensitivity or communication, and PK, as a form of nonmuscular influence on a system (guided, perhaps, by ESP scanning of the environment). I shall now look briefly at these two lines of development.

Observational theories. The currently dominant versions of the observational theories are those proposed by Schmidt [140], [141], [145] and Walker [187], [188]. I am not prepared at the moment to offer a detailed assessment of these theories, especially their formal aspects (which I leave to physicists to appraise), although, in II.A.3., I criticize Walker's naively atomistic phenomenology. I refer the reader to Millar [97], however, for a good survey and discussion of the various versions of the observational theories.

Although they exhibit certain startling features, such as reliance on retrocausation, the observational theories also have certain advantages. One is that they purport to account for the apparently critical role played by observation of feedback in experiments like those conducted by Schmidt. According to the observational theories, subjects can exert a psi influence only on random events and only if they receive feedback of the result of their efforts. Thus in order to influence the output of an RNG, a subject must receive feedback at some point about how he has scored. It does not matter whether the feedback is received minutes or years later. All that matters is that the subject later learn by ordinary sensory means what the previous output of the RNG was.

Notice that the observational theories do not merely *permit* a kind of retrocausation; they actually *require* it. The subject's PK effort, for example, is effective only after observing feedback of earlier results. On this view, a PK effort made *during* target generation but before observation of feedback will be totally ineffective.

Another apparent advantage of the observational theories is that they offer a kind of *unified psi theory* by reducing all categories of psi to just one—namely, PK. To quote Millar,

[With respect to PK] the observational theories give . . . the picture that the subject hears the tones which were generated by a pure-chance process some time before. At the moment of feedback he causes the RNG at the time of generation to become biased in such a way that he hears more hits. It is one of the great strengths of the observational theories that by addition of only *one plausible postulate, namely that the brain contains at least one pure-chance process which determines, in part, the subject's guessing behaviour*, that the cognitive forms of psi can be readily (and quantitatively) assimilated to the same model. Suppose that a subject performs a card-guessing test: after each trial a computer tells him whether or not he was right. If the computer generates the targets in a deterministic way then these can not be affected by PK; so that to secure correspondence between target and guess and hence to be informed at the time of feedback that he had a hit, the subject must direct his PK onto his own "internal RNG" which determines his choice at the time he made his guesses. To put it another way, *ESP is simply a special case of time-displacement PK in which the subject's earlier guessing behavior plays the part of the RNG* ([97]: 309, emphasis added).

This approach is ingenious, but I am not convinced, for one thing, that the postulate on which the reduction of all psi to PK depends is defensible. At this point, it is not clear to me what is meant by saying that some brain process determines guessing behavior. If this requires that there be some *mechanism* in the brain which produces guesses of a certain type, then the postulate is not only implausible but unintelligible for reasons I explore in II.A. (especially II.A.2.).

Ignoring this difficulty for the moment, another virtue of the observational theories is that they appear to explain how psi can be *selective*. Broad (in 'Normal Cognition, Clairvoyance, and Telepathy', in [23]) examined in detail how, on a perceptual model of ESP, it was virtually impossible to understand how a person could identify one card and distinguish it from adjacent cards in a sealed or otherwise intact deck. But on the observational theories, this is no longer a problem. All that is required is that the subject receive feedback of individual hits. Thus, if the subject learns that he correctly guessed, say, the 6th card down, this permits him to influence by means of retroactive PK his guess at the previous time.

As parsimonious as all this sounds, I confess I can make little sense of it. Consider, first, the case of the reduction of ESP to retroactive PK. The observational theories ask us to concede that

(a) Subject S's observation of feedback of a hit

is causally necessary for

(b) Retroactive PK on a previous brain state of S;

and that (b) is causally necessary for

(c) S's making the correct guess,

which is causally necessary for

(d) Recording of the hit (by a computer);

and that (d) in turn is causally necessary for

(a) Subject S's observation of feedback of a hit.

On this view, the computer could not inform the subject of a correct guess unless the guess was already made. This is plausible enough. But the observational theories also maintain that the subject cannot exert the appropriate PK effort unless the correct guess is already made and recorded. So, making the right PK effort both *presupposes* and *causes* the earlier correct guess (or observation of feedback, etc.). Now I do not see, frankly, how these states of affairs are jointly possible. I do not see how the making of a correct guess can be both a necessary causal condition of, and also the result of, the same subsequent PK effort.

In order to appreciate what is wrong with saying that some event E is both causally necessary for and also caused by some other event E', let us consider one way in which such a claim wreaks havoc with our conceptual scheme. I want to argue that acceptance of this feature of the observational theories forces us to reject certain assumptions which we have no other reason to reject, and which in fact have considerable antecedent plausibility.

Let a be the name of the random event caused and presupposed by the retroactive PK activity of a psi source, and let b be the name of this PK event. Then if 'Cxy' means 'x causes y', the observational theories claim

(1) Cba & Cab

But when (1) is added to two other perfectly respectable assumptions, a manifest absurdity results. One of these is simply that causal relations are transitive,

(2) (x) (y) (z) $[(Cxy \& Cyz) \supset Cxz]$

The other is that nothing (except possibly God) can be the cause of itself. Hence, restricting ourselves (plausibly) to the domain of events we can assert

(3) (x) (y) $[Cxy \supset x \neq y]$

But now, we may note that an instance of (2) is

(4) (Cba & Cab) $\supset$ Cbb

and that (4) and (1) yield

(5) Cbb

But an instance of (3) is

(6) Cbb $\supset$ b $\neq$ b

and (6) and (5) give us the intolerable result

(7) b $\neq$ b

So (1)-(3) together give the result that an event is not self-identical. And I submit that if any of these statements is to be rejected, the most plausible candidate is (1). Proponents of the observational theories might suggest that we reject (3) instead. But the *only* reason for doing so would be to retain (1). (3) has considerable antecedent plausibility, while (1) has none; so this suggestion is hardly persuasive.

The only way I can see to avoid this seemingly vicious circle of having an event E cause and be caused by another event E' is to take a step which the observational theories would not sanction. We must first observe that in order for subject S to make an appropriate retroactive PK effort (say, on his brain, in an ESP test), the following conditions must be satisfied.

  (i) A target T is generated;
  (ii) S guesses correctly that T is the target;
  (iii) S learns after his guess whether he guessed correctly.

Now, since S's PK effort is directed to an earlier state of his own brain, and not on the target generator, satisfaction of condition (i) is not a causal consequence of that PK effort. Rather, the satisfaction of condition (ii) depends on what S does later, since, by hypothesis, the brain state producing the guess of T is at least partly a random occurrence, while the generation of T is not. But satisfaction of condition (iii) requires that condition (ii) be satisfied, and this is where the vicious circle enters. Condition (ii) must be satisfied in order that S make the appropriate PK effort later. But satisfaction of (ii) is also a *causal consequence* of that same PK effort.

Now, if proponents of the observation theories merely required that subjects be given feedback of targets, and *not hits*, the vicious circle and its attendant problems could be avoided. That is, suppose we required, not that condition (iii) be met in order for the subject to make his PK effort on his own brain, but only that

  (iii') S learns after his guess that T was the target.

By replacing condition (iii) with condition (iii'), we seem to have a way of breaking the circle—or at least one sort of circle. Whereas (ii) is a necessary causal condition of (iii), it is *not* a causal condition of (iii'). So when we substitute (iii') for (iii), we get a much different and less paradoxical-looking *causal sequence*. Let us say that condition (iv) is

  (iv) S uses PK on his brain so that he guesses target T.

When we review our original set of conditions, the observational theories posit the following sequence:

$$(ii) \rightarrow (iii) \rightarrow (iv) \rightarrow (ii)$$

But with the new conditions we get the sequence

$$(i) \rightarrow (iii') \rightarrow (iv) \rightarrow (ii)$$

Here, satisfaction of (ii) is not (paradoxically) a non-trivial causal requirement of its own satisfaction. We do not need to interpose (ii) between (i) and (iii') when describing the situation's *causal* history. Rather, (ii) goes between (i) and (iii') only when describing the sequence of events with respect to their actual temporal ordering, without reference to which events were causally necessary for which. What this seems to show is that the causal order of events is not necessarily the same as their temporal order. The correct causal sequence for our revised set of conditions, as we have seen, is

$$(C) \quad (i) \rightarrow (iii') \rightarrow (iv) \rightarrow (ii)$$

while the correct temporal sequence is

$$(T) \quad (i) \rightarrow (ii) \rightarrow (iii') \rightarrow (iv)$$

But this is the correct temporal sequence *only* by hypothesis. We simply happen to be considering a case where S's guess precedes certain events but not others. The causal history represented by (C) is, however, indifferent to the temporal placement of S's guess relative to other events. Depending on the sort of case we are considering, the temporal ordering could be different from that of (T), even though the causal ordering remains that of (C). For example, we could have the *precognitive* ordering

$$(T') \quad (ii) \rightarrow (i) \rightarrow (iii') \rightarrow (iv)$$

We could also have the temporal ordering

$$(T'') \quad (i) \rightarrow (iii') \rightarrow (iv) \rightarrow (ii)$$

where S's guess *follows* S's PK influence on the guess. This might correspond to a case where, after learning the identity of the target, S's PK effort causes S to guess correctly at a later time—let us say, long after S has forgotten what the target had been. So, while the discrepancy between sequences (C) and (T) may conflict with our supposition that causes must precede effects, we cannot object to (C) on grounds of circularity.

Now whether this general maneuver is acceptable to the observational theories depends, among other things, on whether it is essential that the subject learn through feedback that his guess is *accurate* and not simply that he learn what the target is (whether or not he then knows that he has guessed correctly). The first alternative, as we have seen, leads to a clearly unacceptable causal picture. Proponents of the observational theories have apparently not appreciated the potential importance of these two interpretations of the role of feedback. Or, they may be clear about it, and content with the first alternative and its seemingly vicious circle. For example, Schmidt states openly,

> . . . a person can predict a future event only if he (or some other person who acts as a psi source) gets later feedback on the accuracy of the prediction ([141] : 228).

And, in the passage quoted above, Millar also emphasizes that the subject learn that he scored a hit.

In any case, despite this fuzziness in the exposition of the observational theories, there is reason to think that the afore-mentioned escape route is not open to them. We can see why, by reviewing the causal sequence posited by those theories in the case of PK. There, the conditions to be satisfied are

(1) Target T (say, a $+ 1$ or -1) is randomly generated;
(2) T is recorded;
(3) Subject S receives feedback of T,
(4) S uses PK to cause generation of T.

The correct causal ordering for this situation is

$(1) \rightarrow (2) \rightarrow (3) \rightarrow (4) \rightarrow (1)$

and here, satisfaction of (1) is both causally necessary for and a causal consequence of satisfaction of (4). Thus, this sequence is circular just as the sequence

(ii) → (iii) → (iv) → (ii)

was, in the case of our original set of causal conditions for ESP. But unlike that case, in the PK case we have no way to break the circle. The random event—in the PK case, generation of T—is both a cause and effect of some later PK effort, and unlike S's guess in the ESP case, we cannot deprive generation of T of its role in causing the PK effort. The observational theories apparently require that the random event which is to be affected be the same event which is necessary for the PK effort. But this suggests why, in the ESP case, learning of *hits* (not just learning target identity) is essential after all. Only that condition would require a causal loop exactly like the one required in the case of PK. This means that, in the case of ESP, the random event—S's guess—must be causally necessary for S's subsequent PK effort. But then we cannot replace condition (iii) with (iii'), since it would rob S's guess of its role as a causal condition for (iv): satisfaction of (ii) is necessary for satisfaction of (iii), but not for (iii').

I should add that Schmidt does not, as the above objections suggest, insist on feedback of individual hits. Unlike Walker, Schmidt maintains that the appropriate feedback can be of a statistical kind, so that S's receiving feedback that he is scoring at a certain rate is all that is causally necessary for S to make the PK effort that causes him to score at that rate. Let us overlook the fact that this position tends to undermine one of the apparent advantages of the observational theories—namely, the ability to explain selectivity of hits (say, in card-guessing tests) through presentation of feedback of individual hits. What matters, here, is that the new causal loop is as viciously circular as the one involving feedback of individual hits. In the case of PK, the new causal loop is this. In order for the subject S to make the PK effort which biases the RNG to produce some scoring rate r, S must receive feedback that he has scored at rate r. So Schmidt's proposal still makes one event—in this case, the RNG producing a certain output at rate r—both a precondition and effect of the same PK effort. The same problem applies, *mutatis mutandis*, to the reduction of ESP to PK.

Now, if these conjectures about the sorts of causal loops required are correct, then I must confess to having a further difficulty about accepting the observational theories. I fail to understand how such theories explain non-chance psi scores. For example, according to the observational theories, in order to make an ESP hit, the subject must observe *having made a hit*. After all, if the subject observes having missed, then it follows that he did not exert the appropriate retro-active PK. Thus, a subject can exert the appropriate retro-active PK on his earlier guessing only after having received feedback of having guessed correctly. This requires a *closed causal loop* according to which the subject's guess (as the result of his later PK effort) is explained *without reference* to his having access to any information about the target inde-pendently of his guess. As I understand these theories, independent information about target identity is *irrelevant* to the outcome of the subject's PK effort (hence, to his guess as well). But then, the theories seem unable to explain why the subject guessed the correct rather than the incorrect target—and, *a fortiori*, why there should be an extra-chance number of correct guesses that is not completely fortuitous.

As we have seen, the following conditions are causally necessary for S to influence retroactively his guessing so that he guesses correctly.

(ii) S guesses correctly that T is the target;
(iii) S learns after his guess whether he guessed correctly.

Moreover, the causal antecedent of (ii) is *not* that S was somehow able to identify the target independently of seeing how he guessed. Rather, the causal antecedent of (ii) is simply

(iv) S uses PK on his brain state so that he guesses target T.

Let us suppose that S makes his guess at time t and that at $t' > t$ he observes feedback of his hit and uses the appropriate retroactive PK. Thus, at time t', S has already guessed, and nothing done at that time can change this. That is why when S guesses *incorrectly* at t, nothing that happens later can rectify the error. But if we ask proponents of the observational theories why the subject guessed the correct rather than the incorrect target, they can give no sort of answer (as far as I can see) that will explain statistically significant numbers of hits. They can say that S guessed target T at t, because of S's PK effort at t' on S's brain state at t, and they can explain the PK effort at t' with respect to S's learning that his guess at T was correct. But then, it appears that significant nonchance scores are fortuitous. S's correct guess does not result from any information S has about the target, gained independently of his subsequent knowledge that his guess was correct. According to the observational theories, the only reason S guesses correctly is that he later made a certain PK effort; and the only reason he made *that* PK effort (and not one that would have resulted in a different guess), is that he guessed correctly. Hence, the reason S guesses correctly is that he guesses correctly. But of course this does not explain why S guesses one way rather than another (since S's guess of T is explained by reference to itself); it also does not explain why he guesses correctly more often than would be predicted on the hypothesis of chance.

An analogous situation obtains in the case of PK. The reason target T (let us say, $+1$) is generated is that S uses PK on the RNG so that a $+1$ is generated; and the reason S uses PK to produce a $+1$ (and not a -1) is that the RNG produced a $+1$ (so that S could receive the appropriate feedback). But there is no room in this causal loop to explain why a statistically significant excess of $+1$s is anything but fortuitous. Schmidt would say that the presence of the 'psi source' S in this causal history changes the probabilities associated with the outputs of the RNG. But it is not merely the presence of S that changes these probabilities. S can effect such changes only if he receives feedback of the RNG output.

But this means that the explanation of the nonrandom output of the RNG is not explained independently of what that output is—for example, simply with respect to the presence of S. But unless we can give such an independent account of the behavior of the RNG, its nonrandom behavior cannot be taken to be anything but a statistical anomaly. As it is, the observational theories claim (in effect) only that the RNG output is, say, +1 because its output is +1.

I am not confident that the foregoing objections are fatal; but I must say that, in the present form of the observational theories, the objections do seem fatal to me. Moreover, if the observational theories are committed (as I suggested earlier) to a mechanistic analysis of guessing, this too would be a fatal feature of the theories.

Another main source of difficulty lies with a general line of reasoning according to which the conventional models of ESP and PK appear unattractive. This line of reasoning has found its most eloquent exponent in Stanford (see, e.g., [157]).

Cybernetic and Psychobiological Models of Psi. According to the cybernetic model of PK, the organism—presumably through ESP—acquires information about the system it wishes to control; and while acting on that system by means of PK, it monitors and guides its activities by means of a continuing supply of information (or feedback). On this view, PK is rather like riding a bicycle or steering a car, since the PK subject is regarded as *acting on* the target system while monitoring the effects of those activities and adjusting its actions accordingly. Thus, PK involves something analogous to both motor abilities and information-processing abilities.

But on the cybernetic model of PK, we should *not* expect PK success to be independent of such things as the complexity of the target system and the speed of target generation. We should expect that intermediate complications of these sorts *would* make a difference to the outcome of a PK task, since they would affect the steps one would have to take to achieve the desired goal; and presumably, the greater the number of steps, or the more complicated or difficult the steps, the more complicated or difficult the associated monitoring activities and the greater the difficulty of attaining one's goal.

Consider the difference between riding a bicycle and riding a tricycle. Of the two, it is harder to ride a bicycle successfully, since the rider cannot count on two rear wheels for support and balance. Speaking more cybernetically, we could say that, for bicycle riding, more data than is needed for tricycle riding must be monitored and processed if success is to be achieved. Altogether, bicycle riding is a more complicated motor and information-processing task than tricycle riding. And if we take this example seriously, as the cybernetic model of PK encourages, then we should expect that for PK, as for bicycle riding, there would be a positive correlation between the complexity of the information to be processed or the system to be controlled and the difficulty of the task to be achieved.

A number of parapsychologists construe the PK data (reported above) as suggesting that PK is unusually, if not completely, indifferent to the complexity of the PK task. We observed earlier that, in Schmidt's tests with RNGs operating at two speeds, the faster speed was associated with a hit rate lower than that associated with the slower speed. We also noticed that, in Schmidt's second experiment in retroactive PK, subjects had a much higher hit rate with targets generated at the fast speed when they observed the target feedback at a slow speed. But although this suggests one kind of correlation between task complexity and PK success, it may not indicate the kind of correlation the cybernetic model suggests—namely, a positive correlation between the complexity of the target *system* and the complexity of the PK task. These facts about Schmidt's high-speed RNG should perhaps be viewed against the data indicating that conditions *during* the test (including the nature of the feedback) matter more to the outcome than conditions during target generation. Schmidt's equivalence hypothesis, we may recall, states (roughly) that, under the same sensory or psychological conditions, the magnitude of PK success will be the same for *any* two output-indistinguishable RNGs. On that view, what matters for PK success is not how complex or fast the process of target generation is. What seems to matter is rather what psychological or sensory conditions the subject finds himself in during the test—conditions that is, that may be only contingently related to the nature of the target system. (It would presumably be instructive for someone [preferably Schmidt, if he turns out to have been the phantom PKer] to conduct an experiment in which subjects make a PK effort on *rapidly played back* targets which were generated at a slow speed. The results could then be compared with those on targets momentarily generated at the slow speed.)

Moreover, not only does the cybernetic model seem at odds with PK's apparent independence from the complexities of the process of target generation; it also seems to conflict with the apparent independence of PK from moment-to-moment *changes* in target system or generation speed, or the subject's (normally-acquired) *knowledge* of these things or of what counts as a success in the test itself (e.g., whether for a certain trial run, the RNG must produce +1s or −1s). An analogy drawn from baseball may help make this clear. If batters could always count on the pitcher's throwing one kind of pitch (say, a fast ball) into the same part of the strike zone, batting averages would be much higher than they are. But pitchers throw different sorts of pitches, and how and where they throw them tends to vary from pitch to pitch. As a result, batters must constantly adjust to rapid changes in the nature and speed of the target they are to hit. And even though they have a brief moment in which to judge what sort and speed of pitch is being thrown and make at least some adjustments, batting efficiency inevitably suffers. However, PK on RNGs seems not to work this way, since moment-to-moment changes in the target seem not to affect PK scores. Moreover, the fact that subjects often do not even know of such changes (at least by normal means) suggests that PK is even less like the baseball example—since the batter adjusts to *perceived* changes in the target.

There is yet another respect in which the data seem not to conform to what the cybernetic model of PK leads us to expect. Bicycle riding, we observed, is a more complicated motor and information-processing task than tricycle riding. But of course there are tasks even more complicated in these respects than bicycle riding—for example, forging a Rembrandt painting. And when we reflect on the difference between bike riding and Rembrandt forgery, we must realize that there is a positive correlation between the complexity of the task and the complexity or sophistication of the organism able to complete it. A human and a chimpanzee can both learn to ride a bicycle, but (to my knowledge) only a human being can forge a Rembrandt. The latter task requires keener and more refined perceptual and motor skills than are possessed by lower primates. Analogously, on the cybernetic model of PK we should expect a correlation between the complexity of the task (i.e., the complexity of the required monitoring and motor—or quasi-motor—activities) and the complexity of the organism required to complete it. We should expect that *some* organisms are too simple to carry out the required activities.

Here, the studies of PK in animals are especially suggestive, since to some extent they thwart our cybernetic expectations. Although the evidence for PK in animals is not nearly as impressive as that for human PK (see the essay by Morris, in Wolman [198], and the surveys by Rush and Schmeidler, in Krippner [84]), some evidence indicates that PK has been demonstrated by organisms seemingly incapable of the kinds of information processing needed for the task involved—in particular, on the assumption that PK requires monitoring and interfering with the operation of the system to be controlled. For example, tests have been performed on such simple creatures as brine shrimp, cockroaches, and fighting fish. And while the studies completed thus far do not present a solid body of evidence for animal PK, they are provocative enough to warrant further exploration.

To give you an idea of the sort of research being conducted, I shall describe what may be the most impressive study of animal PK to date, conducted by W. Braud [18], whose career in parapsychology was preceded by a 'legitimate' career in physiological psychology. Much of Braud's work during this time concerned the physiology and behavior of fish, and the parapsychological study I wish to report employs some of the techniques he used and developed at that time.

In a series of four experiments, 34 aggressive tropical fish were given a 20-second mirror presentation as feedback for making a hit on one of Schmidt's binary RNGs. The use of mirror presentation as a stimulus is standard experimental procedure in learning experiments with fighting fish. Since quite a bit is known about it, Braud reasonably assumèd that his use of this procedure in parapsychological experiments could be instructively compared with its more orthodox applications. The performance of the 34 test animals was compared with the performance of 34 nonaggressive control fish, for whom mirror presentation is not reinforcing.

The results were not overwhelming (the work was preliminary in any case), but there were distinct differences in the performances of the two groups. The control group scored at chance levels during all four tests. The performance of these 34 nonaggressive fish, over a total of 3,400 trials, yielded a deviation from chance of +6, which is nonsignificant. However, the 34 aggressive fish apparently achieved in 3,400 trials a deviation of +82 (the probability of this being .005). Naturally, experimenter PK is not ruled out in principle. So it is not entirely clear who is responsible for the deviation. One interesting fact, however, may suggest that the fish were the culprits. The experimental group of aggressive fish showed a distinct *decline* effect from the first to the last of the four runs, whereas no decline was observed for the control group. This result is consistent with the well-documented existence of such a decline effect in standard behavioral research using the mirror technique with fighting fish (see Baenninger [2]), and suggests that, in PK experiments, as in more conventional learning experiments, the reinforcement value of the mirror technique tends to decrease over time. On the other hand, since human beings also often exhibit the decline effect in psi tests, the decline during the fish experiments might equally be evidence for experimenter psi.

In any case, no matter what our final assessment of the work conducted with animals thus far, Stanford's position against the conventional models of PK and ESP is hardly outlandish. But my own view is that, though it is forceful, Stanford's verdict may be a bit hasty. To see why, notice first, that Stanford makes two claims, not clearly separated, one of which is stronger than the other. The more modest of the two is (i) that PK violates a cybernetic model according to which an organism acts on a system and guides and monitors its own PK activities by means of (presumably paranormal) feedback loops. But Stanford feels that the data also support the more sweeping claim (ii) that no psychobiological model of PK is satisfactory—that is, that PK is not at all like ordinary motor actions, and that any model of PK based on familiar psychological or biological activities must be systematically misleading. In making this wider claim, Stanford argues that PK seems to be accomplished without *any* form of computation or information processing by the organism involved. I believe, however, that the evidence probably does not support either of Stanford's claims—particularly the stronger.

Let us look first at the weaker claim, that PK cannot be modeled cybernetically. This amounts to the denial that, during PK, the organism guides and monitors its actions by means of a continuing supply of feedback. But the evidence seems able to support only the still weaker claim that *if* PK can be modeled cybernetically, the feedback loops involved must be somewhat unusual—not quite like those involved, say, in steering a car (which Stanford treats as a paradigm case of an activity that may be construed cybernetically).

But the data may not support even this strong a claim. Even the results of Schmidt's tests for PK with RNGs seem *compatible* with the view that the subject monitors his PK activities by means of ESP, and that, through ESP, the subject keeps tabs on such things as moment-to-moment changes in the target system and the requirements for success in a given trial run. Apparently, Stanford thinks the data from Schmidt's tests are incompatible with this cybernetic picture, because he assumes that the limitations of mental processes (paranormal or otherwise) are just those of neural processes (see [157]: 204). Stanford is correct in pointing out that no known machine or organism can accomplish by any known means the sophisticated information processing that would be required in such cases by ESP. But that is compatible with the view that mental processes in general—or at least that subset involved in ESP—are much more efficient than those of any information-processing system we know of. And of course one reason for this may be that mental processes are in no way mechanistic. The alleged incompatibility of the cybernetic model with Schmidt's results, and the implausibility of the super-refined ESP information processing required by that account seem compelling, therefore, only from the viewpoint of a rather crude reduction of the mental to the neurological.

Stanford and his sympathizers may, however, protest that certain specific results of Schmidt's PK work cannot be reconciled with the cybernetic model, even if we grant that there may be mental processes that can outstrip the efficiency of any known physiological or physical processes. For example, one apparent fact drawn from Schmidt's work is that

(a) PK success is causally dependent on conditions during observation of feedback of results.

Moreover, since target generation sometimes *precedes* observation of feedback, Schmidt's work suggests that

(b) PK may involve retrocausation.

(a) and (b) suggest further that PK does not rely on monitoring of moment-to-moment changes in the target system, since the conditions which seem to contribute causally to PK success occur *after* such changes have taken place.

Now, as far as I can see (although I am hardly confident about this), the cybernetic model does not require that PK operate in the familiar temporal direction. Once we allow for retrocausal psi functioning, it is presumably open to us to say that the state of a system S at t can be monitored by means of feedback presented at some *later* time t', and that this feedback can guide retrocausal PK influence on S.

Suppose, for example, that S is a binary RNG, and that at t_1 an electron is fired from the radioactive source in S. Suppose, further, that, at $t_3 > t_1$, S generates a random event, and that a recording of that event is made. Again, suppose that, at a much later time, say t_{100}, the recording is played back for a subject, who thus observes feedback of an event which occurred earlier at t_3. Let us say that the feedback shows a hit and that $+1$s count as hits. Finally, suppose that this process of observation triggers an ESP process which, at t_{101}, monitors the state of S at t_1. We can then imagine that the (presumably unconscious) ESP at t_{101} of the state of S at t_1 activates a PK process which interferes with S at t_2 in a way that insures that the $+1$ is registered at t_3. I cannot honestly say that this suggestion makes clear sense to me. But it seems to make no less sense, or to be any the more circular, than the causal mechanisms suggested by the idea of mere retroactive PK. So if we grant the possibility of these latter mehanisms, as opponents of the cybernetic model urge, I think we must be prepared to allow those of my example. Hence, (b) seems compatible with the cybernetic model of PK.

So does (a), for that matter. (a) asserts a correlation between PK success and sensory/cognitive states during feedback. In fact, were it not for the rather dazzling aspects of the fact that feedback sometimes occurs well after target generation, (a) might even lend *support* to a kind of cybernetic view. After all, one of the reasons the evidence for PK supports (a) is that it supports

(c) The probability of PK success decreases as the rate of feedback increases.

As the feedback rate increases, it may well be that it becomes more difficult for the subject to distinguish the individual feedback events, and this sort of negative correlation between difficulty of perceptual task and probability of PK success is just what one would expect on the cybernetic model.

But the information processing occurring during observation of feedback is, presumably, the ordinary sort involved in sensory processes. So some opponents might object that the reliance on observation of feedback does not show that the organism is using ESP to monitor its PK activities; they might contend that PK still appears to operate independently of the ESP feedback loops required by the cybernetic model. But actually, the evidence is fully compatible with the view that successful *ESP monitoring* of PK activities depends (at least sometimes) on conditions during observation of feedback. In fact, there is some evidence suggesting that conditions during testing may activate unconscious psi functioning other than PK. Schmidt's evidence for the importance of feedback, for instance, may be interpreted as suggesting that certain conditions during feedback trigger more successfully than others PK functioning (possibly retrocausal functioning) in virtue, precisely, of activating (or more fully activating) the *ESP* functioning required to gain the needed information about the target system.

Furthermore, I suspect that opponents of cybernetic models of PK have, in rejecting such models, overestimated the importance of the cognitive complexity of the PK task. Stanford and his followers think that, since it seems indifferent to tasks of differing cognitive complexity, PK cannot conform to a cybernetic model—since, on that model, the greater the cognitive complexity of the task, the more difficult it should be to perform or complete it successfully. But that assumption is false. Cognitive complexity proves to be only one of several relevant factors; it may, in fact, not be related in the way Stanford suggests to the difficulty of the task. For example, the nature of the target may be the major factor in determining whether a task is difficult. For example, it is easier to push a bunch of dice around than a car or a boulder, though the latter tasks seem cognitively simpler than the former. An even more relevant kind of example may come from the domain of sport. I am not sure how one would go about determining different degrees of cognitive complexity among various athletic skills. But it is clear that people with highly developed athletic abilities often perform a variety of different tasks with equal degrees of proficiency, *just because they are good athletes.* For example, baseball players may be equally good at hitting, fielding, and base-stealing; and some tennis players are equally good at playing the net and the back court, or returning lobs and passing shots. Novices at these sports, however, or people with little athletic ability, tend to find certain of these tasks easier than others. Now as far as I know, opponents of the cybernetic model have not seriously considered the possibility that, for people with well-developed PK abilities, there may be a whole range of tasks falling within their skills that are comparably easy.

We must also be careful not to assume that there is but one mode of PK influence, even if all modes fit some cybernetic (or psychobiological) model. After all, there are many different ways of moving a bicycle (riding it, pushing it, carrying it), each of which may (as much as any human activity) be analyzed cybernetically, and each of which will have characteristically different features with respect to such things as extent of influence, control over movement, and relevance of cognitive complexity. But for all we know, PK, even if it can be modelled cybernetically, may also have different modes, each of which has analogous sets of characteristically different features with respect to these same parameters. In likening PK to steering a car (or riding a bicycle), Stanford may have failed to consider that, even from a cybernetic point of view, there are alternative ways of accomplishing the task of moving a car (or bicycle) and that these may differ from one another with respect to relevant factors such as those mentioned above. Similarly, Stanford may have failed to consider the full range of ways in which influencing the output of an RNG might be accomplished, and the corresponding importance to these various ways of cognitive complexity of the task.

The case against the cybernetic model of PK does not, then, seem as coercive as Stanford suggests. But even if we abandon this model, we are not thereby committed to renouncing altogether a psychobiological model of PK, as Stanford seems to think. In other words, PK may still be something like a form of action or influence on a system; and it may even involve some kind of information *gathering*, even if it does not involve *monitoring* through feedback. Perhaps, for this reason, the comparison between PK and steering a car is inappropriate, although analogies with other ordinary physical activities may well prove instructive. We might perhaps view PK as an activity less like steering a car and more like giving a car a sudden *push*. A push may initiate changes in the motion of the car, and then again it may not (we may not have pushed hard enough, or from the appropriate angle). Moreover, whether the car does what we want, once we set it in motion, is not necessarily within our control. What this alternative analogy suggests is that we can retain the psychobiological model of PK (while giving up the more specific cybernetic model) simply by abandoning the assumption that PK action on a system is a form of *control*, or continuing control, of that system. It may be more like a kind of brute influence, the results of which need not be fully within our control, but which depends nevertheless on *some* information gathering (e.g., it helps to have some awareness of what we are pushing, before we push it).

In any case, the fact that the evidence for PK suggests

(c) The probability of PK success decreases as the rate of feedback increases

shows that Stanford is not entitled to claim that PK is accomplished without *any* computation or information processing by the organism. Moreover, Stanford seems to have been hasty in claiming that the evidence shows that PK success is independent of the nature and mechanics of the target system and the conditions of target generation. At best, the evidence seems to support a much more modest claim, namely,

(d)   PK success seems independent of the nature or mechanics of *some sorts* of target systems.

It does look as if, when we test for PK using randomly generated numbers, success is a function of conditions during feedback rather than of conditions during target generation (for instance, the speed and nature of the generation process). But it is rather a big step from this to the claim that PK success is independent of the nature or mechanics of target systems *generally*. However, only if this more sweeping claim were true, would we have reason to reject the relatively limited cybernetic model or the broader psychobiological model of PK—and then perhaps, only if conditions during feedback were also irrelevant to the experimental outcome. But the evidence does *not* support this more sweeping claim. If PK success were generally independent of the nature or mechanics of target systems, we should expect it to obtain with a much greater variety of target systems than has so far been displayed. For example, although the evidence concerning PK with dice, coins, and similar devices is difficult to assess and interpret, it is far from clear that these devices and RNGs are influenced with equal ease. Of course, it may also be that the observation of rolling dice is a more complicated feedback activity than the observation of clicks in headphones or needle deflections. But if this is invoked to explain PK success with RNGs, then it probably supports some sort of psychobiological—possibly even cybernetic—view of PK.

If we turn from quantitative studies to consider experiments conducted with such PK superstars as Nina Kulagina of the U.S.S.R. (see Keil, *et al.* [77]), we cannot fail to notice that they seem able to demonstrate PK effects on small objects better than on large ones. Kulagina and others seem to be able to deflect compass needles and to move objects like cigarettes and ping-pong balls; but, to my knowledge, they have not moved large objects like tables and chairs. If, however, moving tables is a more difficult PK task than moving compass needles, it seems unlikely that the difference is due to greater complexity in the *observation* of tables—in the way, say, that complexity of RNG feedback is related to PK success. It seems related more to the kind of system to be affected. In fact, Kulagina appears unable to influence objects placed in a vacuum, and seems to have more difficulty affecting objects made of plastic (above 19 g in weight) than metallic objects in the same weight range. Kulagina herself claims that objects made of gold are more easily affected than those composed of other substances. She also appears to find it easier to move objects placed in certain positions rather than others. It seems relatively easier for her to make cigarettes standing on end move across a table than cigarettes that are placed horizontally on the table.

Furthermore, different PK superstars excel with different sorts of targets. To my knowledge, Kulagina has not been as successful in exposing photographic film as Ted Serios (see Eisenbud [50], [51]), or as successful in bending metal as Silvio.* *Prima facie*, this resembles the distribution of ordinary motor skills. For example, people with small hands will not be able to control a basketball as effectively as those with large hands; and some people wield tennis racquets more effectively than baseball bats or golf clubs. Such facts are obviously connected with relevant differences among different objects and different endowments. In general, PK superstars are not equally successful with all kinds of targets; and the evidence of this is certainly compatible with (and may even support) the view that, in some cases at least, the nature of the target system makes the difference, and that some sort of psychobiological model of PK is required after all.

---

*Silvio is a new superstar metal bender from Switzerland. To my knowledge there are no English-language reports of experiments conducted with Silvio. But those who read German are directed to Bender & Vandrey [15], Wälti [189] and Betz [16].

Similarly, we should be cautious about reasoning from the special features of PK results with RNGs to PK results in general. Thus, in the RNG studies, the relative indifference of PK to moment-to-moment changes in the target system and the conditions there required for success may tell us more about one kind of PK target or test situation than about PK targets or PK in general. Again, it helps to remember Kulagina and other PK superstars. Kulagina seems to make a concentrated effort to get her results, though not as intense as those made, say, by Felicia Parise (see Honorton [66] and Watkins and Watkins [191]). Her PK efforts often exhaust her, resulting in an unusually high loss of body weight as well as dizziness, reduced coordination, various pains, and an increase in blood sugar level; and she often requires a period in which to 'warm up' or attain the appropriate level of concentration. If this sort of effort is needed to influence macroscopic objects psychokinetically, then it would be difficult, presumably, to transfer PK effects quickly from one target to another. In fact, this seems to be the case.

I suggest, therefore, that we not follow Stanford's lead and abandon psychobiological models completely. We have seen that steering a car is not clearly inadequate as a cybernetic model for PK, and that even if cybernetic models are inadequate, other psychobiological models may still prove instructive. The evidence, moreover, does not point conclusively—or even all that strongly—away from psychobiological models, particularly if we broaden our scope beyond RNG experiments. There may well be certain target systems whose nature and mechanics are pretty much irrelevant to PK success with those systems. But viewing the evidence for PK from a wider perspective, this would seem to tell us more about the peculiarities of those systems than about PK in general. Perhaps RNGs are such that they can be affected psychokinetically only by a kind of brute PK influence, controllable only to a very limited degree. This might help explain the erratic and usually non-dramatic nature of the scores obtained using RNGs. Perhaps PK efforts, or psi functioning generally (or even certain ordinary states of concentration or attention), produce something like PK quantum field effects, so that RNGs in a certain region of spacetime will be affected. I am not endorsing these suggestions. Indeed, I am not certain I fully understand them. But I suggest, rather, that instead of entirely abandoning the psychobiological approach to PK, we try to link the peculiar features of RNG test situations with the peculiarities of RNG results. Hence, to the extent that conclusions based on PK tests with RNGs are not generalizable to PK as a whole, and of course to the extent that Stanford's overall line of reasoning is suspect (as I have endeavored to show), much of the rationale behind the observational theories begins to crumble.

3. Clairvoyance

a. The Pearce-Pratt Tests

As the reader is probably aware, clairvoyance experiments have been conducted for many years, and have typically involved such activities as trying to identify or reproduce concealed target objects like drawings or cards. Some early experiments (see, e.g., Coover [32], Jepson [74], Richet [126], and, somewhat later, Carington [28], [29]) yielded apparently impressive results. But the experimental conditions tended to be loose in various ways and the statistical methods employed, sometimes questionable. It was not until J. B. Rhine and associates at Duke University began conducting clairvoyance tests that the experimental methodology began to become acceptably tight.

Undoubtedly the best of Rhine's clairvoyance experiments was the Pearce-Pratt series. I shall summarize these tests only briefly, since they do not represent the sort of recent work to which this volume is devoted, and also because they have been thoroughly explored in the literature (see, e.g., Rhine [118], and Rhine & Pratt [124]). The experimental technique employed may be considered a variant of the *down-through* (or *DT*) technique, a forced-choice procedure in which the subject tries to identify each member of a pack of cards placed face down on a table, proceeding from the top to the bottom card. The variant involved is usually called the *broken* (or *basic*) technique (*BT*).*

Rhine's star subject during his early work at Duke was a young Methodist ministry student, Hubert E. Pearce, Jr. During numerous experiments with Pearce, the experimental conditions were gradually tightened. Eventually, the work with Pearce led to the series in which J. G. Pratt functioned as co-experimenter, now generally considered one of the cleanest and most successful experiments, methodologically, in the history of parapsychology. The tests proceeded as follows.

First, Pearce and Pratt synchronized their watches. Then Pearce went to one building, while Pratt remained in another. Different buildings were used in different series of trials; in some, Pearce was located 100 yards from the building housing Pratt; in other cases, Pearce was 250 yards away. After Pearce and Pratt separated, Pratt would shuffle a deck of ESP cards, keeping them face down; he then placed the shuffled deck on the right-hand side of the table. At a specified time, Pratt would remove the top card and, without looking at the card face, place it face down on a closed book in the center of the table. Thirty seconds later, as arranged, Pearce would record his guess of what the card was. After the card had remained on the book for one minute, Pratt repeated the procedure with the next card; he continued the process until he had run through the 25 cards in the deck.

Pearce made duplicate records of his calls before leaving his building, and Pratt made duplicate records of the order of the cards. Each man sealed one of these records in an envelope. The sealed records were then delivered to Rhine, who acted as experimenter independently of Pratt. The entire experiment was divided into 4 subseries, the results of which

---

*In his summary of forced-choice techniques in Krippner, ([85] : 24-25), Morris describes the *DT* procedure as a variant of the *BT*. The reason for this may be the fact (if it is a fact) that, historically, the *BT* method was used first. But since the *DT* method strikes me as the simpler of the two, I treat the *BT* as a variant of the *DT*. Obviously, nothing important hangs on this.

are given in Table 3 (taken from Tart [167]: 26). Altogether, Pearce made 558 hits out of 1,850 trials.

The most sustained attack on this series of experiments is the one launched by C. E. M. Hansel [62], who proposed an elaborate scenario to show how Pearce could have cheated. Hansel does not argue that there is positive evidence that Pearce did actually cheat. He merely contends that cheating was possible (which, as I argued in I.B.1.c., is not a very strong line, even if the alleged fraud *is* possible). Hansel suggests that Pearce might have left his building during the test, returned to Pratt's building, and then from the room across the hall from Pratt peeked through the transom above Pratt's door. Hansel proposes that Pearce could thus have copied the target order as recorded by Pratt, and then returned to his own building. But as Honorton [65] and Stevenson [162] have observed, not only does the complexity of Hansel's scenario strain credulity, but his drawing of the experimental arrangement does not fit the actual situation. A study of the original blueprints of Pratt's building (which was renovated before Hansel attacked the experiment) makes it clear that Pearce could not have used the room across the hall from Pratt to peek at Pratt's recording of the order of the cards.

Table 3. Results of the Pearce-Pratt series of clairvoyance tests.

Subseries	No. of Runs	Hits Above Chance	Odds Against Chance
A	12	+59	$P < 10^{-14}$
B	44	+75	$P < 10^{-6}$
C	12	+28	$P < 10^{-4}$
D	6	+26	$P < 10^{-6}$
Combined	74	+188	$P < 10^{-22}$

b. Clairvoyance and RNGs

In any case, research in clairvoyance, like research in PK, has come to rely heavily on mechanical methods of generating targets as well as on mechanical methods of recording results. In fact, Schmidt's first experiments with RNGs were clairvoyance experiments (see [134] and [135]). In these tests, the subject was seated before a small box with four colored lamps, below each of which was a pushbutton. The number of trials and hits was recorded by electromechanical counters and, for the purpose of cross-checking, on paper punch tape as well. The lamps remained unlit until the subject pressed one of the buttons. Once a button was pressed, the next radioactive decay particle to reach the Geiger counter would stop a high-speed modulo-4 counter in one of its four positions, and the lamp corresponding to that position would light. The subject's task was to press the button corresponding to the lamp he thought would light next. A hit was recorded whenever the number of the pushed button corresponded to the number of the lamp which lit. Thus, the experiment was designed to test for precognitive clairvoyance. Moreover, various safeguards against cheating and carelessness were incorporated into Schmidt's machine—for example, preventing the subject from making two or more guesses simultaneously.

Schmidt's initial results were very encouraging, and he subsequently conducted two successful confirmatory experiments. In the first, subjects completed 63,066 trials with a scoring rate of 26.1%. Although this seems only slightly above the 25% scoring rate expected by chance, the odds against producing this or a higher score are, due to the large number of trials attempted, approximately 500 million to 1.

The second confirmatory experiment is especially interesting, since subjects were allowed to choose whether they would aim for a high or a low score. In the latter case, subjects would try to push a button corresponding to any lamp that would *not* light next. These decisions were made before the trials were begun, and the two types of test were recorded on tape in different codes so that they could be distinguished in the subsequent computer evaluation. Altogether the experiment contained 20,000 trials. 10,272 of these aimed for a high score, and subjects scored at a rate of 26.8%, 189 hits above chance expectation. The remaining trials, aiming for a low score, produced a hit rate of 22.7%, 212 hits below chance expectation. The odds of obtaining this or a better total score by chance alone is greater than 10^{10} to 1.

As Schmidt recognized, these were not pure clairvoyance tests, since nothing in the experimental arrangement precluded the operation of PK. So for his next series of experiments, Schmidt replaced his RNG with a hidden punch tape containing a random sequence of the digits 1, 2, 3, 4 derived from the RAND tables. With this arrangement, the order of the lamps to be lit was determined in advance of the subject's pressing the button on the display panel. The subject's guess would be automatically recorded, and then one tenth of a second later the next number on the punch tape would be recorded and displayed to the subject by the lighting of the corresponding lamp. As in the previous test, subjects were allowed to aim for high or low scores. Altogether 15,000 trials were completed, 7,091 of which were high-aim trials, and 7,909, low-aim. Again the results were statistically significant. The high-aim trials produced 108 hits above mean chance expectation and the low-aim trials produced 152 hits below chance expectation. The odds of obtaining this or a better total deviation by chance alone are approximately 3 million to 1.

While apparently ruling out the operation of PK, this last experiment could not discriminate between various forms of clairvoyance. If, indeed, clairvoyance accounts for the statistically significant scores, it remains unclear whether the subject used precognitive clairvoyance to determine which lamp would light, or whether he used real-time clairvoyance to 'read' the holes on the punch tape.

c. Pre-Conscious Clairvoyant Interaction

Several studies have been conducted in an attempt to discover physiological measures of psi functioning. Some have sought to measure changes in galvanic skin response and basal skin resistance; typically, these were methodologically not tight enough or statistically insignificant. The most successful have measured blood volume changes and EEG activity. The former seems to provide evidence more strongly for telepathic interaction than for clairvoyant interaction, and will accordingly be discussed in I.B.4.b.

In a test conducted by Tart ([168]), subjects were monitored for several types of physiological changes: various kinds of EEG responses as well as galvanic skin response and blood volume changes. The figures for the EEG and plethysmograph (a device used for measuring blood volume changes— see I.B.4.b.) are statistically significant, though perhaps not coercive. They are especially interesting in light of the fact that the subject guessed only at chance levels regarding when the agent in the experiment had been stimulated with an electric shock. If, in virtue of physiological changes at the time of the stimulus, the figures show that the subject displayed some psi functioning, it therefore appears to be pre-conscious. However, this test should be regarded as a GESP test. Since the stimulus conditions consisted of applying an electric shock to an agent, it is not clear whether the postiive results suggest the operation of clairvoyance or telepathy.

A somewhat less ambiguous experiment was conducted at the Stanford Research Institute by Targ and Puthoff ([165]). Its purpose was to measure EEG activity relative to the flashing of a light in a remote room. The experimenters assumed that EEG responses to a remote stimulus would resemble those obtained under conditions of direct stimulation. Since it is known that when normal subjects are stimulated with a flashing light their EEG shows a reduction in power of alpha activity, Targ and Puthoff hypothesized that a similar change in alpha activity would be observed under conditions of remote stimulation.

The subject was seated in a visually opaque, acoustically and electrically shielded room, and was told that a light would be flashed in the eyes of a 'sender' in another room and that conscious or unconscious awareness of this event might be evident from changes in her EEG output. Overall, there were 7 runs of 36 10-second trials each; each set of 36 trials consisted of 12 periods each of no flashes, 6 flashes per second, and 16 flashes per second, randomly distributed. During the trials of 6 flashes per second, the subject's alpha activity showed a 12% decrease in average power and a 21% decrease in peak power. This reduction was suggestive, but computed to be statistically nonsignificant. The trials with 16 flashes per second more closely approached statistical significance. In these, the subject's alpha activity showed a 24% decrease in average power (P < .04) and a 28% decrease in peak power (P < .03).

I treat this experiment as a test of clairvoyance because the subject's reduction of alpha power occurred even when no sender was present to observe the flashing light. There were two runs conducted without a sender. For the first of these, the subject, H.H., was informed that no sender was in the remote room; in this run, her EEG activity did not vary with the flashing light. In the other run, however, the sender was removed from the room at the last minute, and H.H. was not informed of this event. In this run, the alpha reduction effect was one of the strongest observed. Targ and Puthoff suggest that the failure to get results in the first of these two runs may have been a function of H.H.'s apprehension about conducting the run without a sender.* Moreover, as in Tart's experiment, the subject was asked to indicate with a telegraph key when she thought the light was flashing in the other room; and once again, despite the statistical anomalies of the physiological responses, these guesses did not exceed chance levels of hits.

The experimenters at SRI realize, however, that these results are at best suggestive. Although a follow-up experiment conducted three months later also showed statistical anomalies, and although these anomalies were apparently not dependent on the presence of a sender, the subjects' EEG responses showed an *increase* in power rather than the pre-

*Targ and Puthoff report that, in the last of these two runs conducted without a sender, H.H. emerged from the shielded room and, before anyone said anything, remarked 'I didn't feel anyone in that room. Are you sure there was a sender?' ([164] : 132).

dicted decrease observed previously. Subsequent analysis revealed that the appearance of systematic amplitude changes depended on where in the frequency spectrum the power sums were taken. Although selection of the frequency range to be measured was determined prior to experimentation, the experimenters found that the correlations between EEG response and light flashes would not have appeared in other frequency ranges that might reasonably have been chosen instead (see May, Targ, and Puthoff [93]).

d. Free-Response GESP Tests

A number of psi experiments inhabit a kind of theoretical twilight zone in which it remains unclear whether success should be attributed to clairvoyance or telepathy. Many of the more important such experiments are *free-response* (as opposed to *forced-choice*) tests. In forced-choice tests, like card-guessing tests or clairvoyance tests with a Schmidt machine, subjects are presented with a fixed set of possible targets and are then asked to determine which of the possible targets is the actual target. In a free-response test, however, subjects' responses are not restricted from the start to a predetermined set of possible targets. For example, in one sort of free-response test, the subject would simply be asked to reproduce a concealed target drawing, without being given any idea of what the range of possible drawings was (see, e.g., Carington [28], [29]). These days, subjects in free-response tests are more frequently asked to describe their ongoing mental processes, the reports of which are then typically blind-matched by independent judges against a pool of target objects.

Free-response tests are, from a methodological point of view, inevitably somewhat messy, since the ground rules for comparing free-response material to target objects are by no means clear. (There is also the problem of assigning probabilities to free responses, a matter to which I shall shortly turn.) It is extremely difficult to determine which parts (if any) of a subject's response are extraneous and come from the subject's memories or other unrelated spontaneous mentation, or even (possibly subconscious) guesses or interpretations of what the target is (what Targ and Puthoff call 'analytical overlay'). At the 1978 annual convention of the Parapsychological Association, I attended a discussion group on free-response methodology conducted by most of the leading researchers using free-response techniques. A number of interesting points were raised during the meeting. Some researchers are convinced that subjects' free responses in GESP tests tend to have a *pattern*, usually one in which the first few minutes of response consists of extraneous material, then a brief burst of often highly accurate GESP, and then more extraneous material. In fact, Arthur Hastings (an unusually perceptive man, and perhaps parapsychology's most sought-after independent judge for free-response tests) remarked that just as people in ordinary situations tend to focus on certain features of those situations more readily or more accurately than others, and just as these varying sensitivities and proclivities may distinguish a person's character or psyche, the same is true of subjects' responses to GESP targets. That is, subjects tend to focus on certain aspects of remote targets rather than others, producing something like a psychic signature, just as the different ways people ordinarily observe or perceive events may yield (what we may term) different character signatures.* But just as in ordinary life situations, we do not know how much weight to give a person's report without some idea of the limits or range of his sensitivity, it is correspondingly difficult to determine, before analogous regularities in psi responses are detected, whether a portion of the subject's response results from GESP.†

---

*Targ and Puthoff also attribute this view to Hastings in [164]: 101.

†In his tests in the reproduction of drawings, Carington [28], [29] attempted to compile catalogues of guesses in order to determine the frequencies with which certain objects are likely to be drawn when those objects are not ESP targets. Although one can understand why such a catalogue might be useful in assessing the results of tests in the reproduction of drawings, it is not at all clear that the catalogue could be counted on to be reliable. See Thouless [176]: 48-49, for a discussion of this method; and Hardy, Harvie & Koestler [63], for a report of an experiment that rather dramatically illustrates the pitfalls of testing for ESP through the matching of drawings with target pictures.

The difficulty of separating extraneous from non-extraneous material is especially acute in cases where the subject seems to transform the target material symbolically, or in ways corresponding to his psychological idiosyncracies. Some cases may be very clear—for example, if the target object was a cigar and the subject reported phallic mental images or thoughts about phallic symbols. But the transformations may be much more obscure than this. Of course, this problem in interpretation of free-response reports is not surprising, and is simply an extension of the familiar way in which a person's perception and subsequent report of an event can be colored by his beliefs, mood, and so on.

But even if we could ignore those parts of the free-response material contributed entirely by the subject, it would still be difficult to distinguish partial hits from misses. This is easy to see if we think of GESP information-theoretically, as though there were a GESP *channel* of information in which material being transmitted may be masked in varying degrees by noise. Thus, even if we could identify the 'noise' in the psychic 'channel'—for example, the subject's uncontrolled, irrelevant, or spontaneous mental imagery, or responses to ordinary sensory stimuli—the noise may still mask the target material sufficiently to prevent it from being clearly apprehended by the subject—rather in the way attention is difficult when someone speaks to you in the midst of some sort of sensory bombardment (for example, when someone whispers in your ear while you are experiencing an intense pain). The familiar analogy drawn from information theory is trying to understand what the person on the other end of a noisy telephone connection is saying. Sometimes we fail to hear what he is saying, and sometimes we hear something similar, but relevantly different. This latter case, in which we come *close* to getting the material right, poses the most serious problem for the psi researcher, since, if one could determine whether closeness of response to target was fortuitous, it would be easier to evaluate the significance of free-response material. Blind judging by independent experimenters seems to be the only way to evaluate such material; and although even successful blind judging may not convince the most hardened skeptics, in some cases, successes are sufficiently striking to be taken seriously.

One very important series of free-response tests was conducted at Maimonides Hospital, in Brooklyn. These have been generally regarded as telepathy experiments, but the results, at least in principle, seem equally explainable in terms of clairvoyance. Unlike usual experiments in card-guessing, in which subjects' calls are made in rapid succession, and in which subjects generally report having no outstanding subjective experiences, the Maimonides tests aimed at producing experiences in the subject like those reported in anecdotal cases of telepathic interaction (see Stevenson [161]; also, Gilbert Murray's descriptions of his own apparent telepathic experiences, in Smythies [152]). Moreover, one of the outstanding features of the anecdotal reports is that apparent psi experiences tend to occur when the subject is relaxed or asleep, presumably when arresting external sensory stimuli are at a minimum. For this reason, subjects in the Maimonides experiments were tested under similar (albeit more artificial) conditions.

The original Maimonides experiments tested sleeping subjects, and although several different experimental designs were used (see Krippner et al., [86]-[88], and Ullman et al., [179]-[182]), for the most part they were variations of the following experimental plan. The subject goes to sleep, wired to an EEG machine. When the machine indicates that the subject has entered the REM period of sleep, an agent, isolated from the subject, is alerted to begin concentrating on a randomly selected target object (like a famous painting or a photograph). When the subject has finished dreaming, he is awakened by the experimenter and his verbal account of the dream is recorded. This procedure is carried out for each of the subject's REM periods during the night. Then in the morning, the subject is asked to relate whatever overall impressions he has of the night's dreams. The entire procedure is repeated over a series of nights. When the trials are completed, the transcripts of the subject's remarks, along with copies of the pool of possible target objects, are sent to independent judges who are asked to match each of the subject's verbal reports; they proceed on a blind basis to rank target objects according to their degree of correspondence with the content of the reports. The subject is also asked to match his dream reports with the targets.

Recent variations on this techinque test subjects, not during sleep, but during the artificial state produced in so-called *ganzfeld stimulation*, in which (as you may recall) the subject is sealed in an electrically-shielded sound-attenuated room, listens to white noise in headphones, and looks at a light through ping-pong ball halves covering his eyes (see Honorton [67], [69], [70], Sondow [154], and Terry & Honorton [172]). During the relatively quiet sensory state produced in this way, the subject reports his spontaneous mental activity as part of an attempt to describe the contents of a randomly selected target picture being viewed by an agent in a non-adjacent sound-attenuated room. The subject's reports are recorded via intercom by an experimenter located in the monitoring room adjacent to the subject's chamber. The monitoring experimenter is blind regarding the identity of the target picture. After the subject has given his mentation report, he then ranks the pool of target pictures in order of correspondence to his mentations. A recent variation of *this* method, involving binary coding of the content of the target pictures, has also been employed with some success. The procedure is complicated, and the reader is directed to Honorton [68] for details. Honorton and his associates at Maimonides have tried other variations as well. For example, they have conducted precognitive versions of the basic ganzfeld experiment, in which the target is selected by means of an RNG *after* the subject gives his report. And in yet another recent innovation (from which the data are still being collected), agent and subject try, *before* the experiment, to attain comparable levels of relaxation by simultaneously attempting to influence the output of a biofeedback machine. The point of this effort is not merely to relax both participants, but also (to put it crudely) to see if it may help them to be 'on the same wavelength' and thereby improve psi interaction.

Despite the aforementioned difficulty of distinguishing partial hits from misses, the Maimonides experiments have yielded provocative results. Not only has blind judging been successful in the dream studies, but later studies in ganzfeld stimulation have been successfully replicated at Maimonides and elsewhere (see Honorton [70], Terry & Honorton [172], as well as Palmer's review, in Krippner [85]: 114-116, 120-121; see also Kelly [78], who argues that these results are not as impressive as had been generally believed). Notably, the Maimonides dream experiments have been most successful where subjects have been selected on the basis of successes in previous studies, suggesting (as one might suppose) that the requisite psi abilities obtain in different degrees of refinement and power. Conceding the integrity of experimenters and experimental designs, this difference between the performance of unselected and selected subjects would be considerably more mysterious on the assumption that there was no ESP. However, to my knowledge, there have been no dream or ganzfeld experiments in which the test results of selected subjects have been compared with those of a control group of unselected subjects. Moreover, according to Palmer's recent survey of ganzfeld experimentation (in Krippner [85]: 115), only two of the successful ganzfeld experiments have employed nonganzfeld control groups (Braud *et al.,* [19], and Terry *et al.,* [174]; and of these, only the Braud experiment produced a significant difference between scores in the ganzfeld and control conditions).

In the dream studies, subjects were frequently able to match targets with reports more successfully than independent judges, even when the judges were successful in their own scoring. This disparity is just what one would expect, assuming the subject to be more familiar than anyone else with his own psi experiences and with correlations between them and the targets. Thus a sympathetic interpretation would argue that there *was* telepathic interaction between agent and subject, or clairvoyant interaction between target and subject, and that either the subject did not report all that he could, or that he was unable to verbalize part of his experience (perhaps because he could not express it, or because part of his psi experience was gathered at a subliminal or subconscious level).

The scope of this book (and the limitations of this author) do not permit a discussion of the statistical methods employed to determine the probability of free responses of the sort collected in the Maimonides tests. In addition to the specific techniques used by Honorton, the reader is directed to Morris [99], Burdick and Kelly [26], and Kelly [78]. This last paper is, among other things, a criticism and re-evaluation of received free-response statistical procedures and of tests using such procedures. If Kelly is correct in charging that many free-response tests have employed questionable statistical procedures, and if his proposed re-assessment of some results is on the right track, then parapsychology's score card of successes is somewhat less impressive than it may have appeared to be. It remains worthy of attention, nevertheless.

But ignoring formal issues concerning assigning probabilities to free-response results, and focusing now on the Maimonides dream studies alone, let us briefly consider the correlations obtained between target objects and dream reports. Assuming they do provide evidence of psi interaction, these studies support the widespread idea that, in telepathic (or clairvoyant) interaction, the subject's experience tends to be a distorted or partially correct representation of the agent's experience (or of the target object), and also that the subject often wrongly interprets what he experiences. For example, in a case of telepathy, agent A's experience may be of a man standing before a row of trees. But percipient B might turn unimportant elements of A's experience into important elements of his own—as in experiencing a row of trees with a man behind them in the distance. Or, B might distort elements of A's experience by having an image of a man standing before the bars of a cage. Or, if A experiences a man waving frantically for help, B may have an image or thought of a man waving a friendly greeting.

To take a real case, in one night's experiment, the agent concentrated on a target-print of *Man With Arrows and Companion* (Bichitir), which is a picture of three men in

India sitting outdoors. One holds a musical stringed instrument; the most prominent of the three holds a bow and arrows. The third man has a stick over his shoulder that looks like a rifle muzzle. One minor detail of the painting is a stake with a rope tied around it. The percipient had several dreams that night. In one, he dreamed of three men holding rifles; the scene seemed to be out of a western movie. Three of his dreams that night contained rope, or coiled rope, as a prominent feature; and in another dream, he saw a 'hammock in which there was an awful lot of suspended strings' ([182]: 152). In summing up his impressions of the night, the percipient emphasized cowboy or western themes and rope or strings. He ranked the target picture number 1 out of a pool of eight possible target objects for the night, and gave it a 100 percent confidence rating. If this is a genuine case of telepathic or clairvoyant interaction, it is a good example of the percipient's focusing on obscure details of the target. It is also a good example of the percipient's ability to identify the target when his verbal account contains remarks that are likely to mislead independent judges (e.g., the remarks about cowboy or western themes). For more details, see [182]: 151-53.

In another study, the agent, an orthodox Jew, concentrated on a print of Chagall's *The Yellow Rabbi*, in which an old rabbi sits at a table with a book in front of him. The subject of the experiment was a Protestant. In one dream, he saw a man in his 60s riding in a car. In another he reported 'a feeling of older people. The name of Saint Paul came into my mind'. In another, he dreamt of a professor of humanities and philosophy reading a book. In the summary of his dreams the next morning, the subject reports, 'So far, all I can say is that there is a feeling of older people. . . .The professor is an older man. He smoked a pipe, taught humanities as well as philosophy. He was an Anglican minister or priest' ([182]: 112). The apparent conversion of Jewish images to secular or Christian images is typical of the sorts of apparent distortion that occur in these cases. It has led some researchers to suggest that telepathic information is received uncon-

sciously or subconsciously, and must then surface to consciousness by passing through a filtering system having to do
with one's general emotional, or psychological, background
and dispositions.

The *remote viewing* experiments developed by Puthoff
and Targ at SRI (see [113], [114], [164]; also, Puthoff and
Targ's replies to critics, in *Proc. IEEE* 64 (1976): 1545-1550),
provide further evidence, from free-response material, favoring GESP. Like the Maimonides tests, the remote viewing
experiments have been replicated with some success (see, e.g.,
Bisaha and Dunne [17], Hastings and Hurt [64], Vallee, *et
al.* [183], Whitson, *et al.* [195]). Unfortunately, as was true
with some Maimonides experiments, Kelly [78] has uncovered some questionable methodological procedures in a number of experiments (although these are not always serious
enough to invalidate individual experiments—much less,
repudiate remote viewing experiments on the whole).

The basic double-blind experimental plan of a remote
viewing experiment goes something like this. A pool of
target locations is first prepared, and held by someone not
otherwise connected with the experiment. Each target is
contained in a numbered envelope. A subject is then closeted
with one experimenter; he waits for a prescribed period of
time before attempting to describe the remote target location. In the meantime, a second experimenter obtains a target
location selected randomly from the pool already prepared
(SRI uses a random number function on a Texas Instruments
SR-51 calculator). An outbound team of experimenters then
proceeds by automobile to the target site, having been allowed sufficient time to reach the site before the subject's
narrative begins. The experimenter who remains with the subject is ignorant of the target site and the target pool, and so
can question the subject without worrying about inadvertently providing him with clues as to the identity of the target. The outbound team remains at the target site for a prescribed period, long enough for the subject to complete his
description. The subject's responses are recorded on tape, and
the subject is also asked to make any drawings which he

deems appropriate. Later, after the experiment is completed, the subject is taken to the remote location in order to provide him with feedback. After a number of such trials is completed, the experimental results are then evaluated on a blind basis by independent judges. They are given a randomized set of response packets which include transcripts of the recorded narrative and copies of the drawings, and they are then taken to each of the remote locations. At each location, the judges rank order the packets against the target, from best to worst match.

A precognitive version of this remote viewing procedure has the outbound team visit the site only after the subject has completed his response. As mentioned earlier (I.A.4.), this version of the remote viewing protocol is often more successful than the real-time version. And in a really far out variant of the remote viewing procedure, which in preliminary studies has proved surprisingly successful (see [164]: chs. 1 and 2), the subject is told the geographical coordinates of the target site, but is given no other clue as to the identity of the target. The team at SRI is understandably baffled why this procedure should work with subjects generally ignorant of the conventions of latitude and longitude. These tests, however, are both preliminary and loose and their successes should be treated with caution.

e. The Hypothesis of Trans-Temporal Inhibition

I want, now, to report briefly on a hypothesis recently advanced by C.T. Tart to account for some striking features of data obtained in some of his GESP studies. The tests involved are not pure clairvoyance tests, since, although subjects were to guess the output of an RNG, the output was monitored by the experimenter. If they provide evidence of ESP, therefore, these tests might support a telepathic interpretation. But their interest lies not so much in the strength of the evidence for ESP—at least as determined by the customary measure of deviation of hits from mean chance expectation. It concerns, rather, a certain unexpected *pattern* in the data, quite unlike familiar position or decline effects.

These patterns suggest not only a new way of measuring the presence of ESP effects in data, but also some new ways of conceptualizing psi functioning. Tart's analysis is extremely complicated, and my own brief summary will hardly do justice to the care with which he has interpreted his results. I hope to have indicated in the broadest terms only what he is suggesting; I encourage the reader to go to the source for the full story (see Tart [170], [171]).

To understand Tart's hypothesis, we must first understand a particular approach to analyzing ESP data. Parapsychologists frequently look for evidence of *time-displacement* in ESP scores, since, for some time, they have realized that, while subjects' calls at t may not correspond significantly to targets generated at t, they may correspond significantly to targets generated before or after t. We may, for instance, obtain no above-chance scores when comparing calls at t_i with targets generated at t_i; but above-chance scores may result from comparing calls at t_i with, say, the $(t_i + 1)$th target. This sort of consistent scoring may be taken as evidence for precognitive ESP.

One would think that if ESP were not operating in a precognitive or retrocognitive mode, tests for time-displacement would not reach significance. For example, we should expect calls at t_i to correspond at chance levels only to targets at, say, $t_i + 3$. But when Tart evaluated the data from some of his ESP-learning experiments (see Tart [166]), he found a very unusual pattern of time-displacement. When subjects tended to hit on real-time targets—that is, when calls at t_i tended to match targets at t_i—hitting tended to be correlated with *missing* on the +1 and −1 targets. In other words, calls at t_i tended *not* to match (to an unusually high degree) the $(t_i + 1)$th and $(t_i - 1)$th target. What struck Tart as especially interesting was the fact that significant missing tended to occur only for small temporal displacements. That is, there tended to be fewer correlations between calls at t_i and targets at $t_i + 1$ and $t_i - 1$ (and often $t_i - 2$) than between calls at t_i and targets further removed from the (t_i)th target. Tart also found that the degree of missing on immediately past and future targets was correlated (to a statistically significant degree) with the degree of real-time hitting. The more real-time hits the subject made, the greater number of misses Tart found on immediately past and future targets (even though scores for greater time-displacements continued to hover more closely around chance levels).

This suggested to Tart the existence of some sort of extra-sensory discrimination process, whereby information about the immediate past and future is suppressed in order to enhance the detectability of the desired real-time target. Tart writes,

> What I am postulating, then, is an *active inhibition* of precognitively and postcognitively acquired information about the immediately future and the immediately past targets, which serves to enhance the detectability of ESP information with respect to the desired real-time target. As the inhibition extends over time, I have named this phenomenon *trans-temporal inhibition* ([171]: 15).

This hypothesis benefits from an interesting comparison with the well-known neurological process *lateral inhibition* (von Békésy [185]) in which stimulated neurons send inhibitory impulses to adjacent neurons and receptors. It is this phenomenon which allows us, for example, to feel sharp pointed objects pressed on the skin as sharp pointed objects, or which sharpens the visual perception of edges.* Tart is thus suggesting that, in psi functioning, there is a similar process of *contrast sharpening* achieved through the suppression of ESP information concerning the immediate past and future of the real-time ESP information.

Tart has tested this hypothesis by exploring some of its apparent implications. I shall discuss two of these. Here, Tart's data seem most strongly suggestive of the reality of ESP, since the existence of the predicted additional patterns seems very mysterious indeed on the assumption that there is no ESP.

*Tart also suggests that there may be an analogous phenomenon of *trans-spatial* inhibition in GESP, in which hitting on distant targets correlates with missing on spatially nearby targets.

Still, conclusions must remain tentative, until more data has been collected and analyzed.

Tart's discussion wavers between describing trans-temporal inhibition psychologically (as a process creating *dispositions* or *biases* against calling targets) and more mechanistically (as an information-suppression mechanism). Of the two, the latter most closely corresponds to descriptions of lateral inhibition. But the descriptions are not incompatible. If, for example, information about the identity of the +1 target is suppressed, the subject may develop a bias against calling that target. Tart must be careful here, of course, since the putative relationship between information suppression and bias development is likely to be contingent and not lawlike. In any case, despite this fuzziness in his exposition, Tart postulates that the suppression, at t_i, of the identity of the target at $t_i + 1$ would create a kind of holdover effect; that is, the suppression (and any biases developed at t_i against calling the digit of the next target) would probably linger for a while, thus increasing the likelihood that the subject would *not* call the digit corresponding to the $(t_i + 1)$th target at $t_i + 1$. Since Tart hypothesizes that trans-temporal inhibition is correlated with psi-hitting, he suggests that, when a subject hits at t_i, he is more likely to *miss* on the next trial than if he had not hit at t_i. He reasons therefore, that the data should show fewer hit doublets (i.e., two hits in a row) than would be expected if every trial were independent of the previous one, an effect Tart calls *psi-stuttering*. There is, indeed, some evidence for this in Tart's data: the more subjects showed real-time hitting, the more hitting tended not to occur sequentially.

Tart also reasoned that the effect of trans-temporal inhibition would appear in tests for precognition. He predicted that there would be a similar pattern of missing surrounding hits on whatever future target the subject focused on. Thus, if the subject were to try to guess the targets at $t_i + 10$, we should expect information concerning the identity of the targets at $t_i + 9$ and $t_i + 11$ to be suppressed. Hence, we would expect missing with those targets to accompany hitting on the $(t_i + 10)$th target.

To test this hypothesis, Tart conducted a brief preliminary experiment with Ingo Swann. He did not inform Swann of his prediction; but since he had told Swann about the rudiments of his hypothesis of trans-temporal inhibition, he expected him to have more concern for the identity of the +1 target than others tested in Tart's lab (whose scores provided Tart with his data). Accordingly, Tart expected Swann to show real-time hitting as well as +1 hitting, with missing on the +2 target.

Swann had time to complete only 129 trials, but his results are nevertheless suggestive. He made a total of 21 hits on the real-time target, where only 12.9 would be expected to occur by chance; he also showed some psi-stuttering (but not, in this small sample, a statistically significant degree of it). Swann also made 19 hits on the +1 target, where 12.4 were expected by chance. (In measuring displaced hits, the length of the run decreases with the degree of displacements, thus accounting for the difference in expected hits between real-time hitting and +1 hitting.) But Swann scored only 7 hits on the +2 target, where 11.9 would be expected by chance, and he showed a slightly greater degree of missing on the −1 target.

Although these results are suggestive, the trial sample is obviously much too small to warrant sweeping conclusions, or even to support Tart's conjecture about precognitive trans-temporal inhibition. Also, the results are somewhat confounded by the fact that Swann showed bursts of hitting twice in a row on the +1 target. If Tart were justified in expecting psi-stuttering in his real-time GESP tests, then we should expect psi-stuttering on the +1 target for the same reasons. But again, the number of trials is still too small to enable us to interpret this fact clearly.

In any case, whether or not Tart is correct in all his conjectures about trans-temporal inhibition, his analysis suggests that the presence of psi functioning may be measurable even when the subject's number of hits does not represent a statistically significant deviation from mean chance expectation. Rather than simply measuring the number of hits, we should perhaps consider the difference between hits and *adjacent misses*. If psi-hitting on the (t_i)th target correlates with psi-missing on the $(t_i + 1)$th and $(t_i - 1)$th target, then, when psi is operating, we should find a greater difference between the score on the (t_i)th target and scores on adjacent targets than between the score on some other target in the series and scores on targets adjacent to that—say, targets surrounding the $(t_i + 18)$th member of the series, or between the score on the (t_i)th target and scores on targets *not* surrounding that one.

4. Telepathy

a. Experiments in Card-Guessing

As we saw, some of the experiments described in the section on clairvoyance are best described as GESP experiments, since positive results may also be attributed to telepathy. In fact, as already mentioned, the Maimonides Hospital experiments were regarded as experiments in telepathy. Although, in general, the ambiguity between telepathy and clairvoyance is not circumvented in telepathy experiments, it tends to be overshadowed by another—the ambiguity between telepathy and PK (see I.A.6.); although the latter is also present in clairvoyance experiments, perhaps it does not loom as large.

The evidence for telepathy takes various forms. The phenomenon does not lend itself to quantitative analysis as easily as PK or certain forms of clairvoyance; in fact, parapsychologists have had to muster considerable ingenuity in order to design quantitative measures of its *prima facie* occurrence. Still, despite this difficulty, the most dramatic and conclusive evidence favoring telepathy was, until recently, the card-guessing experiments conducted in England by S. G. Soal with two star subjects, Mr. Shackleton and Mrs. Stewart. Shackleton's results were especially interesting, since they appeared to furnish evidence of a kind of precognitive telepathy (see Soal & Bateman [153] and Broad [24] for details). Unfortunately, Soal's experiments are now shrouded in controversy. His technique was to vary the test conditions between those in which telepathy was permitted and those in which it was apparently excluded. In the former, the agent would turn up, and then look at the face of, a card to be identified by the subject. In the latter, the agent simply touched the back of the card to be identified. It was found that Shackleton and Stewart did very well under the conditions permitting telepathy (the odds against Shackleton's scores, for instance, were 3.88×10^7 to 1), whereas there were no interesting deviations in those tests that excluded telepathy. Moreover, in a different series of experiments with Shackleton, carried out only under conditions permitting telepathy, the odds against getting so many hits (1,679 out of 5,799 calls) were 2.4×10^{63} to 1. Recently however, evidence has surfaced that Soal may have doctored some of his results; * although it may not be conclusive, the evidence has, nevertheless, already cast enough doubt on Soal's experiments generally to oblige us to look elsewhere for persuasive evidence of telepathy. Let us now consider that evidence.

b. Pre-Conscious Telepathic Interaction

We have already considered some of the evidence (I.B.3.c.) for pre-conscious clairvoyant interaction, some of which (like Tart's complicated study) can also be construed as providing evidence for telepathy. The series of experiments I shall now describe are, from a methodological point of view, cousins of those described earlier. They were conducted by E. D. Dean and C. B. Nash (see Dean [38] and Dean & Nash [39]). The experimenters used a plethysmograph to measure blood volume changes in the subject's finger. In the original series of experiments conducted by Dean, an agent in a room adja-

---

*See, for example, the exchange in *Nature* 245 (Sept. 7, 1973): 52-54, as well as Scott & Haskell [148] and Thouless [177]. There are also rumors circulating through the parapsychological grapevine of new, very damaging, and soon to be published evidence against Soal.

cent to that of the subject viewed cards with names written on them. Some names were of persons known only to the subject, others had names of persons known only to the agent, and still others had names selected from the telephone directory. For an additional control measure, there were some periods in the experiment where the agent viewed blank cards. The measurements of the plethysmograph were done on a double-blind basis, and the results showed the subject-names to be correlated with larger vasoconstrictions than were the agent- and neutral-names and the blank cards (the magnitude of the associated vasoconstrictions of all these being about the same).

In a follow-up series of experiments conducted by Dean and Nash, which in general supported the results of the first series, the experimenters confronted a problem which led to some interesting observations. For each of a protracted series of trial runs, the subject was asked to submit five new names, and it proved to be not long before he ran out of names to use. Initially, the experimenters dealt with this problem in subsequent trials by randomly selecting names from the pool already given by the subject. But the results of those trials did not confirm Dean's earlier results. The experimenters then reviewed the successful names used, and found that they were the names of people with whom the subject had been in contact recently, or with or about whom the subject had strong feelings or associations.

Accordingly, Dean and Nash altered the selection process so that the subject-names had at least one feature of strong contact or association, and this time, they found significant vasoconstrictions when the agent viewed names of persons known to the subject. Moreover, they found that the subject showed significant vasoconstrictions when the names viewed were of persons recently contacted by the *agent*, and nonsignificant vasoconstrictions when the agent-names were of people *not* recently contacted.

It may also be significant that one of the names given by the subject was of a person he saw almost every day, and that out of the 43 times the name was viewed by the agent, the subject showed large vasoconstrictions 38 times. Moreover, one of the subject's largest vasoconstrictions occurred when the agent viewed the name of the subject's two-day old baby.

Although the results of these experiments strongly suggest some sort of psi functioning, it is not entirely clear what sort this might be. The most important result may have been the occurrence of large vasoconstrictions associated with the names of persons recently contacted by the *agent*. Had the subject been using clairvoyance to determine the names on the cards—rather then telepathy to monitor the mental states of the agent—presumably the names involved should have meant little to him, and should have had as negligible an effect on his blood volume as the control-names and blank cards. If we must look to some psi ability to account for the success of the agent-names, it seems reasonable to suppose either (a) that the subject telepathically detected the agent's arousal in these cases and responded accordingly, or (b) that the agent's arousal triggered a PK mechanism which caused vasoconstrictions in the subject. Even if we suppose (as we certainly need *not*) that the success of both the subject- and agent-names is to be explained in the same way (rather than, say, telepathy in one case, and PK in the other), the ambiguity between active telepathy on the part of the subject and active PK on the part of the agent persists. The success of the subject-names might be explained either as resulting from the subject's telepathy of the names in the mind of the agent (with corresponding vasoconstrictions resulting from the importance of those names to the subject), or from a kind of PK exercised by the agent on the subject's brain, resulting in the subject's becoming aware (not consciously) of the names on the card.

The reason this series of experiments is regarded as providing evidence for telepathy concerns the subject's vasoconstrictions *at those times* when the agent was viewing cards with names important to the subject, but not important to others involved in the experiment. At the very least, since (as noted in I.A.6.) the distinction between telepathy and PK is not clear even in principle, these experiments suggest some sort of causal relationship between the mental states of agent and subject rather than between the cards and the mental states of the subject. The ambiguity, discussed above, has mainly to do with whether we conceive of the agent or subject as *active*—that is, whether we regard the subject as 'invading' the mind of the agent, or whether we regard the agent as altering the unconscious mental processes of the subject (either by PK on the subject's brain, or by a non-physical process which directly alters the subject's mental states).

c. Hypnogenic Telepathic Interaction

Russian experiments in telepathy were originally intended to garner evidence for materialistic theories of the mind. Soviet scientists hoped to uncover the physical or physiological mechanisms responsible for telepathy; in fact, they hoped to confirm the brain-radio model of telepathy, by finding its electromagnetic origins in the brain. To this extent, their results were somewhat less than hoped for, since their apparently successful demonstrations of telepathy suggest that telepathy is insensitive both to distance and to electromagnetic shielding. Thus, experiments that proved successful at short distances and in the absence of shielding proved comparably successful at long distances and under conditions of shielding.

Among others, A. Dobbs [41] has observed that these unexpected results do not completely rule out electromagnetic theories of telepathy. The evidence for the effects of distance on telepathy, for example, is not precise enough to warrant the conclusion that telepathy does not obey the inverse square law. There is also the possibility that the atmosphere may, for some reason, act as a superconductor for telepathic waves. Moreover, the shielding employed would seem to rule out only familiar forms or wavelengths of radiation. In fact, I. M. Kogan, of the U.S.S.R., has argued that these *prima facie* anomalous results—plus familiar results like the observed low degree of information apparently conveyed in ESP tests—are compatible with the hypothesis that telepathy results from the transmission of extremely low frequency (ELF) waves in the 300-1000 km region (see Kogan [81], [82], [83]; also Persinger [104], [105]). On the other hand, Puthoff and Targ [113] argue that there remain significant problems with this hypothesis.

I prefer not to pursue this issue, since, as I argue in the next subsection, electromagnetic theories can be ruled out *a priori*. The Soviet studies are especially valuable for their novel approach toward demonstrating the reality of telepathy. The premier investigator of telepathy in Russia was the late L. L. Vasiliev (see [184]), chairman of the physiology department at the University of Leningrad. In his earliest experiments, Vasiliev attempted to test for telepathy as' a means of inducing motor responses (like arm or leg raisings) or sensory images. But he rejected these methods because of the difficulty of distinguishing partial successes from misses (as free-response ESP tests have likewise demonstrated).

During the 1920s and 30s, Vasiliev and his colleagues employed numerous experimental designs. A typical experiment ran as follows. The purpose was to determine whether the onset of natural sleep or auto-hypnosis could be accelerated by means of mental suggestion. The subject was alone in a room; and the agent, alone in an adjacent room. The subject was instructed to compress rhythmically an air compression balloon, and to cease this activity with the onset of drowsiness or sleep. The air compression balloon was connected to a kymograph, which recorded the rhythm and intensity of the pressure. The agent used a rotating wheel with black and white disks to determine if he should try to induce sleep in the subject by means of mental suggestion. If the wheel stopped rotating on a white disk, no suggestion was sent. If the wheel stopped on a black disk, the agent immediately began trying to induce sleep in the subject, and would cease when the curve on the kymograph stopped fluctuating. The elapsed time between the stopping of the rotating wheel and the onset of sleep was recorded. This experimental technique was used with four subjects, in the evenings between 7 and 11 p.m., in illuminated rooms. A total of 53 experiments were completed, 26 of which did, and 27 of which did not, involve the attempt to induce sleep in the subject. Without mental suggestion to go to sleep, the average time for the onset of sleep was 17.7 minutes (with an average error of ±1.86 min.). *With* mental suggestion to go to sleep, the average time for the onset of sleep was 6.8 minutes (with an average error of ±.54 min.). It thus took almost three times as long for subjects to fall asleep in the absence of mental suggestion.

In a subsequent and more elaborate series of experiments, the onset of sleep in the absence of mental suggestion was compared with the onset of sleep (with mental suggestion) under conditions both of lead screening of the agent and without screening of the agent. In these, agent and subject were in different rooms separated by several closed chambers; the recording apparatus was in another room adjacent to the agent's. Various precautions were taken against cheating and against the transmission of subtle cues to the subject (see Vasiliev [184]: 140-47). In 29 experiments, 10 were conducted without mental suggestion, and the average time for the onset of sleep was 7.40 min. In 10 experiments with mental suggestion under conditions of screening, the average time was 4.71 min.; and in 7 experiments without screening, it was 4.21 min.

In order to test the sensitivity of telepathy to distance and to rule out completely the possibility of hyperaesthesia of hearing frequently observed in hypnotized subjects, some experiments were conducted from Sebastopol to Leningrad (approx. 1,700 km). Although only two experiments were conducted at this distance (several others were conducted at distances from 25 meters to 7,700 meters), the results were very interesting. Days and times for the experiments were arranged in advance; also agent and the observer of the subject checked their watches, by radio, with Moscow time. The agent, incidentally, also had an observer, but he was ignorant of the purpose of the experiment. On the first day of the experiment planned, the agent became ill and, unknown to his colleagues back at the Institute for Brain Research in

Leningrad, did not attempt mental suggestion. For the planned two hours between 5 and 7 p.m., the subject showed no signs of sleepiness. Two days later, the same subject returned to the laboratory in Leningrad, at 10:00 p.m. At 10:10, the agent began to try to induce sleep in the subject. At 10:11, the subject entered a hypnotic state. At 10:40, the agent tried to awaken the subject. And precisely at 10:40, the subject came out of hypnosis (see Vasiliev [184] : 152-53).

On the whole, Vasiliev's experiments are not described in the kind of detail one would expect from a thoroughly scientific publication. Moreover, the long-distance experiments are clearly preliminary in nature and invite various refinements in design, some of which were already planned when Vasiliev wrote his book. But his experiments are suggestive, nevertheless, and deserve attempts at replication.

d. Theoretical Issues: Telepathy as Energy Transfer

We have considered *prima facie* evidence for different forms of telepathic interaction. Notice, though, that even if this evidence conclusively demonstrates the existence of telepathic phenomena, it affords us no way as yet of deciding whether these apparently distinct phenomena are all instances of some one general underlying process. For example, hypnogenic telepathic interaction may simply be a form of straightforward PK, and telepathic content-simulation (for example, of the kind suggested by the Maimonides Hospital experiments) may be something altogether different, or perhaps a complicated form of PK. On the other hand, it may be that neither should be regarded as a form of PK, and that hypnogenic telepathic interaction is a special form of content-simulation. For example, the two seem analogous in that they both require one person to produce a mental state in another similar to his own. The agent (transmitter) in the Soviet experiments was instructed to 'reproduce with the greatest possible vividness feelings usually experienced when falling asleep, and to associate these feelings with the image of the percipient while mentally conveying the command, "Go to sleep!" ' (Vasiliev [184] : 110). Moreover, as far as the command is concerned, putting someone into a state of hypnotic sleep by a distant command may be similar to commanding a hypnotized person in the same room to go to sleep; in both cases, it is as if an instruction must be properly understood by the subject. And to the extent that the positive results of the plethysmograph experiments point to the reality of telepathy, it seems as though the subject has some sort of pre-conscious awareness of the name the agent is concentrating on. We may not want to go so far as to say that the subject actually *knows* what is in the mind of the agent. But the mental states of agent and subject seem bound to be similar to the extent that they are both focused on the same name. In any event, since the hypnogenic and pre-conscious cases may resemble the content-simulation cases in these respects, and since the sorts of cases which, historically, have aroused the greatest interest in telepathy are just those of apparent content-simulation, let us briefly consider some issues concerning the explanation of that phenomenon.

The position I want to defend in this subsection is that no version of what we may call the *energy-transfer** theory of telepathy (hereafter, *ET* theory) can explain content-simulation. The *ET* theory of telepathy attempts to reduce telepathic processes (including content-simulation) to a certain kind of mechanical physical process between agent and percipient. It holds that telepathy can be fully analyzed as a sequence of events beginning with some state of the agent and terminating in the production of some state of the percipient. Different versions of the *ET* theory construe this process in different ways. For example, to whatever extent mental events figure in this process, such events may be treated as brain states or epiphenomena. Moreover, the *mechanism* of telepathy is usually regarded as a process fitting familiar electromagnetic models, in which the sequence

---

*This is often called the 'brain-radio' or 'radiation' theory. But these terms are usually understood to suggest that telepathy is mediated by some encoding/decoding process. Since, as I argue below, telepathy needn't be modeled after a coding process, I choose what seems to me to be a more neutral, and certainly less abused, term.

of events begins in the agent's brain, continues through some intervening medium between agent and percipient, and terminates in the brain of the percipient. In fact, the typical model for telepathy is that of radio transmission. As Tart has observed (in [169]), this model has some attractive correlations with what appear to be experimentally established facts about telepathy. For example, just as tubes in receivers and transmitters need time to warm up and circuits need time to stabilize, subjects often have to 'warm up' by getting themselves into the appropriate frame of mind for the experiment. Moreover, just as a radio signal will be received from a certain transmitter only when the receiver is tuned to the appropriate frequency, not all pairs of subjects in telepathy experiments seem able to interact telepathically. Also, just as some transmitters are more powerful than others (or receivers, more sensitive), certain people function better as agents (or percipients) than others. And just as radio signals can be distorted by various processes, telepathically communicated material seems to undergo kinds of distortion (as the 'signal', in one of the aforementioned Maimonides tests, of an old rabbi may be distorted into that of a priest). The idea that telepathy can be reduced to some such mechanical process is presupposed by the increasingly familiar assumption that the language of information theory is adequate to express the relevant features of telepathic processes (see Kogan [81]-[83] and Ryzl [130]).

It is possible, I suppose, to offer a mechanistic theory of telepathy which is not a purely physicalistic theory (where we understand the domain of the physical to be the domain of phenomena currently countenanced by orthodox physical theory). In other words, there may be dualistic or idealistic mechanistic theories. But the *ET* theory has usually been couched in the safe terms of current physical theory. In fact, this is part of the appeal of the theory among many who are willing to entertain the possibility of telepathy in the first place. By sticking with familiar physical descriptive categories (rather than attempting to explain telepathy in more metaphysically exotic, if not downright mystical, terms), the *ET* theory displays an attractive scientific and ontological conservatism. I shall, therefore, discuss the *ET* theory insofar as it is a metaphysically parsimonious physicalistic theory. The arguments I deploy, however, presumably apply, *mutatis mutandis*, to other mechanistic approaches as well—for example, the dualistic claim that the causal sequence between agent and percipient has stages in which a mental event produces a physical event (or *vice versa*). In fact, as we shall see, my objections apply to any theory of communication, paranormal or normal, which attempts to characterize communication between persons in terms of nothing more than a causal link between states of persons. Thus they apply, for example, to the Lockean theory that communication begins with an idea in the mind of one person, which gets expressed in (or coded into) language, and which, when heard (or decoded) by another person, produces the same idea in his mind. I shall argue, in effect, that nothing can do the job demanded of Locke's ideas, or demanded of brain states by the *ET* theory.

To oppose the *ET* theory of telepathy is, of course, to attempt nothing new. But appraisals of this theory's merits have usually concentrated on such features of telepathic interaction as its alleged insensitivity to distance or electromagnetic shielding. The *ET* theory's fatal flaw, in other words, is typically claimed to be its incompatibility with the relevant experimental data. But as Dobbs has argued in his very good paper [41], this case against the *ET* theory is quite weak. However, the problems I wish to raise are more abstract than those surveyed by Dobbs, and concern *any* attempt to reduce any form of human communication to processes like those posited by the *ET* theory. The special features of the telepathy case simply throw certain general problems into particularly sharp relief.

First, let us be clear about what needs to be explained by the *ET* theory. The situation we want to explain is one in which a thought of a certain kind in A—let us say a ϕ-thought—produces a similar thought in B. This might be another ϕ-thought or some ψ-thought, where the properties ϕ and ψ are such that ϕ-things and ψ-things would be widely acknowledged to be similar in some salient respect. For example, A's ϕ-thought may be of an old rabbi, and B's thought may also be of an old rabbi, or of a young rabbi, or of a priest. We needn't suppose that B's ψ-thought is anything so tangentially similar to the thought of an old rabbi as would be the thought of a snake charmer or the thought of a clam, even though old rabbis and clams (say) share numerous properties. In the case where A's thought is the thought *that*. . . (rather than the thought *of*. . .), we must characterize the situation somewhat differently. For example, if A's ϕ-thought is the thought that that S is ϕ, then what needs to be explained is how this thought produces, in B, the thought that S is ϕ, or some other thought related to the thought that S is ϕ—perhaps the thought that S is ψ, where the properties ϕ and ψ are as explained above. For instance, A might think that Jones has a fever, and B might think the same thing, or he might simply think that Jones is sick, or that Jones has a headache. Of course these two ways of characterizing thoughts need not be mutually exclusive. A's thought *that* S is ϕ is also a thought *of* S. But the relevant similarities between the thoughts of A and B can be of either sort (propositional or non-propositional).

The major difficulties with the ET theory of telepathy concern its attempt to explain why these sorts of similarities between the thoughts of agent and percipient are not fortuitous. The reason people investigate telepathy in the first place is that there is reason to believe that a person's thoughts sometimes produce similar thoughts in another person—just as A's old-rabbi thought might produce in B the thought of an old rabbi or the thought of a priest. From the point of view of the ET theory, the evidence suggests that the transfer of information from agent to percipient is often distorted by 'noise' or modified by some sort of filtering system. But what is initially of interest to the theoretician is the *ideal* case in which no such impediment to information transfer obtains. The reason, of course, is that even if we knew how one person's thought might, by means of some energy transfer independent of known sensory processes, produce a thought in someone else, we would still need to understand the process by which thoughts of a certain *kind* produce (in others) thoughts of a similar *kind*.

Any explanation of telepathy, then, must explain more than how one person's thoughts may produce a thought in someone else independently of the five known sensory channels. It must also explain how agent and percipient think *of* or *about* the same thing. In other words, it must explain what we may call *semantic* regularities between the thoughts of agent and percipient—for example, that A and B both think of old rabbis, or that they both think of rabbis (never mind their age), or that they both think of men of God. So if the ET theory is a theory of telepathy, it must be able to analyze these semantic regularities as parts of the process of energy transfer between agent and percipient. And to do this, it must (presumably) identify a person's thought with, or causally trace the thought back to, some one of his physiological states—let's say a brain state. But since this theory must explain certain semantic regularities or similarities between thoughts—that is, similarities in the content of thoughts—it must specify not only which brain states are thoughts, but also which brain state-*kinds* correlate with which thought-*kinds*. If the ET theory cannot specify physical regularities corresponding to semantic regularities between thoughts, at the very most it can have explained merely how one person's brain state can produce *some* brain state or other in another person. But the mystery remains, why a ϕ-thought might produce another ϕ-thought, or a related ψ-thought. It is, then, precisely in the search for physiological or other physical correlates to ·semantic regularities between thoughts that the ET theory founders. And it is just at this point, moreover, that the question of the viability of the ET theory goes beyond the question of its compatibility with the experimental data. H.H. Price recognized this difficulty, although he apparently did not see (as we shall see below) that the problems with the ET theory face an entire class of theories designed to explain human communication. Price writes,

> How could a complex proposition or even a complex picture be transmitted by radiation, even if an emotion like fear or anger might be? In the transmission of a message by ordinary telegraphy or wireless, the thought-content of the sender must first be translated into a *code* of some kind, e.g., dots and dashes, or spots arranged in a spatial pattern. Then there must be a series of waves corresponding to these. Then the receiving station reacts to these waves, and translates them back into dots and dashes, or spots; and that again must be translated into words, and finally the words must be understood. Is there any conceivable analogue to all this in the case of Telepathy, especially when we remember that the code of dots and dashes (or whatever it may be) has first to be established by *convention*? ([110]: 113-14).

Price's point is on the right track. But it is not altogether fatal to the *ET* theory, since the energy transfer in question need not be modeled after some kind of encoding/decoding system—in which case, Price's insistence on the system's conventional nature would no longer apply. We need only suppose that brain states can produce similar states in other brains without the mediation of a coding system (perhaps through some as yet mysterious quantum process). Price actually seems to recognize that a coding system is dispensable in explanations of telepathy when he suggests that 'telepathy is more like infection than knowledge' ([110]: 116). The transmission of an infectious disease is a poor candidate for a coding process; yet, when one person catches another's disease, their conditions will be similar in pertinent respects. Of course, we should not take the infection analogy too literally. It does remind us, however, that the *ET* theorist can argue that a person's brain states may, through some process of energy transfer, produce similar brain states in another person without any intervening coding system. They might contend that the brain is a marvelous mechanism, whose intricacies we are barely beginning to grasp, and thus that there *might* be some process in the brain by means of which this kind of energy transfer could occur.

Still, Price comes close to the heart of the matter in emphasizing that the *ET* theory will have difficulty explaining how thought-content passes from agent to percipient. To see why, we must first observe that any two ϕ-thoughts can differ in an indefinite number of ways. Ignoring for the moment the special features of telepathy, let us suppose that A and B are each thinking about an old rabbi. To keep matters simple, let us suppose that both A and B have mental images of an old rabbi. (It is clear enough that old-rabbi thoughts need not involve images at all: B, for example, may recall a vivid verbal description of an old rabbi.) Now, although A and B are both experiencing mental images of old rabbis, it is obvious that their images may differ in various respects. For example, A might be picturing an old rabbi conducting a bar mitzvah, while B is picturing a rabbi eating a pizza and wearing a leisure suit. If we suppose that A's old-rabbi thought telepathically produced B's old-rabbi thought, then what must be explained is how one old-rabbi thought can produce another; the *ET* theory must specify what it is about the brain states of A and B in virtue of which their associated thoughts are thoughts of old rabbis. The *ET* theory must therefore specify physical regularities between A and B's brain states which, as it were, cut right through the (possibly dramatic) differences in the associated thoughts of A and B to whatever it is about those thoughts that makes both of them thoughts of old rabbis (rather than thoughts of something else). And when, instead, B thinks of a young rabbi, or a priest, the *ET* theory must specify physical regularities in the brain states of A and B corresponding to whatever it is about the thoughts of A and B in virtue of which they are, respectively, thoughts of rabbis (never mind their age), or men of God. Here, the regularity which must be explained is this: that one rabbi thought (*simpliciter*), or one man-of-God thought, has produced another thought of the same kind. We must remember that if the *ET* theory cannot specify such regularities between brain states, it cannot explain the most crucial feature of telepathic content-simulation—namely, the striking and (*ex hypothesi*) non-fortuitous semantic regularities between thoughts of agent and percipient. However (I shall now argue), it is impossible that there be any such physical correlates to semantic regularities between thoughts.

In order for the *ET* theory to specify the physical regularities corresponding to semantic regularities between, say, thoughts of old rabbis, the *ET* theory must first specify some brain state (possibly a disjunctive set of states) such that whenever a person is in this state he is thinking of an old rabbi. This, we may say, is the old-rabbi state of the brain, and presumably it is a quite specific state (or set of states), one that differs from a young-rabbi brain state, or a rabbi brain state *simpliciter*, or a man-of-God brain state. If the *ET* theory denies this, it will have no way to specify in causal terms the distinct physical regularities that correspond to the semantic regularities between thoughts. It will be unable to specify the conditions (or the disjunctive set of conditions) under which agent and percipient come to have a certain relevant kind of thought.

But at this point it begins to look as if the *ET* theory will be forced to take some highly questionable (if not utterly unacceptable) stands on some important philosophical issues. To begin with, it seems committed to old-fashioned Platonism—which, at the very least, must be an embarrassment to a view purporting to be ontologically austere and scientific. As we have seen, the *ET* theory must postulate the existence of specific physiological states (or sets of states) corresponding to at least some semantic properties of thoughts. Otherwise, it will fail in principle to specify which state-*kinds* correlate with the semantic regularities between thoughts which by hypothesis must be explained. But then, specific physiological states (e.g., old-rabbi or man-of-God brain states) must correspond to something *in thoughts*, if the *ET* theory is to have any content. Thus, to suppose that there *is* such a thing as an old-rabbi brain state (even if this is a disjunctive set of states) is to suppose that there is some corresponding genuine property (or set of properties) of thoughts in virtue of which a thought is of an old rabbi. But this is to say that there is a property (or set of properties) without which a thought would not be *of* an old rabbi. The more archaic way of saying this is to say that the property (or set) is a thought's old-rabbiness.

However, we have already observed that thoughts of old rabbis take different forms. When one person is thinking of an old rabbi, all that may be happening is that he is remembering or thinking of a verbal description. On the other hand, he might have a mental image of some kind. And none of these things need have any relevant properties in common except that they all function as thoughts of old rabbis. The verbal descriptions or images which, in certain contexts, count as old-rabbi thoughts may be completely different from one another. In fact, thinking of an old rabbi need not even be manifested in an inner episode. One might correctly be characterized as thinking of an old rabbi, not because of something going on inside him, but in virtue of something he is *doing*—say, drawing a picture, or producing a verbal description. If we take this possibility seriously, it becomes completely implausible to suppose that the various ways of thinking of an old rabbi must be linked by a common property (or set of properties). (I pursue this issue further, in II.A.2.) It is more plausible that a person's inner or outer activity qualifies as a case of thinking of an old rabbi (say) in virtue of its *position* in a context. What makes an inner or outer episode an old-rabbi thought is not something intrinsic to that episode.

Some might protest that since the old-rabbi brain state may be a disjunctive set of states, we needn't suppose that the *ET* theory is committed to the Platonic essences of thoughts. A thought (they might say) could be of an old rabbi if it had this property, or that property, and so on. Notice, however, that even if the old-rabbi state of the brain is a disjunctive set of states, not just any old state can be a member of that set. It will have to be a set which itself has a set of distinguishing characteristics, distinct from those of other sorts of brain states. After all, this is needed to enable us to specify the relevant physical regularities corresponding to different semantic regularities in cases of telepathy. The old-rabbi state of the brain must, in principle, be a state whose necessary and sufficient conditions are specifiable. To deny this would be to concede that we could not tell what a person is thinking just by knowing what the state of his brain is. But since, by hypothesis, this old-rabbi state of the brain corresponds to whatever it is in a thought in virtue of which that thought is *of* an old rabbi (and not of something else), the *ET* theory is committed to the view that there *is* an essence to the thought of an old rabbi, and moreover that this essence corresponds to some specific type of physical state or set of states.

Just in case there still beats a heart stirred by visions of the One-Over-Many, I submit the following for consideration. According to the *ET* theory, it is a specific brain state-kind (or set of states) that either *is* or *causes* a certain corresponding kind of thought. Moreover, the physiological characteristics of this state which distinguish it from states corresponding to other kinds of thoughts are the physiological correlates to certain semantic properties of thoughts. We may thus pass from talk of what thoughts are *of* or *about* to talk of what brain states (or sets of states) *represent*. For example, the brain state which either is or causes the old-rabbi thought —the state, in other words, from which future scientists would be able to tell that its owner is thinking of an old rabbi (and not a young rabbi)—is, we may say, the state which represents the thought of an old rabbi (or, perhaps, which represents an old rabbi). We have seen that the *ET* theory must claim that there is some set of necessary and sufficient conditions for a brain state to represent one thing rather than another, since this is the only way it can hope to specify which brain state-kinds correspond to which semantic properties of thoughts. Now, a further consequence of this, which few seem to have appreciated, is that the *ET* theory is thereby committed to a version of a theory of meaning which is, in other guises, transparently implausible. According to the *ET* theory, what the content of a person's thought is—that is, whether the person is thinking of an old rabbi, a young rabbi, or merely a man of God, depends entirely on what state his brain is in. It will not depend on such contextual matters as what the person has been thinking about generally, on whether the person's being in this brain state is a response to something in his physical vicinity (e.g., a remark or some other sort of event), or on how the brain state gets integrated with the person's previous and subsequent overt behavior. This position is analogous to, and as empty as, the view that what a well-formed English sentence-token means depends entirely on its (deep and surface) structure and not on such things as what the conversational and larger social context is in which the sentence occurs, or on how that sentence gets integrated with the rest of the utterer's verbal and non-verbal behavior. In other words, pragmatic elements are as indispensable to determining what a brain state represents as to determining what a sentence means.

In order to develop this parallel between the philosophy of mind and the philosophy of language further, we must make some important observations. To begin with, it is possible that when A is thinking (say) of an old rabbi, all that is happening in A's mind is that he has an image of an old rabbi. But when A is having that mental image, he might instead be thinking simply of a man of God, or for that matter of a person *imitating* an old rabbi, or of the robes worn by rabbis. Just as a picture of a collie may, in different contexts, represent Lassie, or collies generally, or dogs generally, A's mental image of a rabbi may represent different things in different contexts and may thus be a component of different thoughts. And of course some stage-setting is required for the picture of a dog to represent one thing rather than another. Showing the picture to a child endeavoring to learn the alphabet might, for example, be preceded by 'C is for collie', 'D is for dog', or 'L is for Lassie'. Moreover, the picture of a dog can represent different things without there being any corresponding difference either in the arrangement of elements composing the picture or in the set of conditions which produced the picture. But this means that it is not something *intrinsic* to the picture of a dog that determines what the picture represents in a given case. But the situation is no different in the case of A's image of an old rabbi. There may be *one and only one* brain state in A that either is or causes this particular image of an old rabbi, no matter what the context is in which A has this image. If so, then the brain state itself is no less ambiguous than A's old-rabbi image. What A's old-rabbi image is an image *of* for A, and hence what the corresponding brain state represents, will depend on the sort of stage-setting required to fix the representational properties of the picture of a dog. For example, it might depend on whether A has this image (or brain state) in response to the command, 'Imagine to yourself an old rabbi', or 'Imagine to yourself an old man', or 'Imagine to yourself a person imitating an old rabbi'.

Thus, there seems no reason to suppose that a careful and exhaustive analysis of A's brain at a specified time will enable future scientists to discover what A is thinking at that time, any more than a careful and exhaustive analysis of the picture of a dog could be expected to tell us what that picture represents at any given time. Whatever is going on in A's mind in context c might also be going on in A's mind in some significantly different context c', whose difference would be reflected in the fact that we could (properly) regard A as having different thoughts in c and c'. But since neurological or biochemical (or whatever physical) descriptions of A's brain in c and c' might be identical, the representational properties of A's brain state will not simply be a function of physical properties intrinsic to that state. We may put this point differently by saying that, since topologically identical brain states can have different representational properties (since, in other words, there can be a one-many relationship between brain state-kinds and mental state-kinds), representational properties of brain states are not context-independent. The *ET* theory's presupposition that they *are* context-independent is, as we have seen, as unconvincing as the view that representational properties of pictures are context-independent.

We are now in a position to appreciate why the *ET* theory is unable to specify the physiological regularities corresponding to the semantic regularities between thoughts of agent and percipient. Consider, first, a formidable and seemingly insurmountable difficulty with a certain view in the philosophy of language. How, we may ask, can phonemically or syntactically identical strings of marks of sounds mean different things? And how can phonemically or syntactically distinct strings mean the same thing? A familiar answer to this puzzle is to say that the two strings have the same (or different) meaning when the brain states which cause them are the same (or different). We are often told that, when both *A* and *B* say, 'the bill is large', whether they are talking about money or fowl depends on what they are thinking when they utter the sentence; and what they are thinking then gets explained (ideally at least) in physiological terms—i.e., in terms of the states of their brains.

But then we may ask: When are the brain states of *A* and *B* the same? What determines whether they are both in the brain state corresponding to the 'fowl' interpretation of 'bill'? We have already noted that instances of one and the same brain state in *A* may, in principle, correlate with different thoughts, so that the brain state does not itself determine what it represents in any particular case. Whether *A* and *B* are both in the 'fowl' state cannot, then, be a function of properties intrinsic to those states. And to complicate matters further, it is generally conceded (even by physicalists) that *A* and *B* can have brains with different topological properties (or 'wiring' or 'circuitry')* so that there need not be any correlation between the topological (or 'hardware') descriptions of the brain states of *A* and *B* and descriptions

*This is by now a familiar point. Jerry Fodor puts it this way (in [53]: 145): '. . . there is no *a priori* basis for supposing that a parsing of the nervous system according to the psychological function that its parts perform would correspond in any simple way to parsings that are effected in terms of its gross topographical, morphological, or biochemical divisions. . . . The notion of a functional parsing of the nervous system demands the definition of some notion of functional equivalence for sets of neurological states *that may in principle be arbitrarily different in their physical characteristics*' (italics added).

of their mental states. It is possible, in other words, that A and B both be in the mental state corresponding to the 'fowl' interpretation of 'bill' even though their brain states differ topologically—that is, even though the relevant neurological or biochemical descriptions of their brain states differ. But since topologically distinct brain states may be functionally identical, what determines whether the brain states of A and B correlate with the same interpretation of 'bill'?

It is tempting to reply here that similarity between the brain states of A and B may be explained in terms of their structural isomorphism. But this won't help. For one thing, no matter what topological similarities obtain, there is no reason to suppose that a certain common brain structure in A and B (that is, the shared features of the brain states of A and B) uniquely determine a certain set of representational properties, just as there is no reason to suppose that a certain brain state in A uniquely determines a set of representational properties for that state. A common brain structure in A and B may represent different things in different contexts. Suppose that A and B each have only one brain state corresponding to a certain mental image of an old rabbi. Presumably, whatever physiological properties are common to those brain states in one context are common to the two brain states no matter what context they occur in. But, of course, the images themselves—hence, the corresponding brain states as well—needn't represent the same thing in all contexts. So, whether a certain physiological structure common to the brain states of A and B correlates with the 'money' or 'fowl' interpretation of 'bill' is not exclusively a function of properties intrinsic to that common structure; it must be a function, in part at least, of a set of background conditions.

Moreover, how is isomorphism between the brain states of A and B to be explained, if any two person's brains may have different topologies? To say that two brain states are isomorphic is just to say that there is a way of mapping one of the brain states onto the other. However, given the appropriate mapping function, or rule of projection, any structure can be mapped onto any other. This does not mean that no two structures are ever isomorphic. But isomorphism between structures is always relativized to some rule of projection, and these rules are not intrinsic properties of the universe. Just as no property intrinsic to a brain state determines what that brain state represents in a given case, no property intrinsic to a brain state determines which topologically different states it is isomorphic with. Similarly, in geometry, no property intrinsic to a given triangle determines which other geometrical figures that triangle is congruent with. Depending on which rule of projection we choose, a given triangle may be congruent only with triangles with the same horizontal orientation and the same angles, or it may be considered congruent with *any* triangle, or even with squares or lines.

Of course, partisans of this approach to meaning want to say that there is some special way—not just any old way—of mapping A's brain state onto B's. But all this means is that we must change our question—and it is only a superficial change—from 'What determines whether A and B are in the same brain state?' to 'What determines which function maps A's brain state onto B's?', or (since we are looking for some special mapping function), 'In virtue of what, is one mapping function to be preferred over all other possible mapping functions?'. No matter how we pose the question, however, it looks as if isomorphism between brain states, like representational properties of brain states, cannot be separated from the ways in which those brain states are linked to other brain states and to intersubjective contextual states of affairs like bits of overt behavior.

To see why, imagine that there are no relevant physiological differences between the brains of A and B at certain indicated times. We have already seen that topologically identical brain states can have different representational properties, and that, at those times, the corresponding semantic properties of the *thoughts* of A and B are therefore not simply functions of the topology of those states. But then, the special way of mapping A's brain state onto B's likewise cannot simply be a function of the topology of those states, for that special way is supposed to correlate with what is common to the *thoughts* of A and B. Hence, even if the brain states of A and B are topologically *identical*, this would not guarantee that A and B are having the same thought, any more than two instances of the same brain state in A, in different contexts, guarantees that A has the same thought in those very contexts. The reason is the same in both cases, namely, that what a person is thinking at a certain time—and hence, what his corresponding brain state represents at that time—depends not just on the state of his brain, but also on a complex set of relations between him and the world. It is entirely possible that A and B be in topologically identical states, yet give different answers to the question, 'Are you talking about money or birds?' So the only reason we could ever have for saying that the brain states of A and B are similar in some special way is that, in some sense having to do with the ways A and B relate to the world, those states are *functionally*, rather than structurally, identical or similar.

A sophisticated physicalist might protest that the necessary and sufficient physical conditions for a person to have a certain kind of thought are still specifiable in principle, but that they must include the complicated background conditions, or relations between the person and the world that I have been alluding to. The physical mechanisms for having a certain kind of thought will then be spelled out not only in terms of the structure of brain states, but also in terms of the structure of certain other physical states of affairs at the macroscopic level.

But this kind of extended mechanistic approach to meaning leads down an endless spiral. Suppose we *do* consider how the brain states of A and B relate to their behavior (either actual or potential), and suppose that, in answer to the question 'Are you talking about money or birds?', both A and B say (or would say) 'money'. What, we must now ask, determines whether A and B mean the same by 'money'? According to the physicalist, this question must be answered in the same way we answered the earlier question 'What determines whether A and B are talking about money or fowl?'—namely, by reference to the state of their brains. After all, A and B might not both be talking about money when they say 'money'. B, for example, may have intended to say 'bird', but made a verbal slip; or perhaps B really thinks 'money' means what we ordinarily think 'bird' means; or perhaps B is simply lying.

But consider what has happened. We were originally interested in determining when two bits of outer behavior—two utterances—were semantically the same. We explained their sameness or difference by reference to associated inner states. Then, we had to determine whether two distinct inner states were of a certain kind; and we were forced to decide this by reference to further actual or potential bits of outer behavior. And then when asked how to classify these new bits of outer behavior, we once again had to make reference to inner states. But of course the disambiguation of these inner states similarly requires reference to additional bits of outer behavior. And on it goes, the regress, apparently, is fatal. The disambiguation of external states cannot be accomplished by tracing them back to internal states, since these internal states cannot uniquely determine their own application and therefore require their own disambiguation; and that, of course, can be done only by reference to further external states, which themselves are not unambiguous.

The only way of stopping this regress is to claim that some state or set of states, whether inner or outer episodes (or some combination thereof), is *intrinsically unambiguous*— that is, that no matter what its context, it can be understood or taken in one and only one way. In that case, there would be no need for the kind of additional disambiguation that perpetuates the regress. But the idea of a state, inner or outer, that displays its content or determines that it be applied in one and only one way, is, as we have already seen, unintelligible. It is on a par with saying that a picture of a collie (in or out of the mind) can be taken only in one way, or that there is something about the picture that determines that it be used in one way only.

Proponents of physicalist theories of meaning are thus caught on the horns of a terrible dilemma. In their search for a topological, rather than a functional, characterization of sentence-meaning, either they must accept a vicious regress in order to disambiguate the structures they rely on to characterize meaning, or else they must accept the unintelligible notion of a structure (of *whatever* kind, physical, mental, linguistic, logical) that can be used in one and only one way and which itself determines (in a very strict sense of 'determines', permitting only one outcome) precisely what that way is.

We are now in a position to see that proponents of the *ET* theory are in a predicament analogous to that faced by proponents of the physicalistic approach to meaning. Instead of asking when two distinct strings of marks or sounds have the same meaning, we may ask: When are two distinct thoughts both thoughts of the same kind (e.g., when are two qualitatively distinct thoughts both thoughts of old rabbis?)? If the partisans of the *ET* theory are identity-theorists, their answer will be: When the brain states which *are* the thoughts are the same. If they are epiphenomenalists, their answer will be: When the two thoughts are *caused* by the same brain state. In either case, identity of thoughts is ultimately explained by reference to identity of brain states.

Suddenly, the terrain looks familiar. We may ask again: When are two people in the same brain state? Since 'hardware' or topological descriptions of the brains of *A* and *B* need not be the same, and since even topologically identical brain states may, in different contexts, have different representational properties, we must explain brain state similarity or identity (as before) in terms of the causal role, or functional properties, of those states—*not* in terms of their intrinsic structural properties. But then even if we could avoid a regress like that discussed above, this concession would be fatal to the *ET* theory. If the relevant semantic properties of thoughts cannot be explained solely in terms of the internal structural properties of brain states—and must be explained, at least in part, in terms of the sequence of behavior or other background conditions in which those brain states are embedded—then there is no way for the *ET* theory to specify the required physiological regularities to be correlated with the recognizable semantic regularities between thoughts. The very specification of relevant physiological regularities presupposes that there is some way of identifying the physiological correlates of the semantic properties of thoughts, solely on the basis of properties intrinsic to a certain kind of physiological state.

And as if this were not enough, a version of the aforementioned regress plagues the *ET* theory after all. Having conceded that identity of brain states must be explained in terms of the functional properties of those states, then, since those properties cannot be identified independently of the behavior which the brain states produce, at some point we must ask: What determines whether two brain states have produced the same bits of behavior? Just as two functionally identical brain states may differ topologically, and just as two thoughts of the same kind may differ qualitatively, two bits of behavior may differ structurally or topologically even though they are of the same kind (and, for that matter, two bits of behavior may have the same structure, even though they are of different kinds). We have already considered how this applies to linguistic behavior. But it applies with equal force to non-linguistic behavior. For example, *A* and *B* might both be exhibiting the behavior of trying to catch a bus.* However, *A* might be standing at the bus stop smoking a cigar, while *B* is frantically running toward the stop. Moreover, on another occasion, *A* might be standing at the bus stop smoking a cigar, but without trying to catch a bus. On this occasion he might merely be admiring a new sports car across the street. Presumably, the *ET* theory (or one like it) would disambiguate such bits of behavior by rooting them in the appropriate brain states. Thus when both *A* and *B* were trying to catch the bus, the differences in their behavior would be explained as different causal manifestations of a

---

*This example is inspired by a similar example, in N. Malcolm [91].

brain state associated with bus-catching activities. And the underlying difference between two superficially similar bits of bus-stop standing, on A's part, would be explained as the similar causal manifestations of different sorts of brain events. Now, unless the ET theorist makes the unacceptable move of treating these inner episodes as intrinsically unambiguous, he will be brought back to our endless spiral; for, we are forced to ask once again: When are two brain states the same or different?

To sum up, we have seen that neither the semantic properties of thoughts nor the corresponding representational properties of brain states are specifiable independently of background conditions; they cannot, therefore, be identified with any structural states of persons. Moreover, background conditions are no less ambiguous, functionally, than brain states; so the structure of outer episodes also fails uniquely to determine the function of those episodes. In general, both inner and outer states are functionally ambiguous considered only with respect to their topological or structural features. Hence, in telepathy, semantic regularities between thoughts are not reducible to any mechanistic process between agent and percipient.

This is not to say that there are no mechanisms involved in telepathic interaction. There are, after all, mechanisms involved even in ordinary human communication—which cannot be fully characterized mechanistically either. When two people are talking to each other, we can characterize the process partially in terms of certain operations of the vocal organs, eyes, ears, and so on. But what they are thinking about, or what the content of their communication is, reduces to no such operations either of the organisms alone or of those organisms plus some specified context; for, structures (of whatever kind, in or out of the organism) cannot determine their own function.

Thus, even if there *are* physical mechanisms of telepathy, the most the ET theory could show would be how a physiological state in A was, by some currently unknown means, causally linked with some state or other in B. We might discover regular correlations between states in A having certain topological features and states in B having certain topological features (possibly distinct from A's). In fact, some studies of healers provide data of this kind—for example, in cases where the patient's vital signs begin to match those of the healer, or where an increase in energy around a healer's acupuncture points regularly and immediately precedes an increase in energy around the patient's acupuncture points.

But since the semantic properties of thoughts cannot be characterized topologically either as states of persons or as states of persons *cum* context—that is, since they cannot be specified independently of the way in which a person's states are somewhat indefinitely integrated with what Wittgenstein called the 'flow of life', certain interesting questions arise. Perhaps most importantly, in ordinary verbal communication a person's remarks are usually disambiguated within a conversational context by the way in which they fit in with the ongoing behavior of those involved. The relevant information about this behavior is normally supplied through familiar processes involving the five senses. But in telepathic interaction these familiar keys to disambiguation are absent. Telepathic 'impressions' (let us call them) are not typically integrated with any slice of life open to inspection by the five senses. How, then, do the semantic properties of the agent's thought get reproduced in the percipient's thought?

This, I think, is the principal mystery to be solved about telepathy. Even if it were discovered that human brains could interact through some form of energy transfer—say, ELF waves—the semantic regularities between the thoughts of agent and percipient could not be reduced to any such process, and these regularities would remain mysterious. We must still find, then, the telepathic analogues of the background conditions that make ordinary human communication possible.

At this stage, we may well be tempted to entertain some philosophical positions that have not been, to put it mildly, exactly in vogue in modern Western philosophy. For example, we might consider the possibility that human minds constantly (or frequently) interact at some subconscious or unconscious level, and that these interactions provide enough of a context for telepathic communication to occur. This in turn might lead us to consider such hair-raising possibilities as the existence of a world soul or universal consciousness, about which the mystics have often spoken. But these metaphysical speculations must be reserved for another occasion. I want rather to consider certain less exotic applications and extensions of the foregoing discussion to the philosophy of mind.

Part II

A. Psi and the Philosophy of Mind

1. Anomalous Monism

I want now to consider how the objections raised above against the *ET* theory bear on some traditional issues in the philosophy of mind—in particular, how they bear on psychophysical identity theories. It is common practice these days to distinguish two general forms of the Identity Theory. One asserts lawlike correlations between *types* of mental states and *types* of physical states. The *ET* theory is a version of the type-type form of the theory; and although parapsychologists, psychologists, and other scientists dabbling in the study of consciousness often cling, somewhat naively, to type-type theories, this form of the Identity Theory has, for the most part, been abandoned by more sophisticated philosophers in favor of *token-token* versions of the theory.

According to this form of the Identity Theory, every mental state-token is a physical (let us say, brain) state-token, but there need be no lawlike correlations between brain state-*types* and mental state-*types*. My thought that S will ϕ is, then, identical with a brain state of mine, but there need be no lawlike correlations between thoughts of the kind that S will ϕ and any sort of brain state at all. Davidson [36] calls this position *anomalous monism* (hereafter, *AM*). His view is monistic, since he takes all mental events to be brain events. But the relationship between the domains of the mental and the physical remains anomalous—that is, there need be no correlating laws for the two domains.

Some might argue, then, that although my arguments against the *ET* theory weigh against type-type versions of the Identity Theory, they do not touch *AM*. This contention, I want now to argue, is wrong. More specifically, I shall first explain why some of my arguments against the *ET* theory apply directly against *AM*. Then I shall consider further arguments against *AM*, including the argument that *AM*, rather than escaping the pitfalls of type-type versions of the Identity Theory, actually *presupposes* type-type correlations between the mental and the physical, and hence that *AM*, like the *ET* theory, is disguised nonsense.

One of the principal reasons the *ET* theory collapses is that (as I have argued above and will argue from a somewhat different point of view in the next section) mental states can only be characterized *positionally*—that is, with respect to the way in which certain events fit into a sequence of events. If, for example, something specific is going on in *A*'s mind,* (say, the occurrence of an image of a collie), we don't yet know what *A*'s mental state is (that is, what his image is an image *of* for him) unless we also know how *A*'s mental image is incorporated into a sequence of relevant events. The same image may, in different contexts, represent different things. Now *AM* takes *A*'s mental state to be some particular brain state. But if we selected *A*'s physiological state at a given time, and the collie image with which it was allegedly correlated, we might, by placing them in different contexts, properly characterize *A* as thinking about dogs generally or about

---

*I use this example for the sake of simplicity. But we should remember that a person can be in a mental state *m* without there being any particular *experience* corresponding to *m*. For example, every time I brush my teeth, I can be described properly as remembering how to brush my teeth, even though no occurrent mental states of mine (i.e., no memory experience) could properly be described as my remembering how to brush my teeth. Similarly, while discussing football with a friend, I might reach into my trouser pocket for my house key; and although there need be no occurrent inner episode of mine that could be characterized as a memory (or belief) experience concerning my house key, I could properly be described as remembering where my key was (or believing that my key was in my pocket).

Lassie in particular. In one context, for example, *A* might have his image (or be in the corresponding brain state) in response to the instruction, 'Think about dogs'; in the other, the instruction might have been, 'Think about Lassie'. But if it is possible for the brain state corresponding to *A*'s mental image to represent different things in different contexts, then, apart from any context, the brain state itself represents no more than the mere image itself considered apart from any context. To the extent, then, that *AM* construes mental states to be nothing but mere states of persons—to the extent, in other words, that *AM* rests on a static and topological, rather than a dynamic and functional, characterization of mental states—it has reached the same dead end as the *ET* theory. *A*'s mental states cannot be characterized simply in terms of what is happening solely within *A*. But then contrary to *AM*, a particular mental state in *A* cannot be a particular physiological state of *A*.

A similar objection weighs against the extended static and topological view of thinking that identifies a particular mental state with a particular physiological state *plus* a certain specific set of contextual conditions. As we have seen, from a topological point of view, context is as functionally ambiguous as the physiological state with which it is conjoined; placed in a different and *wider* context, it might be correlated with an entirely different mental state. Moreover, as I point out in more detail in the next two sections, there are, in fact, no context-independent preferred descriptions of contexts, hence, there are no context-independent preferred ways of integrating a particular event into its surrounding context.

This objection to a static or non-functional characterization of mental states may be linked with an objection advanced by Wittgenstein [196], [197], and more recently by Norman Malcolm [91]—namely, that we apply radically different concepts of *duration* to brain states and to mental states. Neural firings and biochemical changes in the brain are events whose duration, occurrence, or temporal boundaries can be explicitly measured. In general, however, beliefs, desires, intentions, and so forth—the sorts of things whose instances, according to *AM*, are particular physiological states (or physiological states plus physical contextual states) —cannot be measured in this way. This is not to say that mental states do not last or have duration. It is to say, rather, that many (if not most) mental states—for example, those we treat as dispositional, are simply not the sorts of events or processes for which the making of such measurements is conceptually appropriate in a clear way (see Wittgenstein [197]: paras. 45, 81ff, and Malcom [91]: 257-260). But this shows that mental states generally and brain states are quite different sorts of things, and robs of all antecedent plausibility the suggestion that instances of one are instances of the other.

Proponents of *AM* actually concede that there may be no way of mapping the *predicates* applicable to mental states onto predicates of *any* language used to describe the brain states with which they are alleged to be identical. For example, the predicate '____ is a belief that Jones is a coward' or the predicate '____ is a thought about Lassie' may map onto no predicate in the language of even the most advanced brain science. Therefore, *kind* terms appropriate to mental states may fail completely to correlate with kind terms appropriate to brain states. But as Bruce Goldberg has recently argued [59], proponents of *AM* tend not to notice an important corollary of this fact. Let Ψ be the portion of language used to describe mental states, and let Φ be that portion of language used to describe physical states—in particular, states of the brain. The anomalous monist concedes that the predicate expressions of Ψ need not map onto the predicate expressions of Φ. But, as Goldberg points out, there can then be no reason to suppose that the *referring* expression of Ψ map onto those of Φ. Suppose we correctly say of Smith that he is in a certain mental state-token m, and that m is an instance of believing that Jones is a coward. The anomalous monist grants that there may never be an expression in the language of the physical sciences coextensive with '____ is a belief that Jones is a coward'. In the view of the physical sciences, such a psychological kind term may not mark off a genuine kind; hence, no predicate of Φ needs to correspond to this predicate of Ψ. But if so, then we have no reason to suppose that we shall ever form an expression in the language of the physical sciences having the same *referent* as '*m*'. If the *kinds* of phenomena describable in Ψ fail to map onto the kinds acknowledged in the physical sciences, then we have no reason to suppose that the *objects* to which the predicate expressions of Ψ apply are, or map onto, the objects to which the predicate expressions of Φ apply. If physiology and psychology distinguish different kinds of phenomena—if they do not divide the world into kinds or types in anything like the same way—they may also have entirely different criteria of individuation within their respective domains; in that case, their domains may not divide up into members, or tokens, in anything like the same way. But if so, the anomalous monist can claim no grounds for identifying tokens in one domain with tokens in the other. Having conceded that kinds of mental states may not correspond to kinds of physical states, the anomalous monist must grant that, *in principle*, parsings of physical states need not correlate at all with parsings of mental states. So, in principle, no member of the domain of mental states needs to correspond (or be identical) with any member of the domain of physical states. Thus, *AM*'s assertion of token-token identity between these two domains becomes entirely arbitrary—or else a form of mere wishful thinking. (Whatever appeal remains in the view that mental state-tokens and physical state-tokens are identical is, I suspect, a function of the unrecognized fact that *AM presupposes* type-type correlations between the mental and the physical. Thus, proponents of *AM* tend not to realize that they actually do *not* concede that types of mental states may fail to correlate with types of physical states. I discuss this issue below.)

Hard-core anomalous monists may not be entirely moved by the foregoing considerations. They may argue that our objections show only that we may never get very far with actual psychophysical theories. We may, that is, never be able to achieve an actual reduction of the language Ψ to the language Φ. Even so, they may say, *AM* is able to put forward a substantial metaphysical claim that the objections so far offered leave untouched. The claim runs more or less as follows.

(a) *S* is in mental state-token *m* ⇒ there is some brain state-token *b* of *S* such that without *b*, *S* would not be in *m*.

(a) makes a much weaker claim than the claim of token-token identity. In fact, (a) need not even be a *monistic* claim. It certainly does not assert an identity; it asserts, rather, a kind of causal dependence of *m* on *b*, and thus seems to be an epiphenomenalist claim. Moreover, *b* is a necessary but not a sufficient condition for the occurrence of *m*. This conforms with points raised earlier, since, as we have seen, what mental state a person is in is at least partly a function of context. Since physical or physiological structures are functionally ambiguous, considered only with respect to their topological features, no brain state as such has any intrinsic single function. (a), then, represents a substantial shift away from the already weak identity claim we initially attributed to the anomalous monist.

But we can see why (a) would appeal to some philosophers. It still anchors mental states in physical states; and, while not identifying the two, still refuses, so to speak, to give mental states a life of their own. In other words, (a) seems to be a commendably modest physicalist position, replacing identity between the mental and the physical with mere causal dependence of the former on the latter.

But let us look more closely at (a). In my opinion, it has very little to commend it. According to (a), when *S* is in mental state-token *m*, *S*'s being in *m* is explained in terms of *S*'s being in some brain state-token *b* necessary for the occurrence of *m*. But now we must ask proponents of (a) an embarrassing question: Does it matter, in explaining *m*, what *type* of state, physiologically speaking, the token *b* is a token of? If the answer is yes—as I shall argue it must be, if (a) has anything of interest to say—then (a) is really a type-type view in disguise, and my earlier arguments apply against it. But if the answer is no—if it does not matter what kind of brain state the token *b* is—then *b* can be *any* old state; all (a) asserts, then, is that there must be *some* brain activity for a person to have mental states—perhaps simply that we must be *alive* to have thoughts. Now it is true that my earlier objections do not touch this position. Although so construed, (*a*) is not altogether trivial—for it seems incompatible with certain dualistic and especially spiritualistic views according to which mental processes are autonomous—it is no longer an *explanatory* thesis. It cannot explain, in physiological terms, why *m* occurred rather than some other mental state. Nor would it help explain why *m* is just the *kind* of mental state it is. To do this in physiological terms, we must revert to a type-type correlation view—which is unsatisfactory. In any case, if it does not matter what the physiological features of brain state-token *b* are, then (*a*) promises no physiological understanding of why *m* occurred (rather than a token of a different type), or of what, physiologically speaking, it means to have a thought of type *M*. If Smith is thinking that Jones is a coward, partisans of (*a*) can say no more than that Smith has this thought because he is in *some* brain state or other. They cannot tell us why, physiologically, Smith has this particular thought rather than another thought, or what it is, physiologically speaking, to have (say) a thought that Jones is a coward (or even what it is to have *any* thought about cowards).

Nor can (*a*) provide the foundation for a theory having any predictive utility. In fact, if *b* can be any brain state at all, then (*a*) provides no physiological basis for the science of psychology. We would have no way of describing or predicting, in physiological terms, what mental state a person was or would be in. Understood in this exceedingly weak way, (*a*) is actually contrary to the original spirit of materialism, which was initially conceived as a program for explaining why a person was in one mental state rather than another or what it is (in physiological terms) to be in certain types of mental states, or how on the basis of one's physiological states, we might predict what a person's mental states would be. But these explanatory and predictive features of a materialist theory may be secured only if there are type-type correlations between the mental and the physical.

Actually, these last remarks help to illuminate a fatal presupposition of the stronger token-token identity theories. The problem is that there is no justification whatever for positing an identity between mental state- and brain state-tokens unless type-type identities are presupposed. Consider, for example, a case where A is properly described as thinking about collies. According to token-token identity theories, this thought-token is identical with some brain state-token b—identified, let us say, with respect to some set T of topological features. But at this point we must ask: Can different brain state-tokens having just this set T of topological features correlate with different mental states? Can some brain state-token b' which, like b, is individuated with respect to its being an instance of brain states having the set T of physiological properties, occur with some thought *other* than a thought about collies? If the token-token theorist answers yes (as may be expected of someone who denies type-type correlations)—if, that is, there can be a many-one relationship between mental state-types and the brain state-type individuated by the set T of topological properties—then there is *no reason* to identify A's thought-token about collies with b, since state b', topologically identical with b, can be correlated with a different thought. Thus, the identification of A's thought about collies with b seems completely arbitrary.

It appears, then, that the identification of mental state-tokens with brain state-tokens requires that we presuppose type-type correlations between mental states and brain states. Only thus may we avoid the self-defeating admission of the possibility of a one-many relation between brain states of the physiological type T and types of mental states. But then, since it presupposes a type-type theory, AM proves, after all, to be subject to just the criticisms raised earlier against the ET theory of telepathy.

2. The Myth of the Internal Mechanism

I suspect that many readers will feel uneasy about the stand I have taken against the various forms of the identity theory. Perhaps they rebel against the *a prioristic* nature of my arguments; perhaps they find it odd that purportedly empirical theories should be rejected on non-empirical grounds. If so, I must remind these readers that scientific theories do rest—probably inevitably—on philosophical presuppositions; in that sense, they are really philosophical theories in disguise. (We will see this also in II.B., in connection with the so-called theory of synchronicity, although to call that claim a *scientific* theory, or even a theory, may be unreasonably generous.) Thus the various forms of the ET theory rest on numerous philosophical assumptions, despite their superficially empirical or non-philosophical character. I have been at pains to criticize some of these—for example, the thesis that structures of the brain display their function, or that all thoughts of kind ϕ share some common property or set of properties (a Platonic essence) in virtue of which those thoughts are ϕ, or that there is a set of necessary and sufficient conditions for something to be a ϕ-thought. A theory that rests on such assumptions rests on nothing, and no empirical arguments are needed to demonstrate its inadequacy.

Another probable source of dissatisfaction is harder to dispel. Indeed, I have to work hard to dispel it myself. The problem arises by way of a very natural (but mistaken) assumption—so natural, in fact, that it undergirds the entire field of cognitive psychology, generative linguistics, almost all areas of the brain sciences (in fact a good part of the biological sciences generally), and a great deal of philosophy. But before trying to state the assumption, let me offer some illustrations of the contexts in which we tend to appeal to it. I want the reader to appreciate from the start how fundamental and sweeping a revision our view of human beings and human behavior must undergo, once we abandon this assumption.

Imagine that we are trying to teach someone how to conjugate Spanish *ar*-verbs. Imagine, further, that our student has been unable to do more than memorize the conjugation of the verbs already shown him; he is unable to conjugate any new *ar*-verb presented to him. But after some further instruction, he finds that, for the first time, he can indeed conjugate new *ar*-verbs, and has thus acquired an understanding he did not possess previously. Or, imagine that we are trying to teach a child the color red by teaching him to distinguish red things from non-red things. And suppose that in this process, suddenly, the child clearly understands what to do. The assumption we tend to make in such cases is that something has happened, *within* the person, between the time he did not understand and the time he did. In other words, we tend to explain the newly-acquired understanding in terms of some *associated structural modification* of the person—most would say it was a change in his brain.

Or imagine that Jones, who for many years had been a callous and frivolous person, suddenly has a religious experience that completely transforms his character, so that he becomes a loving, serious, and God-fearing person. We tend to assume that the change in Jones' character must be due to some corresponding physiological change *within* Jones himself (specifically, a change in his brain) produced by the religious experience. We assume that something relevant about the way Jones is put together is different from what it was before. (I say 'relevant' because, after all, Jones must be changing physiologically all the time, whether or not he undergoes a religious conversion.)

Or imagine that one day I see a person whom I recognize as my old friend *A*, whom I have not seen in 10 years. We ordinarily assume that I could not remember *A* were it not for something *within* me (a memory trace) caused by my previous acquaintance with *A*, and that I could not recognize *A* after 10 years were it not for some specific physiological process occurring within me (the process of recognition).

These assumptions, I believe, are entirely false and seriously misleading. Of course I cannot hope to demonstrate in a detailed way how very nearly every aspect of even just cognitive psychology (to take one general field) is based on a mistake, by examining, why these assumptions or their variants are unjustified in memory theory, recognition theory, learning theory, and so on. The general mistake appears in different guises in these and other areas. I shall try instead to analyze the error in its most general and abstract form, and then show how it applies in certain cases. I then leave it to the reader to extend the arguments to other relevant areas in the study of human beings.

The assumption I want to attack may be called the *Principle of the Internal Mechanism* (hereafter, *PIM*). In stating this principle I want, for the sake of simplicity, to insist on a certain terminological restriction. Hereafter, when I refer to the class of *mental states* or *events*, I want to *exclude* such phenomena as sensations and images. Although there is good reason to think that the points I shall be making about thoughts, beliefs, memories, dispositions, instincts, and so on can be made, *mutatis mutandis*, about such things as pains and itches (see Lurie [90]), it would needlessly complicate matters to discuss this entire range of experiences. I shall therefore confine myself to the range of cognitive (or 'intentional') mental states. I don't pretend to have hereby characterized a crisply circumscribed range of phenomena. In fact, I don't believe a neat characterization is even possible.

With this is mind, the principle I wish to criticize may be formulated as follows.

> (*PIM*) It is possible to explain (through some empirical theory) why S is in (occurrent or dispositional) mental state m by reference to some corresponding physiological structure or mechanism b identical with, or causally responsible for, m.

The *PIM* is the backbone of those areas of science whose entire program (like those of cognitive psychology and much of the brain sciences) rests on the supposition that, in principle, mechanisms for at least some human cognitive abilities, or thoughts, beliefs, and so on, are discoverable. Should the *PIM* be false, numerous academic disciplines would thus turn out to have no foundation. Notice, moreover, that the *PIM* is not merely a version of a physicalistic identity thesis. Nor is it an epiphenomenalist principle. It is, rather, presupposed by identity theorists, epiphenomenalists, and even some dualists (e.g., those who insist on the autonomy of the mental in at least some cases, but who permit some physicalistic/mechanistic explanations of mental states).

Although I shall argue that the *PIM* is false, this principle is by no means crazy, and in fact it is quite seductive. The reason for this can be seen clearly in the application of the *PIM* to memory. We tend to assume that I could not possibly remember my friend *A* after 10 years were it not for something (a trace) in me—let us say a modification of my brain —caused in the past through my association with *A*. Otherwise, we suppose, in remembering *A* after all these years we would have causation over a temporal gap. To explain how I remember *A* after 10 years, we must (we suppose) say more than that I used to know *A*. When I remember *A*, therefore, it is presumably because something *persisting* in me links my present memory of *A* to my having known *A* 10 years earlier.

But notice that the appeal to a memory trace is not designed solely to explain how I happen to be in a specific mental state—namely, the remembering of *A*. It is intended to explain how such a state of remembering is *possible* in the first place. The purpose of positing the existence of a trace (or of the structural modification allegedly associated with understanding a new concept, acquiring a new disposition, etc.) is to explain how a certain kind of mental state could *ever* occur—as though without such structural modifications, the mental events in question would be impossible. Without a trace in me—without a physiological representation of *A*— no experience that I now have *could* be a memory of *A*. For example, if after 10 years I call up a mental image of *A*, that image could not be a memory of *A* if it lacked the appropriate causal history linking my present experience to my previous acquaintance with *A*. My image would not count as a memory unless there was some trace in me, caused by my previous acquaintance with *A*, activating that image. Mental images may be possible without such activation, but they cannot then be instances of remembering.

But what if traces *cannot* explain how we happen to be in that particular mental state whose very possibility is putatively insured by that structural modification? In other words, what if the positing of traces cannot possibly explain any particular mental state-token of remembering? If in the explanation of any particular instance of remembering the role to be performed by the trace turns out to be an impossible role, a role nothing could fulfill, then we will perforce have to reconsider our supposition that we must posit such a modification just to demonstrate that states of remembering were possible in the first place. And this is what I shall try to show. I shall argue that any theory in which mental states are to be explained by reference to specific associated physiological structures or mechanisms that produce them is a theory that must rest on one or another false presupposition —specifically, either the Platonic assumption that mental states of type ϕ share some common property (or set of properties) in virtue of which they are of type ϕ, or else the unintelligible assumption that a physiological structure can be intrinsically functionally unambiguous. My discussion will focus almost exclusively on the case of memory. But the arguments apply, *mutatis mutandis*, to other cognitive functions.

The errors underlying the notion of a memory trace* (or more generally, the notion of the structure or mechanism associated with any occurrent or dispositional mental state) are basically just the ones discussed earlier in connection with the *ET* theory and anomalous monism, although the fine details of the mistakes there and here differ somewhat. We have already observed that a given brain structure, identified physiologically with respect to a set T of topological properties, is functionally ambiguous—that is, that topologically

---

*Recently, two sustained attacks on trace theory have appeared in print, those offered by Bursen [27] and Malcolm [91]. They explore in much greater detail (and, especially in Malcolm's case, from a somewhat different point of view) the sorts of criticisms I offer here. If these books were to have the effect they deserve on the intellectual community, many neurophysiologists and neuropsychologists might find themselves out of work. Bursen is more blunt on this point than Malcolm, and charges (correctly) that trace theories are scientific theories only on the surface and that, at bottom, they require that memory is magical.

identical brain states can have different functional or representational properties, depending on how we position them with respect to the background conditions or context in which they are embedded. We also saw that the pretended explanatory power of the ET theory and AM requires the nonsensical assumption that some kind of structure (purely physiological, or physiological *cum* external) is functionally *un*ambiguous—that is, that there is *not* a one-many relationship between the type T of the physiological state and the types of mental states it may be correlated with. And in analyzing the ET theory, I remarked that, in order to identify physiologically some mental state m as being of type ϕ, we must suppose that there are necessary and sufficient conditions for a mental state to be of that type; in effect that there must be some specifiable property (or set of properties) that all mental states of type ϕ share, and in virtue of which a given state is of that type. But that requirement proved that the ET theory rested on an elementary form of Platonism.

Now, the situation is no different if we suppose that physiological structural modifications (of the brain) underlie the acquisition of new memories, concepts, or dispositions. For instance, we can easily expose the Platonic presuppositions of the notion of a memory trace. Recall that a thought of a certain kind (say, the thought of an old rabbi) may take an indefinite number of different forms, having nothing more of relevance in common than the fact that they are of that kind. Thus when I am thinking of an old rabbi, I may be remembering a verbal description, or having an image of a person, or perhaps a more complicated image (say, of a rabbi conducting a bar mitzvah), or perhaps I am just presenting to myself the words 'old rabbi', or perhaps I am imagining these words sung by the Mt. Sinai Hospital Chorale. And of course each of these categories will have innumerable variations as well. The verbal descriptions or the images (for example) can differ subtly or dramatically from one another in their details. But the same is true of any instances of remembering my friend A: there is no one form for this mental state, no one general feature or set of features that any token of remembering A must have. Remembering A

might consist, for example, in nothing more than having any of a number of mental images or different feelings; or it might consist of certain bits of behavior, like producing verbal descriptions of A, or telling anecdotes about A, or reacting in any number of different ways upon meeting A after 10 years. For example, there might be a shock of recognition, or there might be no shock of recognition, not even a feeling of recognition, or no experienced lapse of 10 years at all. On seeing A my sole reaction might simply be to say (or think), 'You owe me $50'. Moreover, remembering A may consist of nothing more than thinking (or talking) about things *associated* with A—say, cupcakes, or the Washington Monument. But if so, then it is clear that one cannot lay down conditions for something's being a remembering of A.

Rememberings of A, then, may come in an endless number of different forms, and need have nothing of importance in common except being instances of remembering A. But behind this diversity of possible forms of remembering A is supposed to be some modification in me (or my brain), something that was not present in those days before I first met A. This is the trace of A. Its existence is supposed to help us understand any particular instance of remembering A. We are to explain the occurrence of any such instance by linking it causally to the activation of the appropriate trace.* But if instances of remembering A need not have any relevant

---

*How the 'right' trace gets activated is a problem that memory theorists tend not to see clearly. They tend to suppose that this can be explained by reference to structural isomorphism between the inner state (the trace) and some other external thing (like a picture of A or A himself). But, as we saw in the case of the ET theory, this idea rests on the untenable claim that isomorphism between two things is intrinsic to those things, and that rests on the unacceptable idea that some structures are functionally unambiguous, that their topologies determine their own representational properties or rules of projection. (How fantastic this idea is becomes clear, if we recall that a brain state does not represent or resemble a person A in the way that even a photograph of A represents or resembles A.)

In the next chapter and in the following section, we shall examine yet another aspect of this mistake—namely, the unacceptable idea that things or events have a preferred parsing.

properties in common save that of being rememberings of A, the trace serves no explanatory function. We may always ask: How can the activation of some particular state b cause any of the variety of things that count as rememberings of A? Where do we find a causal regularity? How can the same state causally explain both my having a mental image of A and my simply saying to A, 'You owe me $50'? If rememberings of A need have no relevant properties in common, then why suppose there is some single trace to whose activation all these rememberings are causally linked? If there is no one thing (no common property or set of properties) to link the trace to, the trace serves no causal role after all. There is no causal regularity to appeal to, since there is no specifiable regularity in the range of possible effects of the trace. But if there is no such regularity, if *anything* experienced or done by a person may, in the right context, count as a remembering of A, then the posited A-trace explains none of these things.

The trace theorist might respond by saying that there are different traces for different *kinds* of rememberings of A. But this won't help; in fact, it starts the trace theorist on an endless regress. These subsets of rememberings are no more linked by a common property (or set of properties) than were the various things that originally counted simply as rememberings of A. Mental images of A, for example, no more need a set of common properties than do the different possible ways of imagining an old rabbi. The image could be of A as a young man or old man; it could be an image of a portrait of A, of A's front, or profile, or A's eyes, or face; the images could be rough images (like stick drawings) or more detailed (like photographs); they could be in color, black and white, or perhaps just in shades of blue; and so on. And so the question again arises: If the members of some subset of rememberings of A need have no relevant properties in common (save that of belonging to that subset), why suppose they are causally linked to the same thing?

Here a certain objection is likely to occur to some readers. They might argue that paradigm cases of causal connections exhibit the same diversity of effect that memory traces have, and these paradigms (they would say) are not thereby rendered suspect. For example, the triggering of dynamite may have various kinds of effects. We can use dynamite to blow up a bridge, a house, or a person; and each of these classes of effects will cover a great variety of phenomena. Dynamite explosions may be loud or muffled, messy or neat, etc. And here, the diversity of possible effects of dynamite is no reason for saying that the triggering of dynamite is not the cause of such effects.

Although this is an important objection, it misses a certain crucial point about the putative effects of memory traces. Despite their diversity, the various things caused by the triggering of dynamite are still explosions. But manifestations of the activation of memory traces needn't have *anything* of interest or importance in common except being instances of a certain type of memory. (They will, of course, have in common an infinite number of irrelevant or trivial properties, such as, being things, or being self-identical.) In advance of any actual triggering of dynamite, we can say that in all probability it will produce an explosion. But we cannot say in advance *how* a person will display a certain kind of memory, once the appropriate trace is activated. Thinking about a Schubert piano sonata, or tuberculosis, or loose jello, for example, might count as manifestations of remembering A, if (say) these were things somehow associated with A. So the alleged parallel does not obtain.

At this point the trace theorist is faced with a fatal dilemma. It arises because he must somehow avoid the fatal Platonic assumption that all instances of a mental state type ϕ share a common property (or set of properties) in virtue of which they are of type ϕ. Grasping one horn of the dilemma, he must, in order to sidestep the Platonic assumption, concede that there may be a one-many relationship between the trace and the kinds of things that are to count as rememberings of A. But in that case, since the rememberings of A are not themselves connected by a set of necessary and sufficient conditions for being a remembering of A, the trace (as we have seen) can have no explanatory power. If there is no specifiable property (or set of properties) that something must have in order to be a remembering of A (and not something else), then there is nothing in any actual remembering of A to link the trace to.

Seizing the other horn of the dilemma, the trace theorist can avoid positing a one-many relationship between the trace and the possible forms of its causal consequences by saying that each remembering of A (i.e., each token of remembering A) is causally linked to its own unique trace. In this way, he avoids supposing that there is a property (or set of properties) common to rememberings of the same type. But this alternative still robs the trace of any explanatory power. If each remembering of A has its own unique associated trace, then first of all the positing of traces does not explain the general *ability to remember A*, since rememberings of A may take different forms. But one reason theorists initially posited the existence of traces was to explain how we could ever have such a general ability. Thus, positing a different trace for each manifestation of an ability fails to explain how the ability itself is possible. Moreover, the second horn of the dilemma assigns to the trace just the functional uniqueness that, in the context of the ET theory, we saw was unintelligible. Memory traces are now linked one-one with particular manifestations of rememberings of A; the trace is the causal antecedent of only one specific token m of remembering A — it *cannot possibly** be causally linked to any different human experience or behavior (including other rememberings of A having no properties in common with m and even non-rememberings of A). The trace theorist must say that m's trace cannot possibly be causally linked to mental state-tokens of different types or different kinds of tokens of the

---

*The type of possibility here is empirical rather than logical. That is, the trace theorist is committed to saying that as a matter of empirical fact (i.e., given the laws of this world) the trace cannot have more than one associated effect, although there may be possible worlds in which some trace t has an effect it doesn't have in this world.

same type, since to say otherwise would be to allow the possibility of the one-many relationship between the physical and the mental to which the retreat to this horn of the dilemma was originally designed to avoid. If the trace can cause other sorts of human responses or behaviors (including nonmemory responses), then it does not explain any of the different effects it may have. But if the trace is to be causally linked with only one token of one type of mental state or behavior (as the theorist must now say), then we are back to the untenable position that a (brain) structure or mechanism can have one and only one functional role, no matter what the context is in which it is embedded.

As a matter of fact, there are numerous places where the trace theorist is committed to the existence of intrinsically unambiguous structures or mechanisms (no matter what the details of his theory). I have already suggested that the appeal to unambigous structures is inevitable at the point where the theorist must explain how the appropriate or right trace gets activated in any particular case of remembering. But the same difficulty appears much earlier in the theory, simply in virtue of supposing that some state of the brain is to do one and only one thing—say, uniquely represent A. After all, if my A-trace could represent someone or something besides A, then it may cause me to remember something besides A; in that case, we could not explain why I remember A and not someone or something else by appealing to the trace.* But (as I observed earlier) a brain structure (of whatever kind) can no more represent in virtue of features intrinsic to

---

*The theorist might protest that the A-trace is causally linked with remembering A in just those cases where the brain is in some *further* state s, and in this way he might try to show how the admittedly functionally ambiguous trace could represent A and not something else. But this move obviously pushes the same problem back a step, since the A-trace and s taken *together* are as functionally ambiguous as the trace alone. If the theorist denies this, he is again positing the existence of intrinsically unambiguous structures. But if he agrees, then the new state (A-trace & s) no more explains remembering A than did the original trace.

it one thing only than can a photograph (imagine A's photo appearing in a book under the heading 'Human Being', or 'Caucasian', or 'Man with Receding Hairline').

The trace's representational properties are supposed to be exclusively a function of its topological properties, those properties of its physiological or physical structure in virtue of which the trace represents what it does and not some other thing. But what a thing a represents is never strictly determined either by its own properties, or by its properties conjoined with those of some context c in which it is embedded. Context c will be just as intrinsically ambiguous as representing object a. If a and c are both physiological structures (like brain states), both will be functionally ambiguous for the reasons already discussed. And if c is something like a societal or conversational context, it will be ambiguous in a different way. How c should be characterized will always be relative to some point of view from which the characterization of c makes a difference. It has no intrinsic characterization. We must somehow describe the context, or pick it out, if only to say what it is that a must be conjoined with in order to represent what it does in c. But how we describe the slice of life we are taking to be a context is not something forced on us by features of that bit of life itself. We must make a decision about how to parse and label it, and there will always be different ways of doing this, each one reflecting some distinctive point of view (recall the familiar philosophical example of describing the same episode as turning on a light, or flipping a light switch, or alerting a burglar). But since nothing about c demands that it be described in one and only one way (since, that is, there is no absolutely, context-independent preferred description of c), we do not, by conjoining a with c, avoid the intrinsic ambiguity of a itself. In fact, even if c were another brain state, it would have no intrinsic or context-independent preferred parsing. (I shall pursue this point in the next section.)

In order for one thing to represent another, then, it must occupy some position in a bit of history; it cannot represent anything independently of a context. But what gets represented is never rigidly fixed by the bit of history within which we consider it. Since there is no one context-independent preferred description of any context in which *a* is positioned, there will also not be one context-independent preferred description of *a*'s relations to its context. But if there are in principle different ways of relating *a* to its surrounding context, then although *a* needs a context in order to represent anything, what we take it to represent, or whether it represents anything at all, will depend on which relations we choose. Independently of any context, or reason for choosing one set of relations over another, there is no preferred choice. When we adopt the *PIM*, however, we adopt the position (in effect) that there do exist intrinsically unambiguous physiological representations—for example, traces of objects (as of *A*) or representations of concepts (like that of the color red). But (to stick with memory traces) if even a photo of *A* does not intrinsically represent *A*, then no brain structure can or will.

At this point, some might try to salvage the *PIM* by shifting from memory traces to *instincts*. Surely, they might say, the *PIM* is not false for all cases, since even relatively simple organisms (like insects) have instincts, and instincts may plausibly be identified with (or causally traced back to) certain associated (and presumably persisting) structures or mechanisms in the insect's nervous system. If this is plausible in the case of insects (they might ask), why not in the case of humans?

I would say, however, that this is *not* plausible even in the case of insects. The problems here do not concern the representational properties of internal structures; but, as with memory traces, the claim rests on a form of Platonism, since it requires that instinct-mechanisms be connnected causally with a class of effects united by some *common property*. Take, for instance, the instinct to survive. This instinct seems to be exhibited by creatures on all levels of the evolutionary scale. But how is it expressed? Among insects, we may say that it is expressed in the insect's search for food, in the construction of nests, in avoidance behavior under certain conditions, and even in aggressive behavior under others. In other words, even in its most rudimentary manifestations, the instinct to survive can take a variety of forms, which (like remembering A) need not be linked by any relevant common property (or set of properties) except the property of being an instance of the instinct to survive. There need be no set of necessary and sufficient conditions for something's being an instance of the instinct to survive. But then, the structures or mechanisms whose activation allegedly causes the instinctive behavior (like the memory trace whose activation allegedly explains remembering A or the ability to remember A) do not after all explain the instinct. In neither case is there some regularity or property common to the effects of the structure or mechanism to which we can causally link that structure or mechanism.

Furthermore, just as memory trace theory faced a fatal dilemma once it was forced to concede that effects of the trace needn't share any relevant common properties, a similar fate confronts instinct-mechanisms. Suppose we identify some putative instinct-mechanism i with respect to a set T of topological features. We may now ask: Is the relationship between i and the kinds of causal consequences it may have one-many or one-one? If it is one-many, then, since the kinds of consequences needn't share some Platonic essence or common property for which we can state necessary and sufficient conditions, there is no causal regularity we can specify, and i, then, has no explanatory power after all. But if we say the relationship is one-one, then, since instincts are manifested in different kinds of ways, we must concede that i no longer explains the instinct as a whole. Moreover, to causally link i to only one specific token of the instinct is to take the untenable position that i is functionally unambiguous—that is, that i cannot correspond to, or causally explain, more than one token of one type of behavior. But since what kind of behavior a bit of behavior is will be a function of the set of background conditions in which it is embedded, this position works no better for i than it did for the memory trace. In neither case can we classify the effect of the structure simply in terms of the properties of that structure, and independently of the properties of the situation in which the effect is produced.

Applying these conclusions to the range of physiological mechanisms posited in cognitive psychology (e.g., in learning theory, in recognition theory, or in theories regarding having beliefs and thoughts), some important morals for the philosophy of mind emerge. Of these, two are of immediate benefit. First, appeals to a persisting physiological structure or mechanism—to explain *abilities* or *dispositions* to react or behave in certain ways (ascribed to persons or other organisms)—will not work, since nothing can be specified among its possible effects to which the structure or mechanism may be causally linked. And second, appeals to a physiological structure or mechanism—to explain, not a class of experiences or behaviors, but only tokens of some type of experience or behavior—will fail as well. Either the structure or mechanism may be identified with, or causally linked to, tokens of various types of states or different kinds of tokens of one type—in which case nothing is explained (since these diverse states need have no properties in common); or it can be identified with, or causally linked to, one and only one token of only one type of state—in which case the putative structure or mechanism is an impossible object.

From the point of view of any viable explanatory theory, abilities, instincts, dispositions, thoughts and beliefs are all in the same boat. They all have manifestations which (like my ability to remember A) need not be linked by any relevant specifiable common property (or set of properties). But then, since we have already seen that no structure or mechanism explains an ability, disposition, etc., whose manifestations are linked by no common property (or set of properties), the only causal antecedents to which we need appeal, in explaining abilities, dispositions, etc.,—if we need appeal to any at all—will be episodes in the organism's history. Once we grant that changes in a person's cognitive abilities need not correspond to any internal structural change in the person, we can admit that these abilities are simply brute facts about the organism for which certain kinds of 'why?' questions are no longer appropriate. If so, then to explain how I can remember A, we need appeal only to certain events in my past. Similarly, when we consider changes in disposition (e.g., Jones' conversion from being frivolous to being serious), we need say no more than that the change makes sense relative to a certain episode in Jones' life (his religious experience, say). Here then, we may abandon the search for a further explanation in terms of something happening within Jones himself (e.g., within his brain). Nothing of that sort could explain the change.

Many readers will no doubt blanch at my suggestion that we stop seeking explanations of abilities, dispositions, etc., in terms of underlying physiological structures or mechanisms. Some may protest, for example, that, since we obviously do not remember *every* event in our past, we must do more than explain present rememberings in terms of past experiences; in particular, we must appeal to some persisting physiological modification produced by the relevant past event. I concede that more *can* be said than that certain events in my past enable me to remember A now. But granting the foregoing objections, I would argue that we should not appeal to internal mechanisms. What we *can* say is that certain events in my past, involving A, were particularly intense or important at the time and that I tend to remember intense or important events. (In fact, even on memory trace theory we must explain why some past events and not others produce traces.) Or perhaps I am simply a person able to do certain things rather than others. I might remember A's phone number but not his name, because I have an ability to remember numbers and not names. Here, we explain my remembering A's phone number in terms of other regularities of mine, like my ability to remember numbers generally. But that general ability is a fact about me for which no structural explanation (say, in terms of memory traces) exists or can exist.

Another objection, bound to be raised sooner or later, is that studies in cerebral lesions and the like show that mechanisms for at least some abilities and dispositions *do* exist.

After all, my opponent would say, we can alter or impair cognitive abilities and even one's character by altering certain parts of one's brain. These (they would contend) are cases in which changes in a person's mental states are explainable as due to corresponding physiological changes. But it seems to me that such cases really show very little. The loss of a cognitive ability after a brain lesion does not show that there is (or was) some brain mechanism for the lost ability. All it shows is that the persistence of a person's abilities, dispositions, etc., requires maintaining the general integrity of the organism. The falsity of the *PIM* is compatible with the fact that we can alter a person's occurrent or dispositional mental states by making physical changes in him. All the rejection of the *PIM* demands is that we stop our search for specific structures or mechanisms within the organism, by which to explain the abilities, dispositions, etc., in question.

To see this, suppose that after damage to a certain very specific region of the cortex, a person S loses his ability to remember numbers, though his other mnemonic abilities (like his ability to remember names and faces) remain unimpaired. Would this show that a certain brain structure or mechanism b in S had been the cause of S's ability to remember numbers? I would say not, and to see why we need only review the points raised against the trace theory. Suppose, for argument's sake, that we identify the brain structure or mechanism b whose activation is allegedly responsible for S's ability to remember numbers, and suppose that b is identified with respect to a set T of topological properties (i.e., that we give a 'hardware' description for b). Consider, now, what sorts of things may be manifestations of remembering numbers. S may demonstrate his ability to remember numbers by speaking, writing, or by pointing to numbers (say, on a chart), or by pointing to a collection of things the sum of whose members is the number remembered, or (say) by tapping his foot in order to imitate a horse counting with his hoof. So first of all there is an unlimited number of ways S could demonstrate his ability to remember numbers. Moreover, a given token of this ability—for example, pointing to a number on a chart—need not serve as a token of remembering a number. What in one context counts as an instance of remembering a number may, in another context, count as an instance of something else. Perhaps the number *S* points to is the only red number on the chart, *S* having been asked to identify which number is red. In that case, our familiar dilemma appears again. The brain structure or mechanism *b* can, when activated, cause an indefinite number of different states and behaviors, which are not intrinsically tokens of remembering numbers, and which need not be linked by any common property (even when they are instances of remembering numbers) save that of being instances of remembering numbers. Thus as before, no particular token of *S*'s remembering a number belongs to a specifiable causal regularity in the range of *b*'s possible effects; so the association of *b* with that token is arbitrary. And as we have seen, the only way to avoid linking *b* with tokens of different types of abilities, or with different kinds of tokens of the same type, is to make *b* the sort of thing which can cause one and only one token of one type of effect. But since any of *b*'s effects may be instances of any number of types of effect, this amounts to assigning an impossible role to *b*.

That we can alter a person's mental states by altering the organism does not, then, demonstrate the possibility of physiologically mechanistic explanations of a person's mental states. Whatever structure or mechanism we isolate can never correspond in the right way to the mental state or class of mental states it is alleged to explain. To repeat: If the structure or mechanism can be identified with, or cause, tokens of various types of mental states or different tokens of one type, then since these various states need have no properties in common, the structure or mechanism (considered simply as a bit of hardware) has no explanatory utility. And if it can be identified with, or cause, only one token of only one type of mental state, then we are attributing a role to the structure or mechanism which nothing can fulfill.

I am not, by the way, saying that we must *supplement* appeals to such things as episodes in a person's life with appeals to such things as brain mechanisms. I am saying, rather, that appeals to such things as brain mechanisms *add nothing* to our reference to the episodes in the person's history. We have seen, after all, that appeals to brain structures or mechanisms confer on those putative items either no explanatory role, or else an impossible role.

Rejection of the *PIM*, however, does not force one to conclude that a person's physiological constitution is *irrelevant* to what that person's mental states are. For example, we needn't deny that brain size and complexity of brain topography (e.g., convolutions) are proportional to intelligence (whether or not this is a fact). Rejection of the *PIM* requires only that we stop looking for something *in* the organism, some bit of hardware, which (or the activation of which) accounts for the particular mental state (occurrent or dispositional) we want to explain. We must abandon the search for a certain kind of explanatory *unit* (like a brain structure) more fundamental than the organism itself. Organisms do indeed differ from one another, and some of their physiological differences may be causally connnected with some of the psychological differences between them. For example, to take a simple case, we can admit that the difference between Einstein's intelligence and that of my cat is the result of the difference in their brains. But to admit *this* is not to grant that there are physiological mechanisms that explain the various features of, say, Einstein's intelligence. Moreover, as far as changes in a person's character or mental states are concerned, things can happen to an organism in light of which the alteration of its behavior or mental life makes sense. And these may be highly specific things, like Jones' religious experience, my previous acquaintance with A, or damage to a certain region of the brain. But to suppose that we must look further *within* the organism for specific explanatory structures or mechanisms is just to commit the very mistakes I have been laboring to expose.

The supposition that we *must* look further is no more than an article of faith, based (it seems to me) on a reluctance to admit that certain sorts of facts might be ultimate facts, not capable of explanation by further dissection and analysis. There is no compelling reason to suppose, either in this area of inquiry or others, that explanation by analysis should be able to continue indefinitely. Now without trying to provide a recipe for discovering where, in any inquiry, we should stop the process of explanation by analysis, I submit that a perfectly good place to stop is just where further analysis can only rest on false or absurd presuppositions.

When we begin to take this possibility seriously—and also the fact that nature has no intrinsic structure which it presents to us, but that we instead parse slices of history in different ways for different purposes (see II.A.3. and II.B. for relevant discussions of this) we shall be drawn to a somewhat different view of life than the one that makes the *PIM* seem plausible. I don't believe I am up to the task of describing this alternative in great detail (since I am still in the process of discovering what it is). But I may be able to indicate how it forces us to revise our conception of what thoughts or mental states must be.

To be seduced by the *PIM*, we must take a certain broad view of what thoughts or mental states are, and of what it means to endow such things with content or meaning. In general, we must believe that thoughts and mental states are certain kinds of *things*; that, in principle at least, we could formulate an ontology in which thoughts or mental states had a place. There are many ways of doing this. For example, we could say that thoughts are brain events, or immaterial mental structures, or even propositions (construed as abstract logical structures). And of course such views may be held with varying degrees of sophistication. We might take thoughts to be brain events, at the same time granting that our mentalistic vocabulary is theoretically defective—that mentalistic terms do not divide the class of mental states in any philosophically or scientifically acceptable way (see, e.g., Davidson [36], Dennett [40]). From this viewpoint, it is our working set of mentalistic categories that fails to provide us with well-defined or definable terms; the domain of the mental may itself remain capable of being divided into well-defined categories. Moreover, since thoughts or mental states are individuated with respect to their content or meaning (e.g., we speak of the thought or belief *of*, or *that___*), it is easy to treat thoughts and mental states as things; we need only suppose that, at least in principle, we can specify the content or meaning of these things clearly and exhaustively. Although (we might say) we still lack sufficiently refined theoretical machinery for the task, nothing prevents us, in principle, from getting it done.

I want, now, to suggest that this general outlook is profoundly and entirely mistaken. We have already considered one reason for this judgment—namely, that mental states do not fall into classes united by any common property (or set of properties). Classes of mental states are simply not neat in a manner susceptible of scientific treatment. But unlike those who take this lack of neatness as a characteristic only of our mentalistic *vocabulary* (or conceptual categories)— hence, a problem that can be solved by the appropriate conceptual development—I have been suggesting that this lack of neatness is a fundamental feature of mental *phenomena*, and that our categories are already somewhat neater than the phenomena to which they apply. When, in the inescapable process of abstraction, we arrive at such categories as remembering (believing, wishing, etc.) that *p*, we inevitably foster the illusion that the range of phenomena under discussion is, in principle, isolable and specifiable—if not by our current stock of categories, then by more adequate future categories. And this illusion is reinforced by our actual success in using these categories to describe or predict human behavior. We tend to forget that the process of abstraction which generates our supply of mentalistic concepts is merely a prerequisite for communication. But there is no reason to suppose *a priori* that any mentalistic vocabulary is anything more than a communicative tool. In particular, there is no reason to suppose *a priori* that either our mentalistic vocabulary or the domain to which it applies must be anything more than fuzzy.

In fact, when we recall that inner episodes, bits of behavior, and sentence-tokens have content, meaning, or significance only with respect to their position in a certain parsing of life, and when we recall further that the position of an experience, bit of behavior, etc., with respect to its context is not inherently a clear-cut matter, it becomes more difficult still to cling to the view that the domain of the mental—mental states as well as their contents—is anything but fuzzy. The range of possible parsings or descriptions of a context (we must remember) is as unlimited as the range of possible perspectives we can take on life itself. There is simply no one correct way (or one context-independent correct way) of positioning an experience or bit of behavior against its context. Moreover, the language in which we make our parsings and specify context or meaning is subject to the same intrinsic ambiguity as the thing whose meaning or content we are specifying. In individuating mental states (or behaviors, sentences, etc.) there cannot ever be a point at which we can fall back on something intrinsically unambiguous. (In my view, this difficulty has not been sufficiently appreciated by those who think we can give the meaning of a sentence S with another sentence—for example, one stating the truth conditions for S.)

Although this is not the whole story, once these points begin to sink in, the meaning or content of a person's state or behavior will no more seem to be a discrete or in principle specifiable thing than, say, the *humor* or *sensitivity* of a bit of behavior. A person's behavior is seen as humorous, for example when it is integrated in a certain way with its surrounding history. Thus a remark is funny when related to something that preceded it, though not to any and every thing that preceded it. A remark's humor is a *positional* property of the remark,* not something inherent in it. It is entirely possible that two people A and B regard remark r as funny—but not in exactly the same way—even though they

---

*I owe this terminology to Bruce Goldberg, and prefer 'positional' to 'relational', since the former term suggests that the humor of a remark depends on how we position it in its context and on what we bring to our understanding of the context, whereas the latter seems to suggest more that a remark's humor is a static and intrinsic feature of it and its context. The term 'relational' has a long philosophical history. I wish to avoid as far as possible whatever misleading associations its use may entail.

both could be properly described as having understood the joke. Given A's history, interests, and his own brand of perceptivity, r might have nuances, overtones, or a kind of complexity and richness that it does not have for B, or even for the joke-teller C, given the different perspectives they bring to the situation. Although these different sets of nuances, etc., are not intrinsic to r; they are also not mere appendages to the (essential) humor of r; indeed, the humor of r is nothing without them. In fact, there *is* no essential humor to r, even in just those contexts in which r is funny. r is, first of all, funny only in virtue of its position in a context; in another context it might not be funny at all. Moreover, since there is an endless number of equally legitimate or correct perspectives, attitudes, etc. that we can bring to our understanding of r, there are endlessly different ways of construing r's content. Thus, the question 'What is the humor of r?' has no single— much less a uniquely correct—answer. Since r has no humor independently of some perspective on its context, and since no perspective is intrinsically preferable to any other, not only is r's humor not the sort of thing that can be exhaustively specified, it is not even *one* thing. Certainly, it is not simply a function of any intrinsic features of r.

The same, I would say, is true of the meaning or content of an inner episode or bit of behavior (as I have been urging ever since I.B.4.d.). The meaning or content of what goes on in a person's mind or of what a person does is, like the humor of r, a positional property of that thing. What the inner or outer episode's content is depends on the context in which it occurs. But since life does not come pre-parsed for us—since there are many different legitimate ways to characterize any slice of history—any bit of human behavior or human experience may be meaningful in different ways relative to different characterizations of, or perspectives on, its context. Experiences and bits of behavior have no content or meaning independently of context and perspective on context; but since no perspective from which behavior and experience are meaningful is intrinsically preferable to any other, this content or meaning is not something which behavior and experience simply have. Like the humor of *r*, content or meaning is not just one thing, and is not the sort of thing that can be exhaustively specified.

If we take this seriously, we must construe human history, not as a series of events with a manifest structure or content, but rather as an intrinsically undifferentiated flow of experiencings and behavings that can be parsed and related to one another in various ways, and that reveal different of their aspects from the points of view associated with these different parsings. Just as, from the perspective of one such parsing, we can individuate a certain episode and see it as humorous, we can individuate the things people do or experience and view them as significant relative to other things individuated within the same perspective. But since the content or meaning of an inner or outer episode is a positional property and not something it has intrinsically, we must realize that mental states in general are not context-independent elements in the manifest structure of history; there is no such manifest structure. Mental states exist only relative to some parsing and characterization of the flow of life.

There are, of course, inner mental episodes; I am not denying their existence! And of course some of these can be dated and measured. But such episodes belong to an ongoing flow of inner activity that itself has no preferred parsing. Moreover, a person's mental life consists of more than inner episodes, and when we take *this* seriously, it becomes easier still to abandon the view that mental states and their contents generally are episodes or kinds of discrete *things*. My belief (or memory) that I have a foot, for example, may be expressed in the putting on of my shoes or in my walking from one place to another (even when my inner episodes concern other things, like last night's football game). There needn't be any isolable *state* which we can identify as the belief (or memory). Similarly, my remembering that I have an appointment at noon may be manifest in my rushed behavior all morning, and not necessarily in a recurring memory state. My fear of being psychologically abused may be expressed in my hostile behavior, and not in a specific fear state.

Within the ongoing stream of life we identify various regularities and relate them meaningfully to one another or to specific episodes. That identification, of course, presupposes some way of individuating the elements within the stream. But this will only mark a selection from the endless possible ways of parsing and describing history. Moreover, these regularities themselves have histories, and some will persist longer than others. For example, dispositions may change—as in Jones' conversion from a frivolous to a serious person. And sometimes we can identify what makes the new regularity intelligible—Jones' religious experience, for instance. In other words, Jones' religious experience may be meaningfully related to an identifiable pattern in Jones' behavior. This is not to say that the religious experience *activates* diverse but related behaviors in Jones, as (say) the triggering of a memory trace is supposed to activate diverse things counting as memories of a certain type. It is only to say that we can *explain* (in one sense of this term, roughly equivalent to 'render intelligible') identifiable behaviors or behavioral patterns in someone's life, not by locating activating mechanisms or structures associated with them, but simply by linking these things with others, so as to form meaningful patterns relative to our present interests. This, I am inclined now to think, may be as far as we can ever hope to push causal explanations of human behavior.

I realize these remarks have been sketchy, possibly provocative, and worthy of further exploration. But I cannot pursue these deeper issues here. I shall add only that the idea that all of life and history is an intrinsically undifferentiated flow, which has an infinite number of aspects (no one of which is absolutely preferable to any other), is rather similar to what the mystics have been saying for a long time. But to regard this view as mystical is to miss an important point. The alternative to this position is to say that nature has an intrinsic structure—some built-in division into elements, and that there are fundamental relationships between these elements that their arrangement somehow displays unambiguously. In short, the alternative to this position is really a kind of Tractarian logical atomism. And that, I submit, is a far more fantastic viewpoint than the one I offer in its place.

3. Some Comments on Recent Theoretical Trends

Some of the objections raised earlier against the *ET* theory, anomalous monism, and the *PIM* generally apply also to several theories currently attracting attention in parapsychology. Although many parapsychologists regard these theories as representing promising lines of conceptual development, they are, in my view, nothing more than complicated variants of crude atomistic psychological theories dressed up in contemporary scientific jargon. None represents even a slight conceptual advance over the most primitive atomistic, static, or non-functionalist theories of consciousness, whose errors have been addressed in the two previous sections of this chapter, and I.B.4.d.

One theory which many parapsychologists regard as promising is the attempt by Karl Pribram [107]-[109] to analyze memories, perception, and other sorts of conscious states in terms of *holographic* states of the brain. Many who are interested in parapsychology regard Pribram's work as a revolutionary advance in the study of consciousness, one that might finally lead the way to the long-awaited development of a satisfactory scientific theory of the paranormal. But this seems to me to be completely unjustified. For one thing, Pribram's memory theory is simply a memory *trace* theory with a twist. Pribram is apparently oblivious to the difficulties inherent in the notion of a memory trace. He seems not to realize that traces have no explanatory value (as I have shown in the last section); and he seems also not to understand why it is unacceptable to characterize mental states solely in terms of their topological properties or as the non-positional states of persons (an error to which my discussions of the *ET* theory, anomalous monism and the *PIM* have been devoted). Somewhat innocently, Pribram thinks that some long-standing puzzles about memory and human cognitive functioning may be cleared up by suitably complicating the nature of the memory trace (and similar physiological counterparts), ascribing to it (and these counterparts) the properties of a hologram. For example, he thinks that his holographic model helps to explain how memories may be retained even after excision of part of the cortex; information contained in the brain (he holds) is, like a hologram, contained in any of its parts. But since the content of a mental state—the information alleged by Pribram to be contained in the brain—is not solely a function of brain physiology, his theory cannot be more than an elaboration of an idea already found to be unacceptable. It does not matter how complicated we make the brain states supposed to be identical with, or the causes of, specific mental states. No structure of any kind can do the job that Pribram requires of memory traces; no structure determines its own (or a unique) function, which is why thoughts cannot be characterized topologically. Hence, Pribram fails to avoid the *ET* theorist's fatal error (analyzing function in terms of structure), and more specifically, that of the *PIM*. Moreover, the question of *where* in the brain memories are located (before *or* after brain surgery) arises only if we assume that memories must be somewhere in the brain, or simply somewhere. But once we see that memories (or mental states generally) are not *things*, we will no longer feel compelled to assign them a location. The basis for Pribram's entire neurophysiological program thus comes to nothing.

Of course, parapsychology is a field that invites ambitious and often reckless sorts of speculation, and Pribram's holographic model has inspired various cosmic extensions. The line most commonly taken (see, e.g., Anderson [1]) is that the universe as a whole can be viewed holographically—that is, that every part of the universe contains the information of every other part. In this way, some hope to avoid the problem of explaining by means of some quasi-perceptual mechanism or mechanism of transmission, the awareness of remote information. According to this neo-Leibnizian picture, information about remote parts of the universe is already present in every part. So instead of worrying about the *transmission* of information from remote places (e.g., thoughts, in telepathy), this approach posits something like *resonances* between similar structures—just as Pribram and his followers hope to explain the activation of appropriate memory traces (as in associative memory) by means of resonances between structurally isomorphic states of the brain. But this view, like the *ET* theory, is hopelessly and fatally tied to the *PIM*—and in particular, to the view that the content or meaning of a brain state (i.e., its representational properties) is a function of its structure. But brain structures do not determine their own function (or a unique function); and what representational properties a brain state has depends upon, though it is not strictly determined by, its position in a surrounding context. Hence, resonances between structures cannot explain, for instance, how my thoughts give me access to the similar thoughts of remote individuals, or how a thought of one kind makes me have an associated thought of a similar kind (cf. my discussion of isomorphism, in I.B.4.d.).

Much in the same spirit, E. H. Walker [187], [188] has attempted to analyze the content of conscious states information-theoretically, as constructs of *bits*—as though bits were fundamental or atomic constituents of mental or brain events rather than conventionally defined components, and as though the content of a mental or brain event is simply a function of its intrinsic structure. Many in parapsychology regard Walker's efforts as important and pioneering. But it seems to me that his view is nothing more than an old-fashioned sense-datum theory stated in the language of the electrical engineer and, like Pribram's, basically unintelligible. One reason for this is that, like Pribram, Walker supposes that, in principle, there can be structures in the brain (or mind) that have or determine one and only one function. Of course, this is the error explored in detail in I.B.4.d. and II.A.1. The other main reason goes hand in hand with this one, and involves another mistake, which I have so far only hinted at. One who assumes that brain states have a structure that uniquely determines their content posits the existence of (impossibly) functionally unambiguous structures. He must also suppose, however, that the structure of the brain state (which either is, or causes, the relevant thought) can be determined independently of determining what that thought is. More generally, views like those of Pribram and Walker presuppose that nature has a structure intrinsic to it (whether macroscopic, microscopic, subatomic, or logical) just waiting to be discerned.

To see why this is a fatal presupposition, consider the following. Suppose that Jones is describing his new home to Smith, and that he tells Smith that the tree by his house is taller than the house itself. Let us keep things as simple as we can, and let us try to characterize Smith's subsequent thought that Jones' tree is taller than his house. Let us suppose that what happens in Smith when he has his thought is that he has an image in his mind of a tree rising above a house. Of course thoughts need not be images. We tend rather easily, however, to think that elements of images are clearly manifest. (For those, like Walker, who think that *perceptual* experiences have a manifest structure, we need alter this case only slightly, by construing the image of the tree and house as the mental image Smith has when he *looks* at Jones' house.)

But what *are* the elements of the image? We are assuming that the thought Smith has when he has the image is the thought that the tree is taller than the house. So we might say that the elements of the thought (image) are a tree and a house, as relata of the relation '____ is taller than ____'. But, as we have observed on numerous occasions, this image, set in a different context (that is, positioned in a different sequence of events), could have functioned quite differently from the way it does here, so that we could have characterized Smith as having a different thought. Jones might not have told Smith that the tree was taller than the house. He might have said other things instead, which caused Smith to have the same mental image of the tree and house. But then, we might reasonably have ascribed different thoughts to Smith—for example, the thought (a) that the tree is *to the left of* the house, (b) that the tree is *just* taller than the *roof* of the house, (c) that there is only one tree in the yard, (d) that the tree is near the door, or (e) that there is not a cloud in the sky. In each of these cases, we would parse the image differently from our original parsing. For example, in the case of (a), the relation between the elements of the tree and house would be '___ is to the left of ___', and, in (b), (c), and (d), respectively, the roof, yard, and door would be elements. Thus, we cannot determine what elements a thought has independently of determining what the thought is—once we grant the functional ambiguity of the structures we take to be identical with, or the causes of, thoughts. How we parse a thought (a bit of mental history) will depend on what we take that bit of mental history to be (in the context supplied). Since one and the same inner episode can serve an indefinite number of different functions, no one of which is a context-independent preferred function, it can have an indefinite number of parsings, no one of which is preferred independently of a given context.*

This fact is fatal to physicalistic theories like those of Pribram and Walker. To see why, we need only imagine Smith having mental image m and being in brain state b in several different contexts, contexts in which we would regard Smith as having different thoughts while he had one and the same image (e.g., contexts where Jones says to Smith that the

---

*Analogously, in the case of perception, Jones may have been calling Smith's attention to any of a number of different things while Smith looks at the house. Here, we might properly characterize Smith as perceiving different things, even though phenomenologically, nothing need be different for Smith. Thus, if Jones had said to Smith that there was not a cloud in the sky, this could be what Smith perceives, even though his mental image remains the same as in our original case. This is one reason why it is unacceptable to maintain that the elements of a perceptual experience can be determined independently of specifying a context in which the experience occurred, and thus why perceptual experiences are not merely constructs out of elements in a sensory manifold.

tree is near the door, or to the left of the house). Now we have seen that Smith's mental image may be parsed into different constituent elements depending on how it functions. But then we cannot parse *b* into constituent elements independently of determining what that function is. To see this, suppose we were not sure whether the functionally ambiguous image of the tree and house correlated with Smith's thought (a) that the tree is to the left of the house or (d) that the tree is near the door. How would we determine, then, what *b*'s structure was? We could not claim that there is one and only one way to parse *b*. That would be a concession that even the unique parsing of *b* was functionally ambiguous, and thus that the content or set of representational properties of *b* (or *m*, for that matter) was not a function of *b*'s structure after all. So that concession would be fatal to any theory that attempts to analyze thoughts in terms of hardware descriptions of the brain. Presumably, then, we must say that we parse *b* differently, depending on how we analyze its position in a sequence of events, or the function of the mental image correlated with it. For example, one parsing of *b* would give us the brain structure for '___ is to the left of ___', and another, the brain structure for '___ is near ___'. But then the structure of *b* cannot be something about Smith's brain that simply presents itself to us. We could not then assign *b* a structure independently of assigning it some role or position in a sequence of events, or slice of life. Since a brain state does not determine its own function—since it may function differently in different contexts—it may have more than one structure or correct parsing. Since brain states have no intrinsic function, therefore, they have no intrinsic or manifest structure.

Even apart from these considerations, the claim that brain states have a manifest structure is completely implausible. Any ordinary physical object may be parsed in different ways for different purposes. For example, a human hand may be considered to be composed of skin, bones, tendons and nails, or fingers, knuckles, palm and back, or perhaps cells of different sorts, or collections of atoms. And no one of these parsings is intrinsically preferable to the others. Similarly, a brain state may also be parsed in different ways—for example, into atoms, cells, neural nets, etc.—no one of which is intrinsically preferable to any other. So not only is it a mistake to suppose that the structure of a brain state can be determined independently of determining its function; it is also a mistake to suppose that a brain state has one and only one structure.

The idea that nature has a manifest structure takes many forms and appears not only in connection with theories of consciousness. I want, now, to examine its role in the so-called theory of *synchronicity*.

B. The Theory of Synchronicity

1. Introduction

The past few years have seen the re-emergence (or resurrection, depending on your point of view) of an idea—it hardly deserves its usual title of 'theory'—associated mainly with C. G. Jung (see [75]). Roughly, this is the idea that some events occur together, *not* due to any causal connections between them, or between the group of events and some common causal ancestor, but simply in virtue of similarities in the *content* or *meaning* of the events. The attention now being lavished by parapsychologists on the idea of acausal but meaningful connections—synchronistic connections—between events stems, as far as I can see, from two main sources. First, many (following Jung) have turned to the notion of an acausal connecting principle (as Jung put it) in the hope of finding a way of explaining the experimental data of parapsychology, one more promising than mechanistic accounts of psi functioning, especially those positing the existence of physical carriers of psi information. The idea here is that if correlations between (say) a subject's calls and targets on ESP tests represent acausal connections, then we needn't bother looking for the kind of causal chains that have so long eluded parapsychologists. The other—and probably the main—reason for the interest in synchronicity is that many people feel that things happen to them in the course of living that have a kind of significance or numinosity which, while not amenable to orthodox causal explanation, is not really fortuitous either, and in fact seems to point to something profound about the workings of nature. Standard causal accounts may, perhaps, be given for each individual event within a meaningful group of events, but the unusual significance of those events *taken together* demands, it seems, an account of its own.

Let us consider a hypothetical, but typical, example. Suppose I am walking down the street with a friend, feeling arrogant about the way I seem to have my life under control. I joke flippantly and callously about how easily I have been able to manipulate people to get what I want. And at one point I remark to my friend rather smugly, 'See, life isn't as big a deal as you always seem to think. You just take things too seriously'. And suppose that at that very moment a large scaffold falls from the building we are passing, missing me by only a few inches. Imagine, moreover (to give this fictitious episode its appropriate religious completeness), that the apparently cosmically perfect timing of the scaffold's fall so impresses me that I become at once a contrite and much more serious person, awed by the enormity and precariousness of life and imbued with a sense of preciousness in every moment. And suppose, finally, that this change in my attitude leads to improved relationships with others and to an enhancement in the general quality of my life.

Now ordinarily we would assume that there is no connection—much less a causal connection—between my glib behavior and the falling scaffold. No doubt we could give separate causal accounts explaining why the scaffold and I happened to (almost fatally) cross paths on the sidewalk. We would mention such things as that my friend and I were taking the direct route from location X to our intended destination, location Y, and that the scaffold had not been properly secured, so that a strong gust of wind (say) caused it to fall when it did. But to someone impressed by the apparent appropriateness of what happened, such independent causal accounts might not suffice. A further matter seems to require explanation—namely, the appropriateness of the falling scaf-

fold to my behavior. We might characterize it as a coincidence, a *meaningful* coincidence. But according to the theory
of synchronicity, that would not mean that it was a mere
chance occurrence that happened to occasion great surprise
or some other intense feeling or reaction. In fact, meaningful
coincidences are not supposed to be chance occurences at all.
Nor on this theory are they occurrences upon which we simply impose an interpretation or point of view which renders
them meaningful for us. The meaning in a meaningful coincidence is instead supposed to transcend any such limited
human perspective. This meaning is supposed to exist objec-
tively and independently of any human psyche. Jung claims,
in typically obscure passages, that synchronicity is a 'factor
in nature which expresses itself in the arrangement of events
and appears to us as meaning' ([75]: para. 916, emphasis added), and 'Synchronicity postulates a meaning which is
a priori in relation to human consciousness and apparently
exists outside man' ([75]: para. 942). Thus meaningful
coincidences are supposed to instantiate some sort of non-
causal natural principle that explains the numinous appropriateness of particular events for particular lives.

Perhaps the person most responsible for recent interest
in synchronicity is Arthur Koestler ([79], [80], [63]). Not
only has he sparked new interest in Jung's views; he has also
focused attention on the related views of the Lamarckian biol-
ogist, Paul Kammerer. I do not intend this chapter to be a
scholarly examination of these different accounts of the idea
of acausal connecting principles. Although I will inevitably
have some things to say about Jung, my interest here is in
the *very idea* of there being a principle in nature (acausal or
causal) which links events in terms of their meaningfulness.
I want to consider whether such an idea is even intelligible,
no matter how we dress it up.

In [63], Koestler observes that we often accept non-causal
principles in physics as fundamental principles of nature—for
example, the Complementarity Principle, or Pauli's Exclusion
Principle. These require that the universe exhibit certain
kinds of order (e.g., that no more than one electron can 'oc-

cupy' an atomic 'orbit'), even though this order need not be manifest in causal chains. Koestler then asks why, if acausal principles may be scientifically legitimate, we should not also regard as legitimate something like Jung's principle of synchronicity (according to which nature is governed by relationships of meaningfulness or significance between events). Koestler never answers this question, as though its rhetorical nature suffices to legitimize the notion of synchronicity. But the question does have an answer, and the answer has two parts. First, synchronistic or meaningful connections are not, as Jung and Koestler allege, clearly acausal. And second, even if they *were* acausal, not every putative principle of organization in nature rests on the same presuppositions, and in some cases the presuppositions involved are false, or at least suspicious.

I shall address both parts of this response to Koestler's question. I shall argue that synchronistic connections count as acausal only on a certain kind of pre-Humean conception of causality, and that even on this view of causality the idea of synchronicity may presuppose a causal cosmology. And with respect to the idea that nature is organized around meaningful relations between events, I shall argue that this idea is a causal view in disguise (and not the radical thesis it is claimed to be), and moreover that it rests on an unintelligible notion of what it is for an event to have meaning, or what it is for a description of an event to be a preferred description. These two lines of thought run together, and I shall not try to keep them entirely separate.

2. How Synchronistic Explanations Work

When we ask *why* a certain event or group of events occurred—when, in other words, we request an *explanation* of the event or events, we may mean to ask different sorts of questions. Sometimes, when we request an explanation of an event E, we are asking for the *cause* of E; in such a case, we say we have explained E when we have specified its cause E'. In this way we might explain why Jones drove his car into the telephone pole—by locating the cause of this event (for example, a failure in the car's steering mechanism, or Jones' having fallen asleep at the wheel). In other contexts, however, we say that what explains event E is, not another event, but a law, principle, or regularity of some kind which systematically links E with other and possibly diverse kinds of events. Thus, by appealing to the laws of gravitation, we might explain why both apples and leaves from the apple tree fall to the earth. Or, we might similarly explain why tenure was refused to someone who has published a great deal but granted to someone who has published little, by pointing out that the tenured members of the department retain only those people they like.

Many philosophers would argue that explanations of this last sort, given in terms of regularities or principles, are really disguised causal explanations, either because they are incomplete unless buttressed by explanations in terms of causes, or because we must ultimately explain causally why such regularities obtain in the first place. I prefer not to try, here, to settle the issue of whether or not some regularities in nature are ultimate and demand no further causal component or account (although in discussing the *PIM* in the previous chapter I *have* maintained that, in some cases, the appeal to mechanisms underlying certain regularities is unwarranted). For our present purposes, we need only observe that many have thought that there are ultimate regularities or principles for which certain kinds of 'why?' questions —those asking for causes—are not appropriate. Candidates for such regularities or principles are usually considered to be *framework* principles, like the Exclusion Principle or the conservation laws in physics. And what matters here is that Jung and his followers apparently regard the principle of synchronicity as falling within that class. Explanations of meaningful coincidences in terms of synchronistic connections are supposed to be ultimate in the sense that no fact of nature is deeper than the synchronistic link itself, so that we need not seek an explanation of why this link obtains. Now, whether or not there are ultimate framework principles, I shall argue that synchronicity could not be one of them, and that in fact synchronistic explanations are really only ill-disguised causal explanations.

As John Beloff [11] has recently observed, one reason Jung seems not to have noticed this is that he took as his model for causal connections something like energy transfer or the propagation of an effect in space and time. He took causal connections to run in the familiar temporal direction, and also to involve something like a spatiotemporal link between cause and effect. For Jung, then, causal explanations of macrophysical phenomena required an actual *link* between cause and effect, the (physical or metaphysical) glue between events the claims to whose existence Hume so vigorously denounced as lacking empirical content. But since, from Jung's perspective, meaningful coincidences (as in precognition) did not display the spatiotemporal links or temporal directionality associated in his mind with causal connections, Jung reasoned that the sort of explanation needed would differ from that used in science to explain causal connections. Therefore, Jung sought something like an ultimate, noncausal framework principle of meaningfulness; and he looked to his archetypes to provide a set of transcendental descriptive categories that would render intelligible—if not exactly systematic—otherwise mysterious but numinously impressive connections between events. In this way, he hoped to account for meaningful relations between events without forcing them into the deterministic causal mold he regarded as appropriate for the scientific explanation of macrophysical phenomena. Jung felt that the principle of synchronicity would help incorporate apparently unrelated events into a larger picture in a way that would allow us, first, to make more sense out of the totality of events, and that would reveal, secondly, a fundamental fact about how nature works.

We can perhaps get clearer about the nature of synchronistic explanations by considering how they both resemble and differ from the following rather simple paradigm. Suppose we are attending a party, and notice that Jones is not talking to anyone. Suppose Jones spends most of his time standing silently among the guests, occasionally exhibiting a transparently forced smile, and occasionally speaking a few reluctant words in response to remarks made by other guests. And suppose that Jones speaks with a voice virtually without inflection, that tends to discourage others from pursuing conversation with him. Suppose, finally, that Smith tries to start a conversation with Jones, saying 'Jones, it's good to see you! How have you been?', and that Jones replies flatly, 'Fine', and then turns and walks away. How might we explain Jones' action here? One sort of explanation would focus on the causal origin of his remark or behavior, perhaps by grounding it in a state of his brain. In this way we would try to explain Jones' behavior by reference to the physiological state which produced it.* Or, we might specify another sort of causal condition—the fact, for instance, that Jones felt that Smith had an insincere smile on his face, or that he had to go to the bathroom but was embarrassed to admit it. But in some contexts we might be seeking a rather different sort of explanation. For example, we might explain Jones' behavior toward Smith by specifying some appropriate behavioral regularity of Jones', without providing a proximate cause of the behavior itself. Thus, we might say that Jones is unfriendly; and in this way we link Jones' response to the rest of his party behavior so as to make sense out of his total behavior at the party.

Viewing Jones' behavior as basically unfriendly, however, may lend only a limited degree of systematicity to our overall observations of Jones. Suppose Jones is not always as aloof as he was at the party. If we viewed him as basically unfriendly, we might thus find it difficult to integrate his party behavior with his warm and friendly behavior on other occasions. So it might occur to us that we would understand him better if we characterized his behavior differently— possibly as a manifestation of *shyness* rather than unfriendliness. This move *would* allow us to link Jones' party behavior

*The reader will recall that in II.A.2. I argue that such a proposed explanation is no explanation at all.

with his superficially different behavior on other occasions. Perhaps Jones was simply feeling more intimidated at the party than on those occasions where he felt comfortable enough to display some warmth and friendliness.

Synchronistic explanations of meaningful coincidences both resemble and differ in important ways from this sort of explanation of Jones' response to Smith. As far as the similarities are concerned, proponents claim that the value of discerning synchronistic connections is that it permits us to relate even superficially different sorts of events in ways that make them into an intelligible package, just as the description of Jones' behavior as an example of his shyness lends order to seemingly diverse sorts of behavior (friendly and unfriendly). Seeing Jones' party behavior as a manifestation of shyness enables us to see significant *patterns* in it which we simply do not illuminate by viewing that behavior as merely unfriendly. Or again, we might find more order in a person's behavior if we see him as *obsequious* rather than *eager to please*, or *insecure* rather than *boastful*, or *apathetic* rather than *lazy*. And in a similar way, the descriptive categories appealed to in synchronistic explanations are supposed to illuminate order underlying otherwise apparently diverse phenomena. Jung believed that his archetypes afforded the descriptive categories needed for this task.

The differences between synchronistic explanations and our explanation of Jones' behavior are as important as their similarities. One important difference lies in the fact that the descriptive categories employed in synchronistic explanations have no predictive utility. In contrast, once we see Jones' party behavior as a manifestation of shyness rather than mere unfriendliness, we are better able to predict how Jones might behave in various hypothetical circumstances where we have some idea of how intimidated he might feel. But synchronistic explanations, explanations that specify how apparently unconnected events are meaningfully related, are viewed as correct or justified for reasons other than their predictive utility. In fact, synchronistic explanations are not supposed to exhibit that kind of generality. They are not intended to explain persisting regularities in phenomena, as our explanation of Jones' party behavior as a manifestation of shyness explains regularities in Jones' overall behavior. Synchronistic explanations apply only to specific clusters of events, and are supposed to explain only how the components of the cluster are meaningfully related. Thus, when we look for the meaning of the falling scaffold relative to my frivolous behavior, we are trying to understand something about this particular concatenation of things. We are not looking for a pattern in nature which, in general, links falling scaffolds to frivolous behavior, as our explanation of Jones' party behavior illuminates general patterns between Jones' overall behavior and circumstances in which Jones is placed.

Having now observed that synchronistic explanations are not supposed to uncover patterns in certain kinds of events generally, but are instead intended only to point up meaningful relationships between specific events, we should observe further that there are, in principle, different ways of relating phenomena meaningfully to one another. We may ask, then, what determines which construal of meaningfulness is the correct one, in any given case. And here is where we get to the heart of the theory of synchronicity. According to Jung, one description of a cluster of events is to be preferred over others, because the meaningfulness of that cluster is somehow *written* into it—somewhat as unsophisticated identity theorists tend to regard the content of thoughts (or the representational properties of brain states) as somehow written, or displayed, in the manifest structure of the brain. Thus, the archetypal description of meaningful coincidences is preferable to other construals of meaningfulness, because the former can be 'read-off' the events themselves, whereas rival descriptions are merely contingently imposed on the events by human interpretations.

I shall return to this point shortly. But I want first to observe that, even if we ignored the conceptual muddles to which this chapter is devoted, Jung's thinking is enormously confused. As Koestler observes, Jung frequently writes, notwithstanding his protestations to the contrary, as though (in his pre-Humean sense of 'cause') the archetypes somehow cause meaningful coincidences between events. Moreover, since they are inherited propensities or patterns of human thought, Jung's archetypes seem linked essentially to *contingent* features of human experience and evolution; they seem not to ground meaningful coincidences in anything *transcendental*, or independent of human consciousness. Thus, if it is possible for human thought to evolve so that certain archetypes do not obtain—for example, if humans were hermaphroditic, so that the symbol of the great mother might have served no archetypal function—then appeals to archetypes are not appeals to natural principles that transcend the accidents of evolution (in particular, the evolution of human conceptual systems).

Furthermore, as Beloff correctly observes, the experimental data of parapsychology does not force us to look for noncausal explanations. First of all, the interesting correlations between subjects' calls and the order of ESP cards (or the nonrandom behavior of RNGs) seem to have no connection whatever with Jung's archetypes. But even if we ignore this—and it is, after all, a problem only with Jung's version of synchronicity—it is only on the pre-Humean view of causality according to which cause and effect are connected by a kind of glue that such correlations could not count as causal. If, say, an RNG exhibits nonrandom behavior only in the presence of a subject making a PK effort, then it seems fair to say that the subject's effort or presence is a causal condition of the nonrandom behavior; that is, the nonrandom behavior would not have occurred *but for* the subject's presence. Only when we demand old-fashioned spatio-temporal contiguity between cause and effect might the subject's presence or effort not be regarded as a causal condition of the nonrandom behavior of the RNG.

I do not, however, want to fret over the details of Jungian scholarship, or even the application of synchronicity to the experimental data of parapsychology. The size of the first task would not be commensurate with the quality of the material, and the second task would not take us to the heart of the problem with the notion of synchronicity. I want, rather, to consider what sense can be made of saying that there is a principle in nature that links events in terms of their symbolic or meaningful connections with one another. And let us consider a case that Jung regarded as a paradigmatic synchronistic occurrence. In 1909, Jung visited Freud in Vienna, and at one point asked him his opinion of ESP. Although Freud later changed his mind on the subject, he did not, at that time, accept ESP. Jung narrates the curious incident that occurred then (reported in Jung [76] : 152).

> While Freud was going on in this way, I had a curious sensation. It was as if my diaphragm was made of iron and becoming red-hot—a glowing vault. And at that moment there was such a loud report in the bookcase, which stood right next to us, that we both started up in alarm, fearing the thing was going to topple over us. I said to Freud: "There, that is an example of a so-called catalytic exteriorisation phenomenon."
>
> "Oh come," he exclaimed. "That is sheer bosh."
>
> "It is not," I replied. "You are mistaken, Herr Professor. And to prove my point I now predict that in a moment there will be another loud report!" Sure enough, no sooner had I said the words than the same detonation went off in the bookcase.
>
> To this day I do not know what gave me this certainty. But I knew beyond all doubt that the report would come again. Freud only stared aghast at me. I do not know what was in his mind, or what his look meant. In any case, this incident aroused his mistrust of me, and I had the feeling that I had done something against him. I never afterwards discussed the incident with him.

The standard interpretation of this unusual occurrence is that the explosions represent or symbolize the explosive nature of the archetypal father-son relationship, or perhaps the clash between Jung and Freud on the subject of ESP, or the impending schism between them (to which this incident may have contributed).

Let us suppose that PK is not responsible for the explosions, and that nothing done either by Jung or Freud caused the sounds to occur. Proponents of synchronistic connections ask us to believe that although there may be no causal link between Jung or Freud and the sounds, nevertheless there is a description of the incident (a) that is justified by an appeal to certain principles built into nature and relationships intrinsic to or manifest in the situation being described, and (b) that explains *why* the explosions occurred.

It is important to see how strong a claim Jung is making when he maintains that meaningful connections are built into nature. He is not advancing the unobjectionable claim that there are kinds of natural laws governing meaningful relationships between events. For example, it is presumably a fact of nature that, in general, animals act instinctively to protect themselves, and in a sense that fact concerns meaningful relations between events—say, one animal's aggressive behavior and the apparently threatening behavior of another. But as I observed above, synchronistic explanations lack this kind of generality. They apply only to specific clusters of events and are not valued for their predictive utility. What allegedly justifies one (the archetypal) ascription of meaningfulness over others is the belief that the very arrangement of events *displays* its own inherent meaningfulness—so that we can 'read-off' the correct interpretation from the structure of the situation itself; other interpretations, then, are only *imposed* on those events.

But the idea that meaning may be 'read-off' from events is no more tenable than the view that the content of a person's thought can be 'read-off' from his brain. In fact these views are false for similar reasons. Both fail to recognize the sort of stage-setting required for something to be meaningful, or put another way, the context-dependence of relations of meaningfulness. And in the case of synchronicity, this error helps obscure the fact that synchronistic explanations must, after all, be *causal* explanations. I shall try to demonstrate this rather abstractly, first, and then consider the matter again in a more picturesque form.

3. Meaning and Context

The first thing to grasp is that the inventory of events in world history is not absolute, or something that history itself simply displays. If we take a temporal slice of history and try to parse it into events, we are bound to realize that, independently of a context that fixes what we are looking for, no parsing is preferable to any other. Thus (to take a simple case) World War II may be treated as one event (for some purposes), or as a complex arrangement of events (for others); and these events, like the European and Pacific Campaigns, may be further parsed into additional events. But without a reason for parsing a slice of history, there is no reason for dividing it up one way rather than another—for example, into fine-grained rather than coarse-grained divisions. Independently of a context in which the parsing of a slice of history s matters, the question 'How many events are there in s?' makes no sense. Similarly, apart from a guiding set of purposes and interests, there is no answer to the question 'How many things are in this room?'

Nature, then, does not dictate how we individuate events. She does not have a structure waiting to be discovered, which transcends *any* perspective or point of view we might have. How we divide a bit of history depends on the purposes for which events are being individuated; it is always part of an overall decision to view a certain slice of history one way rather than another. Thus, the parsing of a time-slice into events or elements is not an activity conceptually independent of the decision to take a certain perspective on that bit of history.

But meaningful relations between events obtain only relative to some parsing of history into the events so related. Hence, meaningful relations between events themselves presuppose a context relative to which the parsing of the relevant portion of history is appropriate. Consider again the exploding sounds in Freud's bookcase, and suppose we agree that the sounds symbolize the clash occurring between Jung and Freud on the subject of ESP. The point I am making is that nothing intrinsic to this situation determines that the clash between them is the element of the situation that the sounds represent. The decision to regard the clash as an element is part of an overall decision to regard the sounds as symbolic of the clash. It is not made independently of the decision to compare the sounds with the clash. After all, the sounds could have been compared or symbolically related to many other things—e.g., concurrent pistol shots elsewhere in Vienna, or perhaps particular *words* spoken by Jung and Freud having explosive phonemic properties, or perhaps a particular remark (like 'That is sheer bosh') made in the course of the dialogue, or perhaps a violent gesture made to accompany that remark. Had any of these comparisons seemed worth making instead, the explosive words (say), or the remark, or the gesture (rather than the clash), would have counted as an element of the situation. And in that case, the sounds in the bookcase would have related symbolically to those elements instead.

Thus, determining the structure and determining the meaning or significance of events are parts of the same package, the former activity enjoys no logical or conceptual priority over the latter. The meaning of events is not simply a function of their manifest structure.* But since the parsing of a bit of history into elements or events is not independent of a decision to view it from a certain perspective—in fact, since events themselves cannot even be identified independently of some way of conceptualizing that portion of history which contains its own criteria of event-individuation —the remarkable similarities or connections between meaningfully related events will always be a function of the way we view that portion of history. But then, since how we choose to view that portion of history will always be a function of the contingent purposes we have at the time, the meaningful similarities or connections between events are *not* built into nature independently of any such perspective or guiding set of purposes.

In fact, this is why such concepts as *similarity* and *relevance* are functional and context-relative, and not structural

---

*Of course this is simply a version of the point made against the *ET* theory in I.B.4.d. and later in II.A.3., except we were there concerned specifically with a slice of mental history.

or context-independent. This point has already been made many times. In I.B.4.d., I observed how, even in geometry, whether two triangles count as congruent is not intrinsic to the triangles, but depends on the rule of projection we choose; in other words, it depends on how the figures function against a set of contingent background conditions in which their comparison matters. I also noted, in I.A.7., that whether or not two verbal performances count as the same joke is not a function of anything intrinsic to those performances, but depends instead on a set of contingent background conditions which presuppose criteria of sameness. And it is easy to multiply related examples. Thus, (a) A's punching B in the mouth and (b) A's making demeaning remarks to B in front of B's fiancée are neither intrinsically similar nor dissimilar. If we are concerned to discuss A's propensity for physical violence, the two events may not count as similar. But they would count as similar if we were interested in identifying examples of A's hostile behavior. Since, therefore, events are not intrinsically similar or relevant to one another, *a fortiori* they are not intrinsically *meaningfully* similar or relevant to one another either.

We see, then, that even the mere individuation of events within a given time-slice is a context-relative or perspective-relative activity; consequently, history cannot intelligibly be said to have a manifest structure. What counts as the structure of a slice of history is tied to some decision about how that bit of history should be viewed. Moreover, grasping this has helped us to see that attributions of structure and meaning are parts of one and the same package. Since meaningful relations between events presuppose some individuation of events (the parsing of history), attributions of meaningfulness —like those of structure—presuppose a perspective from which the parsing is appropriate.

So no matter whether we focus on the elements or constituents of a bit of history or on the meaningful relations between elements, we cannot escape the fact that attributions of either kind (structure or meaning) are inseparable from some perspective on that portion of history. If, furthermore, we recall as well that there are, in principle, numerous ways of interpreting—or assigning meaning to—a given portion of history, we see another reason why attributions of meaning presuppose a perspective on that portion of history—in this case a perspective from which certain interpretations rather than others will count as correct or appropriate.

Relations of meaningfulness, then, are not built into nature, but can be explained only with respect to a point of view or set of background assumptions against which certain interpretations rather than others count as appropriate. But, to put the matter picturesquely, such points of view or assumptions must reside in something. That is, no such point of view can exist, or figure in the actual parsing of a bit of history, without there being an *interpreter* whose point of view it is. But if this is so, then synchronistic explanations (i.e., explanations of the meaningfulness of meaningful coincidences) prove to be kinds of causal explanations after all.

When proponents of synchronicity try to explain, say, the relevance of the explosions in Freud's bookcase to something about the relationship between Jung and Freud, they apparently fail to appreciate how much needs to be explained. For one thing, they must explain why the explosions occurred as and when they did, instead of at a time and place when they would not be jointly meaningful. So the synchronistic explanation must indicate why the sounds occurred when they did—and not, say, a year later when no one was in the room, or perhaps in a bookcase somewhere else in Vienna. Moreover, the explanation cannot be that this was purely fortuitous, and thus that the meaningfulness of the situation was extrinsic to the events themselves and simply imposed on them by a human observer. According to the theory of synchronicity, such meaningful coincidences are not fortuitous. Nor can the meaningfulness of events be explained through some appeal to a general *law* linking (say) archetypal arguments and exploding sounds, since (i) synchronistic explanations are not general in scope in this way, and (ii) such an explanation would be *causal* in nature; it would be an appeal to a kind of causal law stipulating that events of certain kinds tend to accompany one another. Nor can partisans of synchronicity say something even more sweeping and general—namely, that the universe is simply such that events occur in intrinsically meaningful clusters, even though there may be no laws governing specific types of meaningful connections. As we have seen, (a) history has no intrinsic structure or meaning, (b) attributions of either structure or meaning presuppose some perspective or point of view on history, and (c) such perspectives are not autonomously existing things, but presuppose instead an interpreter or consciousness who owns, so to speak, the point of view. But since, according to the theory of synchronicity, the point of view relative to which events are meaningful cannot be a mere human point of view, it seems that the only way to give meaningful coincidences the kind of transcendental or cosmic meaning they are supposed to have is to posit the existence of a cosmic interpreter of history and a corresponding cosmic point of view. But since synchronistic explanations must explain not only the locus of meaningfulness in meaningful coincidences, but also why the events in question occurred in meaningful rather than non-meaningful ways, this cosmic interpreter is presumably the individual (or individuals) responsible for the events' occurrence. The relevant interpreter(s), apparently, can only be the 'author(s)' of those events, and the relevant background assumptions determining which assignments of meaning or parsings into elements are appropriate are presumably his (its, their) assumptions. This is why Beloff [11] suggests (I believe, correctly) that the only way to explain why certain events occur in a meaningful cluster without appealing to causal relationships among those events themselves—and while still avoiding an appeal to causal ancestors in the general human or terrestrial causal network of which those events are a part—is by means of appeal to yet another causal ancestor, *outside* the system of causally related events available for our inspection. Beloff suggests that meaningful connections tend to make sense only in a cosmology where nature is a kind of artifact, or a work of art or drama. We thus explain the meaningful convergence of otherwise causally independent events in terms of something like the activity of a cosmic dramatist, not in terms of anything in the drama itself. But such an explanation remains clearly a kind of causal explanation.

In fact, given that the meaningfulness of meaningful coincidences is not, according to the theory of synchronicity, imposed by an observer on fortuitously converging events, any explanation of why those events are jointly meaningful can *only* be a causal explanation. When we ask why events E and E' occur meaningfully, proponents of synchronicity cannot simply give independent causal accounts for E and E'. That would explain at most why E and E' occur together, and *not* why their joint occurrence is meaningful. But to explain why these events are jointly meaningful, it is not sufficient to say simply that some person happens to find (E & E') meaningful. The meaningfulness must be intrinsic to (E & E') and the convergence of E and E' in space and time must *result* from natural processes relating events with respect to their meaning. And this is a causal explanation.

In fact, it is a causal explanation in very much the same sense as the familiar explanation of why a person but not a parrot or a phonograph can insult me by producing the string of symbols, 'Braude, you're a buffoon'. When a parrot utters these syllables, they have no meaning because they are not organized by the parrot in virtue of their meaning. The parrot is just repeating sounds. But a person can give meaning to the words by intentionally combining them in a certain way in a certain context. So our explanation of why the string 'Braude, you're a buffoon' is insulting when produced by a person rather than a parrot has to do with the different *causes* of the two phonemically identical strings. We might find it amusing when a parrot 'insults' me. But of course whatever meaning we attribute to the parrot's words is imposed by us—from the outside, so to speak, just as two fortuitously combined events may have a meaning imposed on them by an observer. When a *person* insults me, however, the meaning of his words is not simply imposed on those words by an outside observer. His insult is meaningful because of the way his words are produced—namely, with the intention of meaning what they mean. In this respect, the theory of synchronicity parallels a causal theory of meaning. The following situation may help to make this point clear.

4. The Play of Life

Consider the case of a certain drama, written by dramatist D, involving two main characters A and B. And suppose that the story of the play, in synopsis, is as follows. A and B had been rivals in their youth, with A always emerging victorious in their contests (in athletics, school elections, affairs of the heart, etc.). Later, they went their separate ways, lived in different parts of the world, and had no contact with one another. One day, however, B applied for a high position and discovered that his principal rival for the job was A. But this time, unlike the competitive days of their youth, B triumphed and got the job.

We can now imagine the various ways in which the characters (or actors) A and B—and the dramatist D—might interpret the latest contest between A and B, and B's long-awaited victory.

D might give the event a moral or religious interpretation. B, he might say, was a contemplative person who reflected long and hard on his rivalry with A, realizing finally that his own integrity did not depend on the outcome of their contests. Hence, he emerged from his reflections a wiser and stronger person, with a firm and realistic sense of his own value as a human being. Fortified by his wisdom, he had become a person who commanded the respect of others. A, on the other hand, seduced by his early triumphs into a false sense of his own worth, had become conceited and abrasive. Because of his lack of humility, he invited more contempt than respect. Thus, D might conclude, B's victory over A represents a sort of cosmic justice, or instantiates a religious principle according to which people ultimately triumph for their perseverance and integrity, while others (like A) pay, or suffer God's justice, for their ruthlessness and arrogance.

B might provide an equally cosmic but *amoral* interpretation. He might say that his victory over *A* demonstrates that a principle of *symmetry* operates in the universe, in which evil is balanced by good, love by hate, defeat by victory, and so on. *A*, on the other hand, might be somewhat more down-to-earth. *B*, he might say, had throughout his life lost so many important contests to *A* that he was unusually eager to win this one. And *A* would say of himself that he was not as hungry for victory as *B*. He had already won so many of their contests that he felt he could take or leave this one. So, *A* might conclude, the difference in their motivation must have led to *B*'s success.

Some observations about this play and its interpretations are now in order. First of all, each interpretation, in its own way, illuminates the significance of the latest rivalry between *A* and *B*. In some contexts, we might wish to link the story of *A* and *B* with great religious, moral, or mystical themes (imagine this story being told to a philosophy class, or a class in a religious school), in which case *D*'s or *B*'s interpretations would be appropriate. In other contexts, however—for example, in a class in self-improvement or in a business school—we might prefer to connect the story of *A* and *B* with such things as the practical effects of defeat on one's character and self-confidence, or the dynamics of applying for a job. And in this case, *A*'s interpretation might suit our needs instead.

Moreover, not only may these interpretations be compatible with each other, but none is intrinsically preferable to either of the others. If any one interpretation deserves to be preferred, perhaps it is *D*'s, but then only because it is *his* story. He is the one responsible for the details of his characters' behavior, and those details are developed through his own point of view. But that does not make *D*'s perspective transcendental in any interesting sense. *D*'s interpretation has no claim to absolute correctness. In principle, nothing prevents *A*'s or *B*'s interpretation from being deeper than *D*'s, in the sense of tying more events in the play together, or in the sense of giving a conceptual underpinning for *D*'s interpretation, or in the sense of illuminating aspects of the play (or life) not even grasped by the dramatist.

But even more important is the fact that there is literally no sense in the notion of one interpretation of the story of A and B being absolutely or intrinsically correct. This does not mean that no interpretation explains the action of the drama. For example, appeal to a principle of cosmic symmetry does explain the course of the events. But all this means is either (a) that this is one of many ways of interpreting the events, possibly one that ties them together more intelligibly than any rival interpretation (relative to some context in which we have a certain kind of interest in the play*), or (b) that the dramatist had this interpretation in mind when he wrote the play. Of course the point of appealing to a principle of synchronicity to explain events is that something like an interpretation of a drama is, in some sense, *part of nature*; this embeddedness in nature is what renders such interpretations intrinsically correct. They are built into the situation and not merely imposed on events from the outside (cf. the quotations from Jung, in Section II.B.1.).

But in what sense can a particular description or interpretation of events be part of (or embedded in) our analogue of nature, D's play? Suppose we take option (b) above, and justify the interpretation by reference to the mind and intentions of (cosmic) dramatist D. This would give some sense to the notion that that interpretation is preferable to the others. We could then claim, in a certain sense, that the interpretation was built into the situation. But as we have already seen, D's interpretation of the action in the drama is not the only viable one; in some cases, other interpretations might be preferable to his. So option (b) does not help explain how the (cosmic) dramatist's interpretation might be built into the situation in a way that would permit us to 'read-off' that interpretation from the events themselves. Furthermore, although reliance on a cosmic dramatist might appeal to some, as a way of explaining the power or priority of synchronistic explanations, I doubt whether most partisans of

---

*After all, the principle of cosmic symmetry might not be the preferred interpretation in a class in self-improvement, although it might in a class in religious school.

synchronicity would be happy to have their point of view stand or fall with a crudely anthropomorphic theology.

If, on the other hand, we take option (a) above, and construe an interpretation as explaining certain events by tying them together into a coherent pattern, then (as we have seen) many interpretations will explain the actions in the drama. Hence, this option does not indicate a respect in which the interpretation given could be said to be built into the events. In our play, as in nature generally, the facts of the case do not *exhibit* their interpretation, or demand intrinsically, or in every context, that one and only one interpretation be given priority over others. Even if one interpretation is superior to all others, the only respect in which this can be true—having by now eliminated option (b)—is that the others are less illuminating. But—and this is the crucial point—what one interpretation illuminates, and whether it does so more successfully than others, is not a context-independent feature of the situation. How illuminating one interpretation is depends on what we are asking about the events in question, or what we are looking for. If (in the case of our play) we were concerned with the story's moral aspects, D's interpretation would be preferable. But if we were interested in the dynamics of job hunting, A's would be.

Jung, of course, maintained that the locus in nature of the meaningfulness of certain events was the collective unconscious, the source of the archetypes. Superficially, this suggests that there may be another way besides option (b) of making some sense of the claim that a description or interpretation of events is part of nature. But as far as I can see, Jung's maneuver is simply a complicated version of option (b) itself, and does not escape its problems.

An analogy may make this clear. Consider again our drama about A and B. But this time, suppose that the drama is not written by D, or in fact written (in advance) by anyone. Let us suppose that the actors make up the story as they go along, and that the members of this improvisational troupe have more or less the same viewpoint on the action in the drama, so that their individual contributions to this joint creation cohere with one another. I believe this situation parallels Jung's suggestions that the locus of meaningfulness resides in the collective unconscious' repertoire of archetypes. In our drama, the improvising actors are guided by common concepts and a common viewpoint. This is why the action in the play develops as it does—that is, why the characters act as they do and (more generally) why the story line takes certain twists and turns rather than others.

But even here, we are giving a *causal* explanation of how meaningful coincidences occur. Also, our improvisors' viewpoint and the descriptive categories connected with it are no more intrinsic to the drama than was the viewpoint, etc., of the single dramatist D, in our original example. Just as in the earlier case viewpoints other than D's might illuminate aspects of the situation that D's does not illuminate, and just as those other viewpoints might be deeper or more relevant than D's in some contexts, the same is bound to be true of the shared viewpoint of our team of improvisors. There might still be other viewpoints and descriptions of the action that, relative to some context in which we are trying to gain an understanding of the events in the play, will be more illuminating than any viewpoint they may have adopted. Nothing in the action itself demands that it be interpreted in one and only one way. Hence, like option (b), Jung's appeal to the collective unconscious fails to explain how an interpretation of events may be built into nature in a way that gives it intrinsic or context-independent correctness or priority over other interpretations, or in a way that permits it to be 'read-off' the events themselves.

5. Conclusion

Let me now try to sum things up. Synchronistic explanations of apparently meaningful coincidences are supposed to have several crucial features. First, in specifying how events are meaningfully related, such explanations are supposed to specify relations, or kinds of connections, between events that are somehow intrinsic to their joint occurrence.

Only thus can proponents of synchronicity explain how such meaningfulness is not arbitrary, or context-relative, or imposed on the events by an observer; only thus (they believe) can meaningfulness be construed as a function of fundamental operations of nature. Second, synchronistic explanations are supposed to explain why the events in question occurred as they did—that is, why they happened at certain times and in a meaningful way, rather than at other times or in other ways that would not have made them jointly meaningful. And third, explanations of why events in a meaningful coincidence form a meaningful group are not supposed to be causal explanations. These last two demands, however, cannot be satisfied jointly, and the first does not even make sense.

We saw that meaningfulness must be linked to a perspective or point of view. And we saw that a point of view cannot exist independently of an interpreter who (as it were) owns that point of view. That is why explanations of the meaningfulness of certain event-clusters must (if this meaningfulness is not fortuitous) be given in terms of some interpreter(s) of the events who is (are) actually responsible for their occurring when and as they do. But then, despite the protestations of Jung and his disciples, synchronistic explanations prove to be a subset of the set of causal explanations. It is true that the theory of synchronicity rules out explanation by reference to some common causal ancestor. But that constraint cannot be met if we are also to satisfy the requirement that we explain why the events in question occurred in a meaningful rather than a non-meaningful way. And if we refuse to locate the cause of the coincidence in natural history, we must, it seems, posit some sort of causal cosmology. I conclude, then, that the theory of synchronicity is unintelligible and riddled with inconsistencies, and that those who think that an approach like Jung's has promise literally do not know what they are talking about.

There may, of course, be some acceptable way of formulating a theory of meaningful coincidences. But so long as we must explain why events have occurred in a meaningful rather than a non-meaningful way, our explanations will be causal explanations (whether or not the causal chains posited hold among the meaningfully related events themselves). Hence, in rejecting the theory of synchronicity, I am not denying the viability of causal theories of meaningful coincidence. We might, for example, wish to appeal to something like a collective unconscious. Or, we might locate the cause of meaningful coincidences in the minds and intentions of individual persons (i.e., actors in the drama). Perhaps, as I suggested in I.B.2.c., there is a cosmic or externalized analogue of the placebo effect, or of the passive volition of biofeedback control over internal physiological processes. If people who expect or wish for certain things to happen to their bodies are thus able to get what they expect or wish for, we should perhaps leave open the possibility that such expectations and wishes may be causally efficacious on a larger scale. And notice that none of these maneuvers requires that meaningfulness be intrinsic to events, or independent of anyone's point of view. In any case, I am not prepared to pursue these speculations further at the moment. I want instead to emphasize that *any explanation* (and not simply a description) of the meaningfulness of meaningful coincidences must be a causal explanation, as long as the meaningfulness is not fortuitous. The theory of synchronicity thus promises no new kind of explanation after all. It only promises confusion.

C. The Meaning of 'Paranormal'

1. Introduction

As I remarked early in this book, C. J. Ducasse coined the term 'paranormal' in order to divest references to the subject matter of parapsychology of all association with things psychological. The field of parapsychology, he felt, concerned paranormal phenomena—that is, a distinct domain not to be subsumed within some subset of the standard set of psychological phenomena; and he tried (as have some others) to specify what, exactly, that domain is. I wish, now, to address this same issue. I want to see if we can in fact specify what the proper domain of parapsychological research is. In what follows I shall critically examine what seem to me to be the leading accounts of paranormality, and consider some ways of remedying their defects.

2. Preliminaries

Most people operate with a rather vague, tripartite, pre-theoretic distinction between ordinary phenomena, unusual or rare phenomena, and finally, phenomena (whether rare or not) that are downright weird, bizarre, or other-worldly. To some extent, this pre-theoretic distinction matches another distinction of interest to us—namely, the not-so-pre-theoretic distinction between *normal, abnormal,* and *paranormal* phenomena. Since the customary use of the term 'paranormal' and its cognates presupposes this latter distinction, attempts to specify the domain of the paranormal would presumably be less than satisfactory if they failed to preserve these three rather fuzzy categories. And of course we would also expect any such attempt to clarify at least the last of these categories.

However unclear the normal/abnormal/paranormal distinction is pre-analytically, it is nevertheless sufficiently clear to permit us to evaluate proposed accounts of paranormality. We may not be able to decide whether certain borderline phenomena fall into one category rather than another, but I think we have sufficient paradigm cases for each category to lend substance to the distinction. Any account of paranormality incompatible with our classification of these paradigm cases will, it seems, be *prima facie* unacceptable.

I think it is fair to say there is widespread agreement that certain sorts of phenomena are paradigmatically normal. Even the most conservative and eccentric among us probably agree that thunderstorms, sunsets, the movements of the tides, and similar phenomena are normal phenomena. But we also have relatively uncontroversial paradigm cases of abnormal phenomena—for example, certain side-show cases (e.g., a person with two heads, or the half-man/half-woman) as well as such things as cases of microcephaly and situs inversus (a congenital condition in which the position of internal bodily organs is laterally transposed). Moreover, the class of abnormal phenomena is not the same as the class of *unusual* or *infrequent* phenomena, although these classes overlap. Great natural disasters, for example, like floods and earthquakes, or such predictable occurrences as solar eclipses and the passage of famous comets are unusual and infrequent; but they are not typically regarded as abnormal.

Although we do have obvious paradigm cases of normal and abnormal phenomena, it might be needlessly contentious to claim that we have paradigm cases of paranormal phenomena. A correct and more cautious claim would be that we have clear cases of *ostensibly* paranormal phenomena. Examples may be drawn from the experimental evidence studied earlier in this book, as well as from the numerous reports of spontaneous occurrences of apparent ESP, PK, hauntings, mediumistic communications, and so forth. To characterize these as merely ostensibly paranormal is not, of course, to deny their importance. After all, some ostensibly paranormal phenomena might be genuinely paranormal. Nor is it to place them in a kind of ontological limbo. Rather, it is simply intended to acknowledge an interesting difference between the categories of abnormal and paranormal phenomena.

No one doubts that there are abnormal phenomena. No matter how people elect to draw the line between the normal and the abnormal, nobody seriously disputes whether there is a line to be drawn. But people *do* seriously question whether there are paranormal phenomena, rather than (say) merely unusual phenomena explicable in terms of mundane or familiar processes. But whether or not the class of paranormal phenomena is empty, there is considerable agreement regarding what sorts of phenomena are *candidates* for membership in that class. What we must demand of any satisfactory account of paranormality is that it do justice to our classification of certain phenomena as *ostensibly* paranormal. We want our account of paranormality to be such that those phenomena widely regarded as ostensibly paranormal seem *prima facie* to satisfy the account.

One final preliminary point. The terms 'abnormal' and 'paranormal' might be defined in such a way that the set of paranormal phenomena turns out merely to be a subset of the set of abnormal phenomena. On the other hand, these terms might be so defined that the sets of abnormal and paranormal phenomena turn out to be disjoint. It is important to realize that both are legitimate options; but we do not need to decide between them in advance.

3. Paranormality as Scientific Inexplicability

C. J. Ducasse once offered an account of paranormality, which, in more or less disguised (and usually simplified) forms, is probably the one most often advanced by parapsychologists and laymen alike (see [42]). This account is profoundly defective; but its mistakes are instructive.

Ducasse's proposal runs as follows.

(D1) Phenomenon P is paranormal =df (a) the cause of P is not that from which phenomena of that sort ordinarily result, and (b) the cause of P is nothing yet known to the natural sciences as capable of causing a phenomenon of that sort.

One apparent virtue of (D1), which Ducasse acknowledged, is that it permits the domain of the paranormal to change with time, as the scope of science inevitably widens. Thus, phenomena regarded at one time as paranormal might come to be regarded later as either abnormal or normal. I think we can agree with Ducasse that this seems to be a virtue of (D1). Such a shift in perspective appears to have occurred with respect to solar eclipses, hypnotism, and various electromagnetic phenomena, and presumably will happen again with respect to some phenomena now regarded as ostensibly paranormal.

It is not clear, incidentally, what Ducasse regarded as an *abnormal* phenomenon when he proposed (D1). If he had a definite view at all, it was probably something like this. Unlike paranormal phenomena, normal and abnormal phenomena are both explicable by current science, and the difference between normal and abnormal phenomena has to do with the difference in their frequency of occurrence. But as I observed in the previous section, more than this needs to be said if we are to do justice to the pre-theoretic distinction between the merely infrequent and the abnormal.

In any case, (D1) has serious defects. Consider clause (a). The motivation behind this clause, and for that matter behind Ducasse's emphasis on the *cause* of the phenomenon in question, is reasonably clear. The *manifestations* of paranormal phenomena may be indistinguishable from those of ordinary phenomena. Sometimes, for example, pictures just fall off walls, for a variety of humdrum reasons. At other times a magician might make the picture fall, and although the causes may not be humdrum, they are nevertheless ordinary mechanical causes, not even remotely likely to disrupt the body of our scientific theories. But a picture made to fall by means of PK may be observationally indistinguishable from the ordinary event or from the handiwork of the Amazing Randi. What would make the PK case paranormal would have to do with the cause, and not the manifestation, of the event in question.

But despite the reasonableness of Ducasse's emphasis on causes, clause (a) is problematical. The problem is that it requires at least *two* causes for the type of phenomenon to which P belongs: (i) that from which such phenomena ordinarily result, and (ii) that from which such phenomena paranormally result. But of course some sorts of phenomena, even if they can be produced in more than one way, may be sufficiently unprecedented that there is no cause at all from which they *ordinarily* result. This would presumably be true in the case of such relatively uncommon phenomena as ostensible possession and poltergeist manifestations (what is the *ordinary* cause of objects flying across a room *without visible signs of agency*?). Moreover, some sorts of ostensibly paranormal phenomena (e.g., apparent telepathic and clairvoyant interaction) may *not* have more than one cause, and their sole cause may be what inclines us to regard them as paranormal in the first place. In my view, we can best avoid these difficulties by ignoring clause (a) altogether, and treating clause (b) of (D1) as expressing the substance of Ducasse's account. Let us, then, consider the following.

(D1′) Phenomenon P is paranormal =df the cause of P is nothing yet known to the natural sciences as capable of causing a phenomenon of that sort.

But even this trimmed definition is not satisfactory, since the phrase 'yet known to the natural sciences' is crucially ambiguous. Suppose that some phenomenon P is, in principle, causally explicable in terms of current scientific theory, but that no one has discovered what the explanation is. Since such human limitations may be displayed with respect to both familiar and exotic phenomena, this state of affairs hardly constitutes sufficient grounds for regarding P as paranormal. It satisfies (D1') however, if (D1') is construed loosely enough—when, that is, 'yet known to the natural sciences' is understood to mean something like 'yet known to *anyone* in the natural sciences'. But at very best, the case described is one in which we are entitled to regard P as *ostensibly* paranormal. So in order to disambiguate (D1'), and also to avoid the danger of obliterating the distinction between the ostensibly and the genuinely paranormal, let us recast (D1') to exclude this sort of case. What Ducasse probably had in mind is something like:

(D1'') Phenomenon P is paranormal =df P is in fact causally inexplicable in terms of current scientific theory.

Although (D1'') avoids the difficulty just discussed, it too is seriously flawed. The history of science may be regarded as a saga in which observed anomalies periodically force the scientific community to alter or abandon prevailing theories. But even when we consider those anomalous occurrences that occasioned the most profound changes in scientific theory, we find that they were not regarded at the time as ostensibly paranormal. During the twilight of Newtonian physics, for example, scientists grappled with numerous phenomena that the then current theory simply could not handle (for example, the anomalous advance of Mercury's perihelion, the so-called 'ultraviolet catastrophe', and the negative results of the Michelson-Morley experiment). Nevertheless, they were not for that reason regarded as sufficiently bizarre (or whatever is required) to be taken as ostensibly paranormal. Thus, the important error involved in linking paranormality merely to scientific inexplicability is that it leads to the highly counter-intuitive result that all scientific anomalies are paranormal.

4. Paranormality and Basic Limiting Principles

To his credit, Ducasse eventually abandoned his account of paranormality in favor of one offered by C. D. Broad. Broad's definition is in some ways a decided improvement

over (D1) and its revisions, but it also has serious defects.
The most exhaustive presentation of Broad's view appears
in [23] (in 'The Relevance of Psychical Research to Philosophy'*); it is also sketched in his *Lectures on Psychical
Research* [24]. To understand Broad's view, we must first
master a key concept in his account—namely, the notion of
a *basic limiting principle* (hereafter *BLP*).

Broad's *BLP*s are called *limiting* principles because they
specify restrictions or limitations on the way things can be,
or can be known. And they are called *basic* because they are
supposed to lie at the very foundation of our conceptual
system. Broad writes, 'They form the framework within
which the practical life, the scientific theories, and even
most of the fiction of contemporary industrial civilization
are confined' ([24]: 3). *BLP*s are thus not merely laws of
nature. Although, according to Broad, there may be borderline cases in which we cannot tell whether we have a *BLP* or
a natural law, in general *BLP*s are more basic to our conceptual system than laws of nature. *BLP*s are, in fact, *presupposed* by our natural laws (in a sense to be explained below).
It is precisely because we share certain *BLP*s that our natural
laws (and hence our sciences) take certain forms rather than
others.

Broad's taxonomy of *BLP*s differs with his different accounts, and even in his rather thorough exposition in 'The
Relevance of Psychical Research to Philosophy', he does not
claim to have offered a complete list of *BLP*s. Rather, he
offers some examples and assumes we can extrapolate from
these. In the summary of his position in the *Lectures*, Broad
lists the following four *BLP*s, which he seems to regard as
especially important, and which, for the most part, are drawn
or condensed from his earlier and more extensive list.

The first *BLP* imposes limitations on the ways we can
acquire knowledge of another person's thoughts or experiences.

*Reprinted in Ludwig [89] and Wheatley and Edge [193].

(1) We take for granted that a person A cannot know what experiences another person B is now having or has had, except in one or another of the following three ways. (i) By hearing and understanding sentences uttered by B, or reproductions of such sentences, which describe his experiences; or by reading and understanding such sentences written or dictated by B, or reproductions or translations of them. Or (ii) by hearing and interpreting interjections which B makes, by seeing and interpreting his movements, gestures, facial expressions, and so on. Or (iii) by seeing, and making inferences from, certain persistent material objects, e.g., tools, pottery, pictures, etc., which B has constructed or used, or copies and reproductions of such objects ([24] : 3).

The second *BLP* restricts how we can come to know about the future.

(2) We take for granted also that a person cannot forsee (as distinct from inferring, or being led, without explicit inference, to expect on the basis of regularities in his past experience) any event which has not yet happened ([24] : 3-4).

The third *BLP* restricts how we can cause changes in the physical world.

(3) We take for granted, too, that a person cannot *directly* initiate or modify by his volition the movement of anything but certain parts of his own body ([24] : 4).

The fourth *BLP* concerns the dependence of mind on brain and, more specifically, survival after death.

(4) We take for granted that, when a person's body dies, the personal consciousness, which has been associated with it and expressed through it during his lifetime, either ceases altogether or, if not, ceases to be able to manifest itself in any way to those still living on earth ([24] : 4).

With this partial list of *BLP*s, we are in a position to consider Broad's definitions. First, Broad offers the following definition of a phenomenon's abnormality.

(D2) Phenomenon *P* is abnormal =df *P* seems *prima facie* to conflict with a well-established law of nature, but *not* with any *BLP*.

Broad remarks that sometimes abnormal phenomena do not really conflict with any laws of nature, but can be explained in terms of existing laws *and* certain unusual boundary conditions. On the other hand, he says, sometimes abnormal phenomena show us that laws have exceptions, or that we need to supplement or revise our original set of laws.

Before considering what Broad says about paranormality, we should at least note that his account of abnormality is not entirely satisfactory. Many phenomena widely regarded as abnormal (e.g., Siamese twins, situs inversus) are characterized as such even though they do not seem *prima facie* to violate a natural law. And since it is not (as we have seen) satisfactory to link a phenomenon's abnormality to its frequency of occurrence, the concept of an abnormal phenomenon remains somewhat obscure.

We need not dwell on these difficulties, however. Our present concern is to see if we can find an account of paranormality that countenances as ostensibly paranormal those phenomena widely regarded as such, and that at the same time does *not* countenance as ostensibly paranormal those phenomena regarded as merely abnormal. Given the way Broad chooses to characterize abnormality, his account of paranormality is what one would expect.

(D3) Phenomenon *P* is ostensibly paranormal =df *P* seems *prima facie* to conflict with one or more of the *BLP*s, and not merely with some well-established law of nature.

(D4) Phenomenon *P* is genuinely paranormal =df *P* in fact conflicts with one or more of the *BLP*s.

The advantage of Broad's account over Ducasse's is that Broad requires that paranormal phenomena run up against something more fundamental than—or at least something in addition to—the dictates of science. But his account still does not go deep enough; it suffers from a pernicious lack of generality or abstractness. Broad has failed to explain what, in general, a phenomenon must conflict with in order to conflict with a *BLP*. In short, Broad's account is of little value in the absence of a general characterization of a *BLP*.

We have already granted that it is plausible to regard the domain of the paranormal as something that may change with time, as our thinking about the world becomes more sophisticated. After all, this is presumably why phenomena, at one time regarded as weird or other-worldly, have come to be seen as more or less commonplace and quite this-worldly. But if the extension of the term 'paranormal' can change with time, we need a general characterization of what a paranormal phenomenon is, regardless of the vagaries of intellectual history. Hypnotism, we must recall, was once regarded by the (British) Society for Psychical Research as a phenomenon to be investigated along with those we now call ESP, PK, etc. But it does not seem to violate any of Broad's *BLP*s. Also, even if we restrict attention to a particular historical epoch, a partial list of *BLP*s will not suffice to explain what the domain of the paranormal is for that epoch. For one thing, Broad's *BLP*s are by no means universally shared even within our own historical epoch, or even among those who agree on what phenomena count as ostensibly paranormal. For example, many people believe they are in touch with the surviving spirits of dead persons, and nevertheless regard this phenomenon as distinct from both the normal and the abnormal. Their rejection of *BLP* (4) thus seems *compatible* with treating such ostensible communications as paranormal. But even if the *BLP*'s *were* universally shared, we would still want to know the *principle* behind a phenomenon's proper classification as paranormal. Since Broad views phenomena as ostensibly paranormal in virtue of an apparent conflict with a *BLP*, we need to know what, in general, a phenomenon must conflict with in order to be paranormal. This means we need a general characterization of a *BLP*, no matter which historical epoch we are concerned with or which set of *BLP*s we now have. Certainly, no mere *list* (no matter how exhaustive) will indicate what a *BLP* is, especially if the items on the list can change as they do in

Broad's different accounts. Explaining the paranormal *by enumerating* instances or types of relevant conflict is rather like explaining what serial music is by providing examples of serial compositions. The question would remain: What makes these compositions examples of serial music? Similarly, we must still ask of Broad: What makes these principles you have enumerated examples of *BLP*s?

Some may wish to make Broad's account more general by saying that paranormal phenomena violate one or more of *whatever* it is that science presupposes (and that forms the framework of our lives and theories). Beloff may have had something like this in mind when he wrote

> A phenomenon is, by definition, paranormal if and only if it contravenes some fundamental and well-founded assumption of science ([10]: 353).

But this won't do. It takes too great a step in the direction of generality. After all, we presuppose much more (in science and in life) than the sorts of principles Broad lists as *BLP*s, which seem equally to form part of our conceptual framework, and which are not even *prima facie* violated by ostensibly paranormal phenomena—for example, regulative principles like the laws of deductive logic, as well as general assumptions about such things as the viability of the hypothetico-deductive method, the general veridicality of perceptions, or the existence of other minds, and specific assumptions about, say, the fact of our own existence.

Thus, if paranormal phenomena do violate certain scientific assumptions or presuppositions, then it appears that only one or more members of a *subset* of the things presupposed in science (and life) must be violated in order for a phenomenon to be paranormal. But which subset? Putting the matter this way, we see that we need some way to characterize that subset generally. And this is precisely what the suggestions thus far entertained have failed to do.

Before moving on, consider another troublesome aspect of Broad's account. Are *BLP*s more fundamental than laws of nature? Put another way, is it reasonable to suppose that

*BLP*s are *presupposed* rather than *implied* by scientific theory? The question is both relevant and important, since Broad claims that ostensibly paranormal phenomena seem to conflict with something more fundamental than scientific theory. But if they are merely implied by scientific theory, *BLP*s are not more fundamental; a phenomenon that seems *prima facie* to conflict with *BLP*s may then be in conflict only with one or more of the consequences of scientific laws. And in that case, Broad would have unwittingly committed Ducasse's mistake, linking a phenomenon's paranormality to no more than its scientific inexplicability.*

So the question remains: Do our scientific theories have the form they have (describe the world as they do) because the *BLP*s are taken for granted from the start, *or* are the *BLP*s taken for granted because certain general physical principles or laws are assumed to be true?

Broad would have said that our theories take the forms they do because we already have a pre-theoretic view of the world, of which the *BLP*s form a central part. But there are two ways of construing this stand, one of which is patently false, and the other of which is at very least suspicious (and not simply because the notion of a *BLP* is obscure):

(i) Broad might have been making an historical claim about acquiring ideas. He might have been maintaining that the acceptance of scientific theory follows the acceptance of the *BLP*s. But this, of course, is transparently false, since the *BLP*s are by no means universally held, even among those who accept current scientific theory.

(ii) Thus, it is more likely that Broad was making a claim about what may be loosely termed *the logic of belief*—that is,

---

*Interestingly, Beloff may have reverted to something like Ducasse's position recently in maintaining that a 'phenomenon is said to be paranormal if in one or more respects it exceeds the limits of what, on current scientific assumptions, is deemed to be physically possible' ([9] : xxii). On this view, continental drift would, until recently, have counted as paranormal. Prior to the theory of plate tectonics, the phenomenon was indeed deemed physically impossible. Still, it is very unlikely that continental drift would ever have been regarded as anything but a scientific anomaly.

a claim about the *structure* of a fully articulated world view or conceptual scheme. Broad was presumably maintaining that if we made fully explicit the system of beliefs constituting our total world view, its structure would be such that accepting the *BLP*s was a necessary condition for accepting our scientific theories.

The structure of this conceptual system would apparently *not* be like that of an axiomatic system, with the *BLP*s playing a role analogous to that of the axioms, since the *BLP*s are presumably able to support divergent and possibly even mutually incompatible scientific theories (Copernican and relativistic physics, for instance, seem equally to presuppose Broad's *BLP*s). But within the articulated conceptual system, *BLP*s and scientific theories are nevertheless supposed to have clearly distinct roles. Moreover, the sense in which the role of the *BLP*s is the more fundamental would be that we could abandon or revise our scientific laws or theories without repudiating any *BLP*s. If, on the other hand, we gave up some *BLP*, we would also have to abandon those laws and theories that rested on it; and if we gave up all our *BLP*s, we would be forced to scuttle our entire stock of scientific theories. Furthermore, since the *BLP*s may support rival theories, we would, repudiating our *BLP*s, be forced to jettison an indefinitely large supply of rival theories in addition to the prevailing ones. Perhaps we could abandon Einstein's theory of gravitation without abandoning any *BLP*s; but without our *BLP*s, we would have to abandon not only Einstein's theory, but certain other rival theories as well (e.g., Brans–Dicke's) which rest on the same *BLP*s.

From this point of view, the fact that some people accept prevailing scientific theories at the same time they reject one or more of the *BLP*s is easy enough to explain. Presumably, they simply fail to see the logical connections between those theories and the *BLP*s—they fail to see that the former presuppose the latter.

Although (ii) is a much more plausible construal of Broad's position than (i), it nevertheless rests on the mistaken belief that a conceptual scheme or framework has a discernible logical structure, a structure in which the distinction between a theory's implications and its presuppositions is determinable. Granted, this distinction *can* be made with some precision, but only relative to theories with a well-defined structure of a certain sort. We can distinguish a theory's implications from its presuppositions only with theories whose constitutive statements may be systematically listed and ordered in terms of their logical function and interdependence. But most theories in the natural sciences, and certainly the more informal cognitive structures we call 'world views' or 'conceptual schemes', are too ill-defined and loose-knit for there to be a clear distinction between the theories' implications and presuppositions, or between the basic and non-basic elements of the conceptual schemes. Broad's claim that his *BLP*s lie at the very foundation of our conceptual scheme is, therefore, a difficult claim to assess; in fact, it seems to be false. It is not at all clear that there is *any* set of beliefs sufficiently fundamental and sufficiently widely shared to count as *our* conceptual scheme; and besides, even if the *BLP*s were universally or almost universally shared, their importance relative to the rest of our beliefs need be neither clear nor the same for everyone.

Actually, I find it far from clear that science is connected in any interesting way at all to Broad's *BLP*s. It may be that some specific theories presuppose certain of Broad's *BLP*s. For example, perhaps our theories of perception rest on certain presuppositions about how information about the world can be acquired. However I must confess that, since they appear to deal with certain forms of information-acquisition only, I find our theories of perception compatible with the possibility that there are extra-sensory or non-sensory modes of information-acquisition—in short, compatible with ESP. In any case, I can't see why our acceptance (say) of the theory of relativity or of quantum physics rests on our acceptance of any of Broad's *BLP*s. Relativity, for example, seems to be compatible not only with Broad's four *BLP*s but with their denials as well. Broad may simply have assumed uncritically that the admission of genuine psi phenomena would automatically wreak the deepest havoc in science. In fact, this seems to have been a widespread and long-standing assumption in parapsychology itself. But it is less true today, due primarily to the efforts of such influential investigators as Schmidt (see in particular [140], [141], [145]), Walker [187], [188] and Dobbs [41], who have been trying to reconcile backward causation and other puzzling features of psi phenomena with the traditional framework of contemporary physics. In any case, the major weaknesses of Broad's account of paranormality are independent of whether or not our scientific theories actually rest on any of Broad's *BLP*s.

5. Paranormality and Consciousness

Still, Broad was on to something. Reasonable criteria of paranormality undoubtedly concern more than mere scientific inexplicability. But what? An interesting clue may be found in a recent paper by Michael Scriven [149]. Scriven was concerned, there, to explain (among other things) what it is for a phenomenon to be *supernatural*. But since his use of the term 'supernatural' seems to match pretty closely the use in parapsychology of the term 'paranormal', we may ask whether Scriven's account manages to provide suitable criteria for paranormality.

Following the spirit, if not the letter, of Scriven's analysis, a phenomenon may be said to be paranormal if it satisfies three conditions.

(D5) Phenomenon *P* is paranormal =df (a) *P* is inexplicable in terms of current scientific theory; (b) *P* is *so* different from those events we understand as to belong to an *order of existence* not recognized by science; (c) *P* exhibits some manifestation of consciousness, like agency or personality.

The purpose of condition (b) is to require that paranormal phenomena be *especially* unusual from the scientific point of view, and, moreover, that the respect in which they are unusual is (to use Scriven's terms) one of 'exceptional idio-syncrasy' or 'generic difference'. These expressions, however, as well as Scriven's term 'order of existence', are really too vague to be satisfactory. Moreover, the term 'order of exis-tence' is presumably tailored to fit Scriven's discussion of the class of *supernatural* phenomena, phenomena that fall (as Scriven puts it) outside the natural *order*. But I think we can state with somewhat more precision what *we* need in clause (b) for an account of the paranormal, whether or not it is what Scriven was trying to convey.

To say that P is especially unusual from the point of view of science is at least to say that scientific explanations of P demand new descriptive categories or new concepts. This hardly suffices, of course, since we must sometimes develop new concepts in order to explain phenomena that, however novel, are not 'especially unusual' in the sense here required (or intended by Scriven). This was recently the case, for example, when, in developing the theory of plate tectonics to explain such things as the intense geological activity along certain contentintal coastlines, scientists introduced such new concepts as *plate subduction*. So for a phenomenon P to be especially unusual in the required sense, it cannot merely be the case that scientific explanations of P demand the use of new descriptive categories or new concepts. It must, in addi-tion, be true that the employment of these new categories causes major ripples elsewhere in the conceptual pool. In order to explain P scientifically, we must transform or amend, in some major way, science as we know it. So perhaps condi-tion (b) may be recast as follows.

(b′) P cannot be explained scientifically without major re-visions elsewhere in scientific theory.

Condition (c) of (D5) is perhaps the most interesting com-ponent of that definition. Its inclusion in (D5) acknowledges that extreme strangeness is a necessary but not sufficient con-dition of a phenomenon's paranormality. Since manifesting consciousness is another necessary condition, (D5) leaves open the possibility that some phenomena may be extremely strange but not paranormal. This corresponds nicely to our classification of certain strange phenomena investigated in physics and astronomy (such as black holes and quasi-stellar objects).

But despite these attractive features, (D5) seems vulnerable to criticism. Its three conditions appear to specify the domain of the parapsychological, rather than that of the paranormal.* Since the former is presumably a subset of the latter, it may be better to regard conditions (a) and (b') as specifying the domain of the paranormal, and condition (c) as indicating which subset of the paranormal is the parapsychological.

But this maneuver is not quite enough. As we have observed, the remaining conditions (a) and (b') are at best necessary rather than sufficient conditions for a phenomenon's paranormality. There may, in fact, be many phenomena, which we would *not* want to classify as paranormal, but that would satisfy (a) and (b'). Suppose (quite plausibly) that phenomena observed in the vicinity of black holes, or connected with certain subatomic processes—or, for that matter, ordinary cases of human volition—satisfy conditions (a) and (b'). Intuitively, many would not regard such phenomena as paranormal, no matter how intractable they may be from the point of view of science. But doubtless, they would regard it as paranormal if a tree turned to stone overnight, or if it rained blood, or if a television set turned into Leonard Bernstein. Wherein lies the difference?

At this point, some may protest that the category of phenomena we are really interested in *is* that of the parapsychological. These other phenomena (they might say)—raining blood, trees suddenly turning to stone—are simply members of the class of abnormal phenomena. After all, abnormality

*Cf., Beloff '. . . paranormal phenomena. . . almost invariably occur in connection with a human person. Now there is no a priori reason why this should be the case. One could conceive of a world in which inanimate objects took an occasional paranormal holiday during which they behaved entirely capriciously ([10]: 362; see also Beloff [141]: 291).

is exhibited in varying degrees: some phenomena are more abnormal than others. Raining blood may be more unusual than any phenomenon connected with black holes, but it is still only a highly abnormal phenomenon, and clearly more abnormal than situs inversus. In fact, perhaps the category of the paranormal is spurious. Perhaps what we need to articulate is only a distinction between normal, abnormal, and parapsychological phenomena. But in that case (say these critics), our revised (D5) is what we want after all.

There is something eminently reasonable about this line of thought. In fact, it gains plausibility when we reflect that, though a tree's suddenly turning to stone is surely at least abnormal, it would be something else again if the tree began instead to talk or sing, or if it began to reach out malevolently for passers-by. And notice, a singing or grasping tree would presumably be manifesting consciousness in some way.

This approach to the problem, however attractive it may be from the point of view of theoretical simplicity, probably does not appease the nagging suspicion among some that between such phenomena as those connected with black holes (or deep scientific anomalies generally), and such phenomena as raining blood and trees turning to stone, there is a difference worthy of categorization. Readers who do not share this suspicion may, I suppose, stop here. But for those who do, let us consider some suggestions for improving (D5). (For those who care, I personally stop having intuitions one way or the other at this point.)

6. Some Possible Solutions

When we consider what might separate the exotic phenomena connected with black holes or subatomic processes (no matter how deeply scientifically anomalous) from such things as television sets turning into people or its raining blood, it is tempting to think that the relevant difference lies in some *subjective* factor. Raining blood (say) would thwart our ordinary expectations about meteorological phenomena, not to mention those of which blood is a component, whereas phenomena connected with black holes conflict with none of our familiar expectations. Although members of the scientific community may have certain expectations about what they will encounter in deep space, in general the really odd phenomena investigated in astronomy violate no *familiar* expectations. We simply have no familiar expectations about such recondite aspects of nature. However odd they may be from a scientific perspective, black holes can at most only thwart certain specific scientific expectations. This does not mean that there could be no paranormal phenomena involving black holes. If, for example, a black hole were to sing 'You Are My Sunshine', then this would thwart everyone's expectations concerning the behavior of celestial objects, including those of the astrophysicist. Moreover, while some people, even sizeable groups, may actually expect trees to do such things as suddenly turn to stone, such expectations hardly characterize the human community generally. And it is this large community whose attitudes and expectations we are presumably concerned with in this context.

It may, then, be a promising move to add a condition to (a) and (b') of (D5) which would capture this apparently subjective aspect of paranormality. Such a revised definition might look like this.

> (D6) Phenomenon P is paranormal =df (a) P is inexplicable in terms of current scientific theory; (b') P cannot be explained scientifically without major revisions elsewhere in scientific theory; (d) P thwarts our familiar expectations about what sorts of things can happen to the sorts of objects involved in P.

The addition of (D5)'s condition (c) to (D6) would then give us a definition of 'Phenomenon P is para*psychological*'.

Our new condition (d) perhaps captures what was most valuable in Broad's account of paranormality. Broad relied on *BLP*s not simply because he believed that paranormal phenomena violate something more fundamental than scientific theories, but apparently also because he believed that what such phenomena violate is intimately tied to general beliefs about, and dispositions with respect to, our familiar environment. Without trying to distill these expectations into something like a list of *BLP*s, it seems clear that we do expect familiar objects to do certain things, and to exhibit certain sorts of characteristics rather than others.

But it is probably a hopeless task to specify such expectations in a way that permits us to draw a clear line between abnormal and paranormal phenomena, especially if we want our statement of these expectations to be sufficiently general to reflect the attitudes of appropriately large portions of the human community. This fuzziness about our expectations, however, is inevitable and not surprising; in fact, it accounts in part for our difficulty in deciding how to classify certain phenomena. The fuzziness of condition (d), then, is not a fatal flaw in (D6). We needn't demand that an account of paranormality enable us to classify decisively any phenomenon in question. There is no reason to suppose that the concept of paranormality is that clear. It would be enough if our account captured the criteria normally used to classify phenomena as paranormal, even if those criteria are less precise than we would like.

But condition (d) also makes the concept of paranormality more relativistic than (I suspect) some would like. We had earlier conceded that the domain of the paranormal may change with time. But with condition (d) it appears that the domain may vary even from culture to culture. For example, there may be primitive cultures in which certain movements of tree branches in the vicinity of virgins would be taken to be a kind of lascivious clutching by the tree (rather than the result of the wind); and the members of such cultures might expect trees to behave in this way. Lascivious tree behavior, then, would not count as paranormal in such a culture, although it certainly would in ours.

I, for one, do not find this consideration particularly worrisome. It seemed plausible initially to allow the domain of the paranormal to change with time, because of the ways in which our increasing conceptual sophistication influences our attitudes toward and resulting classifications of different phenomena. Our attitudes toward hypnotism, for example, have advanced beyond the stage when 'mesmerization' was seen as sinister. The fact that certain societies may classify certain phenomena, relative to their own conceptual sophistication, differently from the way we do, should be no more problematical than the fact that, at different stages in our own intellectual history, we classified phenomena differently from the way we do now.

Moreover, the words 'normal' and 'abnormal' seem also to be relativistic in this way. In Alaska a heavy snowfall is a normal phenomenon, while in Panama it would presumably be abnormal. It is normal to find carnivorous fish in the rivers of Brazil, whereas this is abnormal in the rivers of Illinois. And we can imagine cultures in which public masturbation is normal behavior, although this behavior would be highly abnormal in most cultures. Offhand, then, it seems that the term 'paranormal' would exhibit a similar relativity of extension.

As reasonable as this seems, however, there is another way of looking at the matter. While it might appeal to our aesthetic sensibilities for the terms 'normal', 'abnormal', and 'paranormal' to be equally relativistic, there is no reason to insist on this sort of parity. The term 'paranormal' might, in fact, have a fixed extension. We might choose to analyze the term 'paranormal' in the way the term 'miracle' has sometimes been analyzed:

(D7) Phenomenon P is paranormal =df P is *in principle* inexplicable (i.e., by any science).

One consequence of adopting (D7) is that if such phenomena as telepathy and PK are ever explained by some future science, they will turn out never to have been paranormal. They will only have been mistakenly taken to be paranormal.

From the point of view of theoretical simplicity, some may prefer (D7) to (D6). But (D7) does not seem to be a definition of 'paranormal' as this term is most commonly used. It seems to me that most people—including philosophers like Broad and Ducasse—have wanted to allow that phenomena, which at one time count as paranormal, may (or will) ultimately be explained scientifically. If, moreover, we understand the strong inexplicability intended in (D7) to be such that an inexplicable phenomena is *ipso facto* an *impossible* phenomenon (in the relevant sense of 'impossible'), then there can be no genuinely paranormal phenomena. But then (D7) departs too far, perhaps, from the usual use of the term 'paranormal'. We are, of course, free to legislate definitions. The issue to be confronted here, however, is to what extent our prescriptive definitions can fly in the face of common usage. The normal/abnormal/paranormal distinction is neither wholly theoretic nor wholly pre-theoretic, and which definition of 'paranormal' we choose may ultimately turn on how we intend to use the distinction.

Bibliography

The following abbreviations will be used:

EJP	*European Journal of Parapsychology*
IJP	*International Journal of Parapsychology*
JASPR	*Journal of the American Society for Psychical Research*
JP	*Journal of Parapsychology*
JSPR	*Journal of the Society for Psychical Research [London]*
PASPR	*Proceedings of the American Society for Psychical Research*
PSPR	*Proceedings of the Society for Psychical Research [London]*
RP	*Research in Parapsychology*

[1] Anderson, Jr., R.M., 'A Holographic Model of Transpersonal Consciousness', *J. Transpersonal Psychology* 9 (1977): 119-128.

[2] Baenninger, R., 'Waning of Aggressive Motivation in *Betta Splendens*', *Psychonomic Science* 5 (1966): 207-208.

[3] Barber, T.X., *Pitfalls in Human Research: Ten Pivotal Points* (London: Pergamon, 1976).

[4] Basmajian, J., 'Control and Training of Individual Motor Units', *Science* 141 (1963): 440-441.

[5] ___, 'Electromyography Comes of Age', *Science* 176 (1972): 603-609.

[6] Bell, J.S., 'On the Einstein Podolsky Rosen Paradox', *Physics* 1 (1964-65): 195-200.

[7] Beloff, J.S., 'Parapsychology and its Neighbours', *JP* 34 (1970): 128-143.

[8] ___, 'Belief and Doubt', Presidential Address presented at the 15th Annual Convention of the Parapsychological

Assoc., Edinburgh, Sept. 2-5, 1972, in *RP* (1972): 189-200.

[9] ___, (ed.) *New Directions in Parapsychology* (Metuchen, N.J.: Scarecrow Press, 1975).

[10] ___, 'Explaining the Paranormal, with Epilogue—1977' in Ludwig [89]: 353-370.

[11] ___, 'Psi Phenomena: Causal Versus Acausal Interpretation', *JSPR* 49 (1977): 573-582.

[12] ___, 'Backward Causation' in B. Shapin & L. Coly (eds.) *The Philosophy of Parapsychology* (New York: Parapsychology Foundation, 1977): 37-51.

[13] ___, 'Is Mind Autonomous?', (Review of Popper-Eccles [112]), *British J. Philosophy of Science* 29 (1978): 265-273.

[14] ___, 'The Limits of Parapsychology', *EJP* 2 (1978): 291-303.

[15] Bender, H., and Vandrey, R.,'Psychokinetische Experimente mit dem Berner Graphiker Silvio', *Zeitschrift für Parapsychologie und Grenzgebiete der Psychologie* 18 (1976): 217-241.

[16] Betz, H.D., 'Unerklärte Beeinflussung eines elektrischen Schaltkreises durch Silvio', *Zeitschrift für Parapsychologie und Grenzgebiete der Psychologie* 20 (1978): 47-50.

[17] Bisaha, J.P., and Dunne, B.J., 'Multiple Subject and Long Distance Precognitive Remote Viewing of Geographical Locations'. paper presented at Int. Conf. on Cybernetics and Society, Washington, D. C., Sept. 19-21, 1977.

[18] Braud, W.G., 'Psychokinesis in Aggressive and Nonaggressive Fish with Mirror Presentation Feedback for Hits', *JP* 40 (1976): 296-307.

[19] Braud, W.G., Wood, R., and Braud, L.W., 'Free-Response GESP Performance During an Experimental Hypnagogic State . . . ', *JASPR* 69 (1975): 105-113.

[20] Braude, S.E., 'Objections to an Information-Theoretic Aproach to Synchronicity', *JASPR* 73 (1979): 119-138.

[21] Brier, B., *Precognition and the Philosophy of Science* (New York: Humanities Press, 1974).

[22] ___, 'Precognition and the Paradoxes of Causality', paper presented at Conference on Philosophical Issues in Psychic Research, University of Denver, Oct. 27-29, 1978.

[23] Broad, C.D., *Religion, Philosophy and Psychical Research* (New York: Humanities Press, 1969).

[24] ＿＿＿, *Lectures on Psychical Research* (London: Routledge and Kegan Paul, 1962).

[25] Broughton, R.S., 'An Exploratory Study on Psi-Based Experimenter and Subject Expectancy Effects', *RP* (1976): 173-177.

[26] Burdick, D.S., and Kelly, E.F., 'Statistical Methods in Parapsychological Research', in Wolman [198] : 81-130.

[27] Bursen, H.A., *Dismantling the Memory Machine* (Dordrecht, Boston, London: D.Reidel, 1978).

[28] Carington, W.W., 'Experiments on the Paranormal Cognition of Drawings', *JP* 4 (1940): 1-34.

[29] ＿＿＿, 'Experiments on the Paranormal Cognition of Drawings', *PASPR* 24 (1944): 3-107.

[30] Collins, H.M., 'Upon the Replication of Scientific Findings: A Discussion Illuminated by the Experiences of Researchers into Parapsychology', paper presented at the 4S/ISA First Int. Conf. on Social Studies of Science, Cornell University, June 1976.

[31] ＿＿＿, 'Science and the Rule of Replicability: A Sociological Study of Scientific Method', paper presented at AAAS Symposium on Replication and Experimenter Influence, Washington, D.C., Feb. 1978.

[32] Coover, J.E., *Experiments in Psychical Research* (Psychical Research Monographs No. 1) (Stanford: Stanford Univ., 1917).

[33] Cox, W.E., 'The Effect of PK on the Placement of Falling Objects', *JP* 15 (1951): 40-48.

[34] ＿＿＿, 'A Comparison of Spheres and Cubes in Placement PK Tests', *JP* 18 (1954): 234-239.

[35] Crumbaugh, J.C., 'A Scientific Critique of Parapsychology', Int. J. Neuropsychiatry 2 (1966): 523-31; reprinted in White [194] : 424-440.

[36] Davidson, D., 'Mental Events', in L. Foster and J.W. Swanson (eds.), *Experience and Theory* (Amherst: Univ. of Massachusetts Press, 1970).

[37] Davis, J.W., and Morrison, M.D., 'A Test of the Schmidt Model's Prediction Concerning Multiple Feedback in a PK Task', paper presented at 20th Annual Convention of the Parapsychological Association, Washington, D.C., Aug. 10-13, 1977.

[38] Dean, E.D., 'Plethysmograph Recordings as ESP Responses',

        Int. J. Neuropsychiatry 2 (1966): 439-446.

[39] ___, and Nash, C.B., 'Coincident Plethysmograph Results under Controlled Conditions', *JSPR* 44 (1967): 1-14.

[40] Dennett, D.C., *Brainstorms* (Philosophical Essays on Mind and Psychology) (Montgomery, Vt.: Bradford Books, 1978).

[41] Dobbs, A., 'The Feasibility of a Physical Theory of ESP', in Smythies [152] : 225-254.

[42] Ducasse, C.J., 'Paranormal Phenomena, Nature, and Man', *JASPR* 45 (1951): 129-149.

[43] ___, 'Causality and Parapsychology', *JP* 23 (1959): 90-96.

[44] ___, 'Broad on the Relevance of Psychical Research to Philosophy', in P. Schilpp (ed.) *The Philosophy of C.D. Broad* (New York: Tudor Publishing Co., 1959): 375-410.

[45] Dukhan, H., and Rao, K.R., 'Meditation and ESP Scoring', *RP* (1972): 148-151.

[46] Dummett, M.A.E., 'Bringing About the Past', *Philosophical Review* 23 (1964): 338-359.

[47] Eccles, J.C., 'The Human Person in its Two-Way Relationship to the Brain', address presented at the 19th Annual Convention of the Parapsychological Association, Utrecht, Aug. 18-21, 1976, *RP* (1976): 251-262.

[48] Einstein, A., Podolsky, B., and Rosen, N., 'Can the Quantum-Mechanical Description of Physical Reality be Considered Complete?', *Physical Review* 47 (1935): 777.

[49] Eisenbud, J., 'Psi and the Nature of Things', *IJP* 5 (1963): 245-269.

[50] ___, 'Paranormal Photography', in Wolman [198] : 414-432.

[51] ___, *The World of Ted Serios* (New York: Morrow, 1967).

[52] Flew, A., 'Parapsychology Revisited: Laws, Miracles, and Repeatability', reprinted with revisions from the *Humanist* 36 (1976): 28-30 in Ludwig [89] : 263-269.

[53] Fodor, J., *Psychological Explanation* (New York: Random House, 1968).

[54] ___, *The Language of Thought* (New York: Thomas Crowell, 1975).

[55] Forwald, H., *Mind, Matter and Gravitation* (New York: Parapsychology Foundation, 1969).

[56] Frank, J., *Persuasion and Healing* (Baltimore: Johns Hopkins Press, 1961).

[57] Gatlin, L.L., 'Meaningful Information Creation: An Alternative Interpretation of the Psi Phenomenon', *JASPR* 71 (1977): 1-18.

[58] Gauld, A., 'ESP and Attempts to Explain It', in Thakur [175]: 17-45.

[59] Goldberg, B., 'A Problem with Anomalous Monism', *Philosophical Studies* 32 (1977): 175-180.

[60] Green, E., and Green, A., *Beyond Biofeedback* (New York: Delta, 1977).

[61] Greenwood, J.A., 'Analysis of a Large Chance Control Series of ESP Data', *JP* 2 (1938): 138-146.

[62] Hansel, C.E.M., *ESP: A Scientific Evaluation* (New York: Scribner's, 1966).

[63] Hardy, A., Harvie, R., and Koestler, A., *The Challenge of Chance* (New York: Random House, 1974).

[64] Hastings, A.C., and Hurt, D.B., 'A Confirmatory Remote Viewing Experiment in a Group Setting', *Proc. of the Institute of Electrical and Electronics Engineers* 64 (1976): 1,544-1,545.

[65] Honorton, C., Review of Hansel [62], *JP* 31 (1967): 76-82.

[66] ___, 'Apparent Psychokinesis on Static Objects by a "Gifted" Subject', *RP* 1973; 128-131.

[67] ___, 'State of Awareness Factors in Psi Activation', *JASPR* 68 (1974): 246-256.

[68] ___, 'Objective Determination of Information Rate in Psi Tasks with Pictorial Stimuli', *JASPR* 69 (1975): 353-359.

[69] ___, 'Psi and Internal Attention States', in Wolman [198]: 435-472.

[70] ___, 'Psi and Internal Attention States: Information Retrieval in the Ganzfeld', in B. Shapin & L. Coly (eds.) *Psi and States of Awareness* (New York: Parapsychology Foundation, 1978).

[71] ___, 'Replicability, Experimenter Influence, and Parapsychology; An Empirical Context for the Study of Mind', paper presented at AAAS Symposium on Replication and Experimenter Influence, Washington, D. C., Feb. 1978.

[72] ___, Ramsey, M., and Cabibbo, C., 'Experimenter Effects in Extrasensory Perception', *JASPR* 69 (1975): 135-149.

[73] Jensen, A., 'How Much Can We Boost IQ and Scholastic Achievement?' *Harvard Educational Review* 39 (1969): 1-123.

[74] Jepson, I., 'Evidence for Clairvoyance in Card-Guessing', *PSPR* 38 (1928): 223-271.

[75] Jung, C.G., *Synchronicity: An Acausal Connecting Principle* (trans. by R.F.C. Hull), Vol. 8 of the *Collected Works of*

C.G. Jung (Princeton: Princeton University Press, 1973). Also in Jung and W. Pauli, *The Interpretation and Nature of the Psyche* (London: Routledge, 1955).

[76] ___, *Memories, Dreams, Reflections* (ed. by A. Jaffé) (London: Routledge, 1963).

[77] Keil, H.H.J., Herbert, B., Ullman, M., and Pratt, J.G., 'Directly Observable Voluntary PK Effects', *PSPR* 56 (1976): 197-235.

[78] Kelly, J.E., 'Methodological Problems in Free-Response ESP Experiments', *JASPR* 73 (1979): 1-15.

[79] Koestler, A., *The Case of the Midwife Toad* (London: Hutchinson, 1971).

[80] ___, *The Roots of Coincidence* (New York: Vintage, 1973).

[81] Kogan, I.M., 'Is Telepathy Possible'? *(Telecommunications and) Radio Engineering* 22 (1967): 141-144.

[83] ___, 'Information Theory Analysis of Telepathic Communication Experiments', *(Telecommunications and) Radio Engineering* 23 (1968): 122-125.

[84] Krippner, S., (ed.) *Psychokinesis* (New York & London: Plenum, 1977).

[85] ___, (ed.) *Extrasensory Perception* (New York & London, Plenum, 1978).

[86] ___, Honorton, C., and Ullman, M., 'A Second Precognitive Dream Study with Malcolm Bessent', *JASPR* 66 (1972): 269-279.

[87] ___, and Ullman, M., 'Telepathy and Dreams: A Controlled Experiment . . . ', *J. of Nervous and Mental Disease* 151 (1970): 394-403.

[88] ___, Ullman, M., and Honorton, C., 'A Precognitive Dream Study with a Single Subject', *JASPR* 65 (1971): 192-203.

[89] Ludwig, J. (ed.), *Philosophy and Parapsychology* (Buffalo: Prometheus, 1978).

[90] Lurie, Y., *The Correspondence Thesis*, Doctoral Dissertation, Cornell University, 1973 (Ann Arbor: University Microfilms, 1977).

[91] Malcolm, N., *Memory and Mind* (Ithaca: Cornell University Press, 1977).

[92] Martin, M., 'The Philosophical Importance of the Rosenthal Effect', *J. Theory of Social Behavior* 7 (1977): 81-97.

[93] May, E.C., Targ, R., and Puthoff, H.E., 'Possible EEG Correlates to Remote Stimuli Under Conditions of Sensory Shielding', paper presented at IEEE Electro/77 Special

Session on 'The State of the Art in Psychic Research', New York, Apr. 19-21, 1977.

[94] McMahan, E., 'An Experiment in Pure Telepathy', *JP* 10 (1946): 273-288.

[95] Meehl, P., 'Precognitive Telepathy I: On the Possibility of Distinguishing it Experimentally from Psychokinesis', *Noûs* 12 (1978): 235-266.

[96] ___, 'Precognitive Telepathy II: Some Neurophysiological Conjectures and Metaphysical Speculations', *Noûs* 12 (1978): 371-395.

[97] Millar, B., 'The Observational Theories: A Primer', *EJP* 2 (1978): 304-322.

[98] ___, and Broughton, R.S., 'An Investigation of the Psi Enhancement Paradigm of Schmidt', *RP* 1976: 23-25.

[99] Morris, R.L., 'An Exact Method for Evaluating Preferentially Matched Free-Response Material', *JASPR* 66 (1972): 401-407.

[100] Morrison, M., and Davis, J., 'PK with Immediate, Delayed and Multiple Feedback: A Test of the Schmidt Model's Predictions', paper presented at the 21st Annual Convention of the Parapsychological Association, St. Louis, Aug. 8-12, 1978.

[101] Mundle, C.W.K., 'Does the Concept of Precognition Make Sense?' *JP* 6 (1964): 179-198; reprinted in Ludwig [89]: 327-340.

[102] Palmer, J., 'Scoring in ESP Tests as a Function of Belief in ESP', Part I, *JASPR* 65 (1971): 373-408.

[103] ___, 'Scoring in ESP Tests as a Function of Belief in ESP', Part II, *JASPR* 66 (1972): 1-26.

[104] Persinger, M.A., 'Geophysical Models for Parapsychological Experiences', *Psychoenergetic Systems* 1 (1975): 63-74.

[105] ___, 'Response Sensitivity of Human Subjects to ELF Electromagnetic Fields . . . ', paper presented at Int. Conf. on Cybernetics and Society, Washington, D.C., Sept. 19-21, 1977.

[106] Pfungst, O., *Clever Hans (the horse of Mr. von Osten): A Contribution to Experimental Animal and Human Psychology* (tr. C.L. Rahn) (New York: Holt, 1911).

[107] Pribram, K.H., *Languages of the Brain* (Englewood Cliffs, N.J.: Prentice Hall, 1971).

[108] ___, 'Holonomy and Structure in the Organization of Perception', in U.M. Nicholas (ed.), *Images, Perception and Know-*

ledge (Dordrecht: Reidel, 1977).

[109] ___, Nuwer, M., and Baron, R.U., 'The Holographic Hypothesis of Memory Structure in Brain Function and Perception', in R.C. Atkinson, D.H. Krantz, R.C. Luce, and P. Suppes (eds.), *Contemporary Development in Mathematical Psychology* (San Francisco: Freeman, 1974).

[110] Price, H.H., 'Some Philosophical Questions about Telepathy and Clairvoyance', *Philosophy* 15 (1940): 363-385; reprinted in Wheatley and Edge [193] : 105-132.

[111] Popper, K.R., *The Logic of Scientific Discovery* (New York: Harper, 1959).

[112] ___, and Eccles, J.C., *The Self and Its Brain* (Springer International, 1977).

[113] Puthoff, H.E., and Targ, R., 'A Perceptual Channel for Information Transfer Over Kilometer Distances . . . ', *Proc. of the Institute of Electrical and Electronics Engineers* 64 (1976): 329-354.

[114] ___, 'Direct Perception of Remote Geographical Locations', paper presented at IEEE Electro/77 Special Session on 'The State of the Art in Psychic Research', New York, Apr. 19-21, 1977.

[115] Randall, J.L., *Parapsychology and the Nature of Life* (London: Souvenir Press, 1975).

[116] Ransom, C., 'Recent Criticisms of Parapsychology: A Review', *JASPR* 65 (1971): 289-307; reprinted with revisions in White [194] : 401-423.

[117] Rao, K.R., Kathamani, B.K., and Sailaja, P., 'ESP Scores Before and After a Scheduled Interview' (abstract), *JP* 32 (1968): 293.

[118] Rhine, J.B., *Extra-Sensory Perception* (revised ed.) (Boston: Bruce Humphries, 1964).

[119] ___, 'The PK Effect: Early Singles Tests', *JP* 8 (1944): 287-303.

[120] ___, 'Telepathy and Clairvoyance Reconsidered', *JP* 9 (1945): 176-193.

[121] ___, 'Psi-Missing Re-Examined', *JP* 33 (1969): 1-38; reprinted in White [194] : 142-179.

[122] ___, 'A New Case of Experimenter Unreliability', *JP* 38 (1974): 215-225.

[123] ___, 'A Second Report on a Case of Experimenter Fraud', *JP* 39 (1975): 306-325.

[124]   ___, and Pratt, J.G. 'A Review of the Pearce-Pratt Distance Series of ESP Tests', *JP* 18 (1954): 165-177.

[125]   Rhine, L.E., and Rhine, J.B., 'The Psychokinetic Effect: I. The First Experiment', *JP* 7 (1943): 20-43.

[126]   Richet, C., 'Further Experiments in Hypnotic Lucidity or Clairvoyance', *PSPR* 6 (1889): 66-83.

[127]   Rosenthal, R., *Experimenter Effects in Behavioral Research* (enlarged ed.) (New York: Irvington, 1976).

[128]   ___, 'Biasing Effects of Experimenters', *et cetera* 34 (1977): 253-264.

[129]   Rush, J.H., Review of Forwald [55], *JASPR* 65 (1971).

[130]   Ryzl, M., 'A Model of Parapsychological Communication', *JP* 30 (1966): 18-31.

[131]   Sargent, C.L., 'Experimenter Psi-Effects: Retroactive Expectancy Effects', *EJP* 2 (1978): 126-136.

[132]   Schmeidler, G.R., 'PK Effects upon Continuously Recorded Temperature', *JASPR* 67 (1973): 325-340.

[133]   ___, and McConnell, R.A., *ESP and Personality Patterns* (Westport, Conn.: Greenwood Press, 1958).

[134]   Schmidt, H., 'Precognition of a Quantum Process', *JP* 33 (1969): 99-103.

[135]   ___, 'Clairvoyance Tests with a Machine', *JP* 33 (1969): 300-306.

[136]   ___, 'A PK Test with Electronic Equipment', *JP* 34 (1970): 175-181.

[137]   ___, 'PK Experiments with Animals as Subjects', *JP* 34 (1970): 255-261.

[138]   ___, 'PK Tests with a High-Speed Random Number Generator', *JP* 37 (1973): 105-118.

[139]   ___, 'A Comparison of PK Action on Two Different Random Number Generators', *JP* (1974): 47-55.

[140]   ___, 'Toward a Mathematical Theory of Psi', *JASPR* 69 (1975): 301-319.

[141]   ___, 'A Logically Consistent Model of a World with Psi Interaction', in L. Oteri (ed.) *Quantum Physics and Para-Psychology* (New York: Parapsychology Foundation 1975)

[142]   ___, 'PK Effect on Pre-Recorded Targets', *JASPR* 70 (1976): 267-291.

[143]   ___, 'A Take Home Test in PK with Pre-Recorded Targets', paper presented at 20th Annual Convention of the Parapsychological Association, Washington, D. C., Aug. 10-13, 1977.

[144] ___, 'Evidence for Direct Interaction Between the Human Mind and External Quantum Processes', paper presented at Int. Conf. on Cybernetics and Society, Washington, D.C., Sept. 19-21, 1977.

[145] ___, 'Can an Effect Precede its Cause? A Model of a Non-Causal World', *Foundations of Physics* 8 (1978): 463-480.

[146] ___, 'Use of Stroboscopic Light as Rewarding Feedback in a PK Test with Pre-Recorded and Momentarily Generated Random Events', paper presented at 21st Annual Convention of the Parapsychological Association, St. Louis, Aug. 8-12, 1978.

[147] ___, and Pantas, L., 'Psi Tests with Internally Different Machines', *JP* 36 (1972): 222-232.

[148] Scott, C., and Haskell, P., 'Fresh Light on the Shackleton Experiments?' *PSPR* 56 (1974): 43-72.

[149] Scriven, M., 'Explanations of the Supernatural', in Thakur [175]: 181-194.

[150] Shapiro, A.K., 'A Contribution to a History of the Placebo Effect', *Behavioral Science* 5 (1960): 109-135.

[151] ___, 'Factors Contributing to the Placebo Effect', *Amer. J. of Psychotherapy* 18 (1964): 73-88.

[152] Smythies, J.R. (ed.), *Science and ESP* (London: Routledge and Kegan Paul, 1967).

[153] Soal, S.G., and Bateman, F., *Modern Experiments in Telepathy* (New Haven: Yale Univ. Press, 1954).

[154]· Sondow, N., 'Two Ganzfeld Conditions: An Exploratory Study', paper presented at the 21st Annual Convention of the Parapsychological Association, St. Louis, Aug. 8-12, 1978.

[155] Spencer Brown, G., *Probability and Scientific Inference* (London: Longmans, 1957).

[156] Stanford, R.G., 'Experimental Psychokinesis: A Review from Diverse Perspectives', in Wolman [198]: 324-381.

[157] ___, 'Toward Reinterpreting Psi Events', *JASPR* 72 (1978): 197-214.

[158] ___, *et al.*, 'Psychokinesis as Psi-Mediated Instrumental Response', *JASPR* 69 (1975): 127-133.

[159] ___, *et al.*, 'A Study of Motivational Arousal and Self-Concept in Psi-Mediated Instrumental Response', *JASPR* 70 (1976): 167-178.

[160]   ___, and Stio, A., 'A Study of Associative Mediation in Psi-Mediated Instrumental Response', *JASPR* 70 (1976): 55-64.

[161]   Stevenson, I., *Telepathic Impressions* (Charlottesville: Univ. of Virginia Press, 1970).

[162]   ___, 'An Antagonist's View of Parapsychology. . . ' (Review of Hansel [62]), *JASPR* 61 (1967): 254-267.

[163]   Swann, I., *To Kiss Earth Good-Bye* (New York: Hawthorn, 1975).

[164]   Targ, R., and Puthoff, H., *Mind-Reach* (New York: Delacorte, 1977).

[165]   ___, 'Information Transmission under Conditions of Sensory Shielding', *Nature* 251 (Oct. 18, 1974): 602-607.

[166]   Tart, C.T., *Learning to Use Extrasensory Perception* (Chicago: Univ. of Chicago Press, 1976).

[167]   ___, 'PSI: Scientific Studies of the Psychic Realm' (New York: Dutton, 1977).

[168]   ___, 'Physiological Correlates of Psi Cognition', *IJP* 5 (1963): 375-386.

[169]   ___, 'Models for the Explanation of Extrasensory Perception', *Int. J. of Neuropsychiatry* 2 (1966): 488-504.

[170]   ___, 'Improving Real Time ESP by Suppressing the Future: Trans-Temporal Inhibition', paper presented at IEEE Electro/77 Special Session on *The State of the Art in Psychic Research*, New York, Apr. 19-21, 1977.

[171]   ___, 'Space, Time and Mind', Presidential Address, 20th Annual Convention of the Parapsychological Association, Washington, D.C., Aug. 10-13, 1977.

[172]   Terry, J., and Honorton, C., 'Psi Information Retrieval in the Ganzfeld: Two Confirmatory Studies', *JASPR* 70 (1976): 207-217.

[173]   Terry, J., and Schmidt, H., 'Conscious and Subconscious PK Tests with Pre-Recorded Targets', paper presented at 20th Annual Convention of the Parapsychological Association, Washington, D.C., Aug. 10-13, 1977.

[174]   Terry, J., Tremmel, L., Kelly, M., Harper, S., and Barker, P.L., 'Psi Information Rate in Guessing and Receiver Optimization', *RP* (1975): 194-198.

[175]   Thakur, S.C. (ed.), *Philosophy and Psychical Research* (New York: Humanities Press, 1976).

[176] Thouless, R.H., *From Anecdote to Experiment in Psychical Research* (London: Routledge and Kegan Paul, 1972).

[177] ———, 'Some Comments on "Fresh Light on the Shackleton Experiments"', *PSPR* 56 (1974): 88-92.

[178] ———, and Wiesner, B.P., 'The Psi Process in Normal and "Paranormal" Psychology', *PSPR* 48 (1947): 177-197.

[179] Ullman, M., and Krippner, S., 'An Experimental Approach to Dream Telepathy ...', *Amer. J. of Psychiatry* 126 (1970): 1,282-1,289.

[180] ———, *Dream Studies and Telepathy* (New York: Parapsychology Foundation, 1970).

[181] ———, and Feldstein, S., 'Experimentally-Induced Telepathic Dreams: Two Studies Using EEG-REM Monitoring Techniques', *Int. J. of Neuropsychiatry* 2 (1966): 420-439.

[182] ———, and Vaughan, A., *Dream Telepathy* (New York: Macmillan, 1973).

[183] Vallee, J., Hastings, A., and Askevold, G., 'Remote Viewing Experiments through Computer Conferencing', *Proc. of the Institute of Electrical and Electronics Engineers* 64 (1976): 1,551-1,552.

[184] Vasiliev, L.L., *Experiments in Distant Influence* (New York: Dutton, 1976).

[185] von Békésy, G., *Sensory Inhibition* (Princeton: Princeton Univ. Press, 1967).

[186] Wade, N., 'IQ and Heredity: Suspicion of Fraud Beclouds Classic Experiment', *Science* 194 (1976): 916-919.

[187] Walker, E.H., 'Foundations of Paraphysical and Parapsychological Phenomena', in L. Oteri (ed.), *Quantum Physics and Parapsychology* (New York: Parapsychology Foundation, 1975), 1-53.

[188] ———, 'Consciousness and Quantum Theory', in E.D. Mitchell, *et al.* (ed. by J. White), *Psychic Exploration* (New York: Putnam, 1974), 544-568.

[189] Wälti, B., 'Die Silvio-Protokolle 1976-1977', *Zeitschrift-für Parapsychologie und Grenzgebiete der Psychologie* 20 (1978): 1-46.

[190] Warner, L., 'The Role of Luck in ESP Data', *JP* 1 (1937): 84-92.

[191] Watkins, G.K., and Watkins, A., 'Apparent Psychokinesis on Static Objects by a "Gifted" Subject: A Laboratory Demonstration', *RP* (1973): 132-134.

[192] Werth, L.F., 'Normalizing the Paranormal', *Amer. Philosophical Quarterly* 15 (1978): 47-56.

[193] Wheatley, J.M.O., and Edge, H.L., *Philosophical Dimensions of Parapsychology* (Springfield, Ill.: C.C. Thomas, 1976).

[194] White, R.A. (ed.), *Surveys in Parapsychology* (Metuchen, N.J.: Scarecrow Press, 1976).

[195] Whitson, T., Bogart, D., Palmer, J., and Tart, C.T., 'Preliminary Experiments in Group Remote Viewing', *Proc. of the Institute of Electrical and Electronics Engineers* 64 (1976): 1,550-1,551.

[196] Wittgenstein, L., *Philosophical Investigations*, ed. G.E.M. Anscombe and R.Rhees (trans. by G.E.M. Anscombe) (Oxford: Blackwell, 1955).

[197] ———, Zettel, (ed.), G. E. M. Anscombe and G. H. von Wright (trans. by G. E. M. Anscombe) (Oxford: Blackwell, 1955).

[198] Wolman, B. (ed.), *Handbook of Parapsychology* (New York: Van Nostrand Reinhold, 1977).

[199] Wolstenholme, G.E.W., and Millar, E.C.P. (eds.), *Extrasensory Perception* (New York: Citadel, 1969).

Index